Ian W. Shaw is a Canberra-based writer of both non-fiction and fiction. Ian's focus is on the lesser-known incidents and aspects of Australiana, the small pictures which help fill in the larger picture of Australian history. When not reading, researching and writing, Ian's interests are family, friends and football, in that order, but with a limpet-like attachment to the Sydney Swans.

Also by Ian W. Shaw

The Bloodbath
On Radji Beach
Glenrowan

THE GHOSTS OF ROEBUCK BAY

IAN W. SHAW

Pan Macmillan Australia

First published 2014 in Macmillan by Pan Macmillan Australia Pty Ltd
1 Market Street, Sydney, New South Wales, Australia, 2000

Cataloguing-in-Publication entry is available
from the National Library of Australia
http://catalogue.nla.gov.au

Typeset in 12.5/17 pt Fairfield LH 45 Light by Post Pre-press Group
Printed by IVE
Maps by Laurie Whiddon

CONTENTS

LIST OF ABBREVIATIONS

ABDA	American, British, Dutch, Australian Command
AOB	Advanced Operational Base
AWOL	Absent Without Leave
IJN	Imperial Japanese Navy
KLM	Royal Dutch Airlines
KNIL	Royal Dutch Indies Air Force
KNILM	Royal Dutch East Indies Airlines
MLD	Marineluchtvaartdienst Dutch Naval Air Force
MMA	MacRobertson Miller Airlines
NEI	Netherlands East Indies
QEA	Qantas Empire Airways
RAAF	Royal Australian Air Force
RAF	Royal Air Force
RAN	Royal Australian Navy
USAAF	United States Army Air Force
VDC	Volunteer Defence Corps

CAST OF CHARACTERS

Australians

Ambrose, Lewis – Senior QEA pilot operating between Broome and Java.

Archer, Ken – Broome resident and Mobil Oil representative.

Bardwell, Beresford – Former pearler, army reservist and Broome roads board chairman.

Bardwell, Marjory ('Biddy') – Wife of Beresford; telephonist exchange operator.

Brain, Lester – Qantas/QEA pilot and troubleshooter despatched to Broome to oversee the evacuation. A practical, brave and compassionate man.

Caldwell, Keith – RAAF A18–10 flying boat captain; ex-QEA pilot.

Carseldine, Maurie – Broome Shell Oil representative and coxswain of company launch.

Cowie, Inspector James – Senior policeman at Broome; ill at time of attack.

D'Antoine, Charlie – Aboriginal deckhand, *Nicol Bay*; member of an extended family.

Davis, Lieutenant Beau – Former pearler; RAN officer sent to Broome to organise pearling fleet's evacuation.

De Castella, Jock – Broome's Shell Oil representative based at airfield.

Ireland, Andrew – RAAF A18–10 aircrew; active in rescue attempts.

Jolly, Dr Alexander – Broome district medical officer; evacuated from Broome on the day of attack.

Macnee, Harry – First World War hero, captain in Broome VDC, based at airfield during the attack.

Mathieson, Harold – Norwegian mariner and captain of ketch *Nicol Bay*; worked tirelessly to rescue survivors.

Millar, Malcolm – QEA manager who established evacuation operations in Java.

O'Neill, Laurie – Former policeman and Broome native affairs inspector.

Oram, Jim – QEA aircraft steward sent to Broome to organise accommodation.

Palmer, Jack – Beachcomber, finder of 'Dakota Diamonds'

Plenty, Flight Lieutenant Herb – RAAF Evacuee, first to warn of Japanese attack.

Russell, Frank – RAAF A18-10 aircrew and rescue worker post-attack.

Smith, Flight Lieutenant Hamilton – RAAF doctor who arrived post-attack and remained to assist wounded.

Woods, Jimmy – MMA airlines pilot who provided regular Broome air service.

Americans

Dimmock, Captain – USAAF doctor evacuated from Java. Killed at Broome.

Donoho, Sergeant Melvin – USAAF ground crew and evacuee who survived the shooting down of his evacuation aircraft.

Lamade, Lieutenant Jack – USN, and pilot of floatplane stranded at Broome.

Legg, Lieutenant Colonel Richard – Self-centred USAAF officer posted to Broome to oversee US operations there.

Minahan, Lieutenant John – USAAF pilot and diarist seconded to Legg's Broome operation.

Dutch

Blaauw, J.F.P. 'Joop' – PK-AFV, the *Pelikaan*, evacuee shot down and wounded at Carnot Bay.

Doorman, Theo – Y-67 evacuee; young son of senior Dutch admiral.

Hasselo, Flight Sergeant Hank – X-1 pilot who fought back at Japanese attackers.

Idzerda, Sergeant Rudi – X-23 navigator who just made it to Broome before attack.

Juta, Sergeant Henri – Y-67 navigator evacuated from Java with family.

Koens, Elly – X-1 evacuee who escaped with parents and sibling.

Koens, Piet – X-1 evacuee; brother of Elly.

Koens, Simon – X-1 evacuee; aircraft engineer in Dutch Naval Air Force, father of Elly.

Muller, Johan – PK-AFV, the *Pelikaan*, wireless operator; shot down at Carnot Bay.

Piers, Jan – X-1 evacuee who lost his family on Roebuck Bay.

Sjerp, Wing Commander Bastiaan – X-20 pilot who flew his family from Java.

Sjerp, David – X-20 evacuee.

Smirnoff, Captain Ivan – First World War Russian fighter ace, British RAF flight trainer and pilot of the PK-AFV, the *Pelikaan*, shot down at Carnot Bay.

Van Hulssen, Corporal Frits – Y-59 wireless operator involved in Roebuck Bay rescues.

Van Tuijn, Sergeant C.C. – KNIL flight engineer aboard Winckel's aircraft. His family flew with Smirnoff.

Van Tuijn, Johannes – PK-AFV, the *Pelikaan*, evacuee, and son of C.C. Van Tuijn.

Van Tuijn, Maria – PK-AFV, the *Pelikaan*, evacuee, and wife of C.C. Van Tuijn. Shot down at Carnot Bay.

Winckel, Lieutenant Gus – KNIL pilot, tireless in evacuating Dutch from Java and in protecting Broome airfield.

Others

Bowden, Corporal Jimmy – RAF Catalina gunner and non-swimmer who took on Japanese attackers.

Kudo, Warrant Officer Osamu – IJN combat ace who was shot down off Broome.

Miyano, Lieutenant Zenjiro – IJN commander of the Zero flight which attacked Broome and Roebuck Bay.

Broome and Roebuck Bay – 9.15 a.m., 3 March 1942

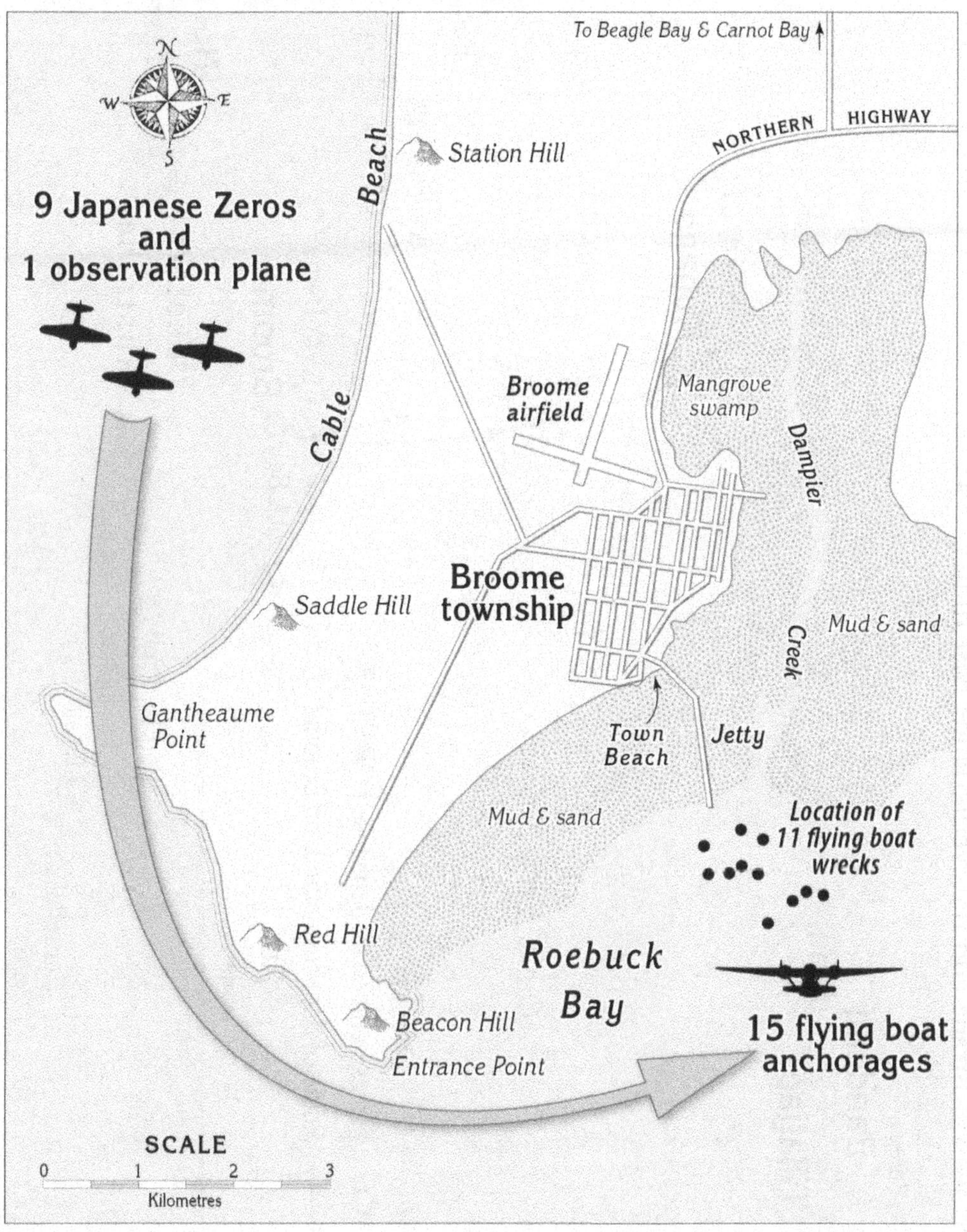

North West Australia and the Netherlands East Indies, 1942

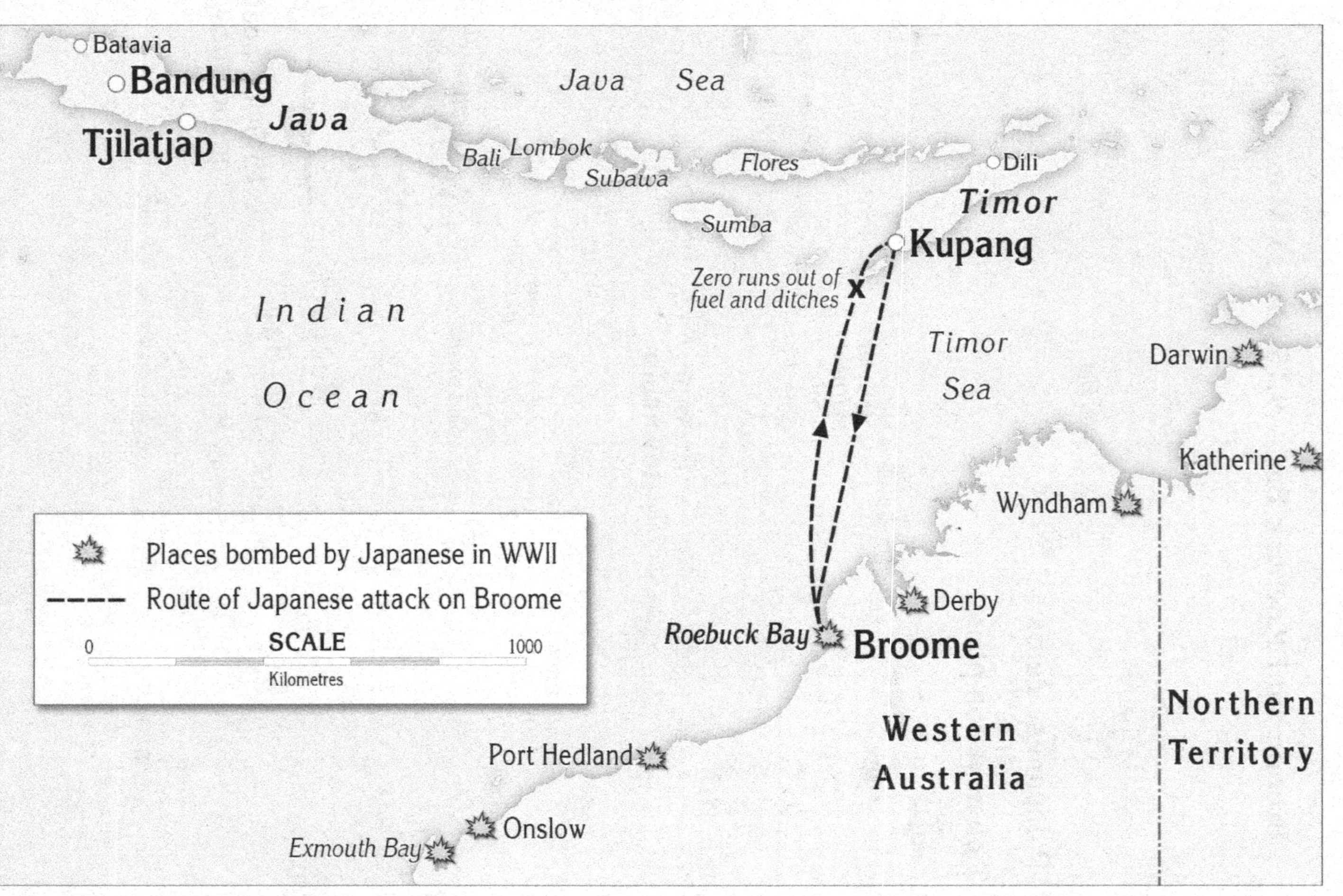

Broome, Saturday. A man's skeleton has been found on Dampier Creek, which runs through the town. It has not yet been identified.

The skeleton, which was found in mangrove swamps, was partially submerged in mud. The skeleton is thought to be that of a victim of the Japanese bombing of Broome in 1942.

Perth *Daily News*, 20 July 1946

PROLOGUE

Roebuck Bay, 9:20 a.m., 3 March 1942

'Elly!'

Standing on the edge of the aircraft 's wing, Elly Koens could hear her mother screaming at her from the flaming water below. 'Elly! Jump, jump now!'

But little Elly refused to jump until she was ready, and she wasn't ready yet. For a start, she knew not to wear shoes into the water, and so she sat down to take them off. Her father and brother yelled out to her again and again to jump but Elly focused on what she was doing, blotting out the sounds of chaos and destruction around her for just a few seconds more. Just as she was preparing to jump, something from the aircraft behind her exploded and she was thrown sideways into the churning sea below. The water closed over her as she sank into the deep.

*

The last few weeks had been hell for the Koens and the other Dutch families who lived in the Netherlands East Indies, particularly for those in Surabaya, the headquarters of the enormous Dutch naval forces in the colony. The Koens had been happily living in a big house with servants. Elly's father Simon was a soldier who flew the big airplanes at the flying boat base. Life had been wonderful for ten-year-old Elly and her older brother Piet.

But now things were different. Just a couple of days ago, her father had told them their house was no longer safe.

Elly would never forget her mother visiting their neighbours, giving one the keys to their car and the other the keys to their home. 'Help yourselves,' she had said, and walked away without looking back.

They couldn't go home to the other Netherlands, Holland as many called it, because of the war raging in Europe. And now it looked like war had reached their home in Surabaya as well. Their maid, their friends and so many people they knew were all leaving as quickly as they could, worried about what might happen if they stayed.

Her father led them to a sugar plantation, and helped them hide in one of the little workers' huts. Elly's father's aircraft had been moved away from its base just outside Surabaya and hidden away on a river where the Japanese couldn't find it.

Her mother had struggled with the changes. They all had. She and Piet had to carry little bags wherever they went, pouches containing a mask and little first-aid items she hoped they would never have to use.

Her father drove them a short distance to a track that led to a river. Under overhanging trees and with branches draped across any parts that might not fit under the trees was a large flying boat, like the ones her father worked with. They joined the people already aboard, finding a place in the main body of the aircraft. More people came on board until Elly thought they would never be able to take off. Late that night and with some difficulty the plane taxied a long way down the river before eventually taking to the air.

Many of the other passengers were women and children and they cried and wailed throughout the flight. It was cold and the toilet overflowed.

They were all relieved when the sun came up and they landed in the middle of a bay whose waters were a most beautiful blue-green colour. Elly's father said that the land was Australia and they were now safe.

Elly saw there was not a lot of water in the bay, but there was a lot of mud and sand, and many other planes. They were all a long way from a yellow sandy beach. In the distance she could see a very long pier and, at its end, a small town.

One of the pilots walked through the plane and told the passengers they might be there for a few hours. He instructed the crew to open all the doors and hatches, even the gun turrets, and encouraged people to go outside, climb onto the wings and floats while the crew took care of everything else.

It was a beautiful morning in a beautiful place, he said. Enjoy the sun, but don't get sunburnt, he added, and watch out for sharks. Elly thought he was pulling their leg, but Piet said he knew there were sharks in this area.

Then she saw the little silver specks in the distance, specks that grew bigger and faster the closer they came. The planes dived down towards the seaplanes in the bay.

And then it was just shouts and screams, explosions and the rat-a-tat from the planes shooting at them. Elly's father, mother and Piet all jumped into the water and called for Elly to follow. There were pools of fire on the water, and people were caught in them. Some of the passengers were hit again and again. Elly heard their screams and saw their blood.

Her mother screamed and her father and brother yelled out for her to jump.

Elly finished taking off her shoes and socks, and arranged them in a neat little pile alongside her. She had one last question. 'Is it cold?' she called out, for she hated cold water.

Before a reply came, another little silver planes swept in and opened fire. Somewhere on the plane, something exploded, and the plane tipped to one side. Elly flew through the air and hit the water, which closed over her as she began to sink. Bobbing back up, Elly paddled to her family who were floating not far from her. Together they surveyed the terror and destruction around them and prayed for deliverance.

*

That day, 3 March 1942, was just one day in a very long war. This date does not mean a lot when compared to the 'Day of Infamy', 7 December 1941, when Japanese fighters and bombers opened the Pacific War at Pearl Harbor, or to the days that marked the end of the war, D-Day, V-E (Europe) Day and V-J (Japan) Day. For most people engaged in fighting the most damaging war in human history, 3 March 1942 may not have even been memorable, indistinguishable from the hundreds that preceded it and the hundreds that followed.

But for those in and around Broome, it was a day that changed their life. The events at Broome and Roebuck Bay brought the war to them. What happened that day showed some people at their absolute best, and some at their absolute worst. It showcased selflessness and selfishness, bravery and cowardice, planned reactions to spontaneous events and spontaneous reactions to planned events.

Above all, what happened that day highlighted the sometimes inexplicable randomness of war, how life or death can be determined by where you sat in an aircraft or whether a current swept you into flames or away from them. The day also reminds us that most of the people caught up in wars are not wearing uniforms.

Elly Koens and her family were among the lucky that day. The Koens would walk away with only some scratches on their bodies belying the deep scars in their minds. Other families were far less fortunate, and were broken by the tragedies of that day. Children who were far too young to understand what was happening perished. And while some families were literally torn apart, others forged friendships that lasted a lifetime. It was a day that Broome would never forget.

The Koens were refugees, evacuees fleeing their home ahead of the invading Japanese, and like many from the Dutch community in the Netherlands East Indies (NEI) who fled to Australia aboard seaplanes, the Koens made the 1000 kilometres flight to escape the Japanese, who were progressing southwards through Southeast Asia at great speed and were seemingly irresistible. Their forces had overrun Hong Kong on Boxing Day, 26 December 1941, and had pushed the American forces in the Philippines into a small perimeter outside Manila. On 15 February 1942, Singapore – the island fortress, supposedly impregnable and Britain's major military base in Southeast Asia – had fallen. The Japanese did not stop at Singapore, invading the Dutch territories of Borneo, Sumatra in rapid succession, and prompting the first major evacuation of civilians from a war zone ever undertaken by air. For the majority of those fleeing the Japanese advance, the first port on the evacuation route was the small Australian pearling port of Broome, and they began arriving there in significant numbers from the last week of February. Among the mix of Dutch civilians and servicemen were significant numbers of Americans, servicemen all, also being evacuated from Java ahead of the Japanese and also uncertain as to their future.

During that first week of March 1942, Broome was packed with desperate souls, many of whom were there only temporarily, evacuees making their way from Broome to the cities and larger towns in the south and southeast of the vast continent. Tragically, many of those who were in Broome on 3 March 1942 would not have the choice to travel further. That day, nine Japanese Zero planes attacked the small town, with a plan to destroy the aerodrome and American planes they believed would be either there or moored in the nearby bay. With no warning and little in the way of defences, the town could only put up minimal opposition. After an attack that lasted just twenty minutes, not a single operational aircraft remained in Broome, either at the aerodrome or at the mooring buoys on Roebuck Bay. The human toll was high both in terms of death and injury, and in the pain that those who survived would carry with them for the rest of their lives.

The Japanese air raid that day was a tragedy for those who were there, whether servicemen or civilians. It was a tragedy for the town as well, and a tragedy for the fleet and the sailors who had created Broome. And yet this tragedy has largely slipped through the cracks of history. History, though, is replete with ghosts, and what happened in Broome on 3 March 1942 is now part of a much wider history. Who then are the ghosts of Roebuck Bay?

CHAPTER 1

The Port of Pearls

By the 1940s, Broome had become a nondescript town on a lonely coast, falling into apathy and sunbleached of its colour and rapidly losing traces of its past.

John Bailey, *The White Divers of Broome*

Broome has always been open to refugees and newcomers, to fortune-seekers and adventurers. In the first few weeks of 1942, however, Broome was just a shadow of its former self. Its glory days as one of the most colourful sea-ports in the southern seas were just fading memories for the few original inhabitants still living there. The small peninsula on which the township sits was one of the first areas of the Australian continent to be visited by Europeans. The buccaneer turned explorer, William Dampier, visited twice, in 1688 and 1699. Roebuck Bay, the inner stretch of water that framed the peninsula, was named after Dampier's ship on his 1699 voyage, while the creek at its head, Dampier Creek, was named in his honour.

Dampier had been singularly unimpressed with what he found in the northwest of the continent, but other Europeans who followed just over 200 years later found riches that Dampier could not have known existed. The waters around the peninsula were home to enormous natural pearl beds. Shortly after the discovery of this underwater treasure, the township of Broome was firstly surveyed and then named after the then-governor of Western Australia, Sir Frederick Broome.

From around 1880, Broome became a magnet for fortune-seekers from around the world. Some sought the pearls, while others prized the shells the pearls grew in; mother-of-pearl was in demand in Europe and elsewhere for use as buttons and brooches, and as inlays in furniture and fittings. Between 1880 and 1920, 80 per cent of the world's pearl shell came from Broome. The town became home to more than 8000 people, every one of them from somewhere else.

The white Europeans learned early on that while the industry itself was attractive, the same could not be said for the process of retrieving the pearl shell from the seabed. At first, local Aboriginal people were hired or simply taken to dive for the shells. As the shallower waters were worked out, the Indigenous people were replaced by those who could dive deeper: Manilamen from the Philippines, Malays and Koepangers from Timor, specifically the area around Koepang (Kupang) in West Timor. The South Asian people were in turn replaced by Japanese divers but many remained in the industry as deckhands on the pearling luggers. The Japanese divers were also better equipped with the new technology that was entering the industry in the form of air pumps and diving suits.

The changing nature of the industry straddled the years when the bottom fell out of the pearl shell market. The disruption caused by World War I was followed by the development of cheap plastic alternatives to pearl shell during the 1920s which, in turn, was followed by the Great Depression. By the late 1930s, pearling luggers were still operating out of Broome, but where they once numbered in their hundreds, there were now merely dozens of craft. The white male Europeans in their white cotton suits were gone, too, replaced by Japanese owners and agents on the luggers and in the shops.

The Japanese dominated the pearling industry, albeit through a series of dummy companies which disguised that dominance; the White Australia Policy was still the law of the land. They also held a strong position in the Broome community as a result of this dominance. They even had their own club in the town, the Japanese Club, housed in one of Broome's largest buildings, and it quickly became one of the most popular venues in town. Broome still has Australia's largest Japanese cemetery; it is the final resting place for around 900 Japanese people who died seeking pearls and pearl shell.

By December 1942, though, the town's population had dropped from a peak of over 8000 to around 1600, of which just 450 were European. The majority were Asian – Chinese, Japanese, Malays and Koepangers – and a large number were Aboriginal and mixed-race residents.

With the decline of the pearling industry came the realisation that Broome was nothing more than an outpost of civilisation on the edge of a vast and empty continent. The only overland connection to Perth was via a track that was rough at best and impassable at worst, especially during the wet season. The railway tracks in the region were as small as the route they traversed was short, from the far side of Broome to the end of the long jetty. They were used by the small steam engine that pulled flatbed carriages out onto the jetty with petrol and other supplies and, on their return trip, the bags of pearl shell that the luggers brought in.

The ships and luggers that used that jetty were Broome's lifeblood until the early 1930s when an airfield was established on the edge of town on the track to Cable Beach. The town's first regular air service began in 1932, connecting Broome and Perth in a trip that took two-and-a-half days. In February 1942, there was a regular passenger and mail service connecting Broome with the cities and towns to the south. The contract to deliver that service had been won by MacRobertson Miller Airlines (MMA) and the pilot assigned to it, Jimmy Woods, was one of the most popular people to visit the town.

The coming of war in September 1939 brought increasing change to Broome; slow, incremental change at first, but small changes that were cumulative. By the end of 1941, virtually all the young men and women from the town had either enlisted in the armed forces or had moved to the large cities in the south to work in the jobs vacated by others who had enlisted. In a small town like Broome, their loss was a major blow.

If the war came to Broome, the town's defence would be in the hands of the local equivalent of a home guard, the Broome Volunteer Defence Corps (VDC). Unfortunately, the VDC was not particularly impressive, on paper at least. Formed in July 1940, it could count on just 30 or so volunteers, who had only six weapons in their armoury, all World War I–vintage Lee-Enfield rifles, with 500 rounds of ammunition for each.

Their leaders were of the same vintage, but all had impressive records from the Great War. Their commanding officer and their intelligence officer, captains Harry Macnee and Lou Goldie respectively, had both served at Gallipoli and on the Western Front, and both had been commissioned from the ranks. Both had served in the 10th Light Horse Regiment, as had the units' drill sergeant, Beresford Bardwell. So far, their activities had been confined to regular training and occasional guard details at the wireless station and the jetty, the main points of strategic interest in Broome. They prepared as best they could but nothing could have prepared them for the fateful events ahead.

*

There was a distinct social order in Broome at this time and those at the top were the families of 'Old Broome' when Broome was the 'Port of Pearls', the town where fortunes were made with the opening of a single shell. By 1942, those days were long gone. The mansions were boarded up or falling down, and most of the luggers had disappeared. The most important people in town were no longer the pearlers but those who had authority rather than wealth; with the passing of the pearl trade came the passing of power from the commercial to the administrative. Those who now exercised that power were Broome's senior public servants, the most prominent of whom were the town doctor and senior policeman.

The town doctor was the English-born Dr Alexander Thomas Hicks Jolly, 32 years of age and married to Margaret with a small daughter. Jolly had only arrived in Broome in July 1940, and was still feeling his way in local society. As well as carrying the designation of resident medical officer, Jolly was also the town's resident magistrate. While time proved him to be a competent doctor, Jolly would never really become part of the town's establishment the way previous doctors had. The town may have been a little too 'frontier' for Jolly and his family, or perhaps he was a little too urban for that particular time and place.

The senior policeman was Inspector James Duff Cowie, a former city detective who had joined the Western Australian Police Force in 1910, and served with distinction since. Cowie was not especially happy about his Broome posting. It was a long way from where the real action was in the south, and the tropical climate had already affected his health through several bouts of dengue fever. Just to confuse everyone, the senior police sergeant at Broome was also named James Cowie – no relation, but enough of a coincidence to regularly raise a laugh.

Another senior bureaucrat was the Broome inspector of Aborigines, the local representative of the state Native Affairs Department. The position was occupied by Laurie O'Neill, a former police sergeant who had spent most of his police career in the northwest, at places like Fitzroy Crossing, where he had been the district's sergeant of police. O'Neill was efficient and popular with both the Aboriginal people he was responsible for and the Europeans he had to negotiate with.

Also close to the top of social hierarchy was Beresford Bardwell. As well as his role as VDC drill sergeant, Beresford also headed up the Broome Public Works Department and was a member of the Broome Roads Board. Beresford and his brother Bernard did not really qualify as 'Old Broome' as they had originally come to Broome around 1910, drawn from their native Melbourne by promises of adventure and riches from the sea. They had some of the former but little of the latter before the Great War broke out in 1914. Beresford enlisted and served with some distinction before being invalided back to Australia in 1918 because of wounds suffered in France. He and Bernard continued their pearling partnership after the war, joined by other family members, and then in 1920 their fortunes improved dramatically.

Beresford was out on one of the company's luggers, going through pearl shells brought up by one of his Japanese divers. Opening one shell, he spotted a pearl the size of his thumbnail. Concerned about what might happen if the rest of the crew saw the pearl, Beresford slipped it into his mouth, and continued opening shells until he could ease away into his cabin where he locked the pearl securely away. That pearl later sold for £4000 (about $700,000 in today's currency), and was one of the most valuable ever discovered in the northwest.

In the mid-1920s, the Bardwells got out of the pearling trade like so many others in Broome, seeing no future for the industry. Unlike many who left pearling, they didn't leave Broome. Beresford and his wife, Biddy (Marjory), had three children – two sons and a daughter – and were determined to stay and make a life for themselves and their children.

In the 1930s Beresford was appointed to the position of harbour master for the port of Broome. When the long jetty there caught fire in 1937, his quick thinking prevented the destruction of the entire structure. When he arrived on the scene, a fire had taken hold in the centre of the jetty. He sent someone away for dynamite, which he used to blow out sections of the jetty on either side of the fire. The jetty was damaged, but it was quickly repaired in a few days.

Finally in the hierarchy of the town, there were a number of 'new' Broomites, families such as the Milners. Harry and Catherine Milner had come to Broome in the 1920s. Harry was an engineer, but in 1924 left that job and went into partnership with Leonard Knight to run the open-air cinema in Broome, the Sun Theatre. They did well. Their family now numbered seven – five daughters and two sons – and, like most in the town, they participated in the town's social life. Catherine was the Girl Guide district commissioner and, through their children, involved in most things that happened in town. Unfortunately, Harry died in 1940. Catherine bought out Leonard Knight, took over the running of the theatre and tried to carry on with her life.

*

In 1941, Australia's defence planners recognised that Broome had another point of *potential* strategic significance – its small airfield. Because it was there, in place, and was being used on a regular basis, Broome's little airfield was designated an Advanced Operational Base (AOB), as were similar small airfields at Wyndham and Derby in the northwest.

A wireless telegraph station was built near the airfield on the same side as the town. Unfortunately, the messages it was designed to send and receive were in code, and no trained operators were available until sometime in 1942. Until then, the military authorities in Broome had to use the civilian telegraph with its copper wires running to the nerve centres of defence in the south.

It was the same with the plans for the airfield. The proposed upgrade would only be to the extent that it could handle two medium-sized aircraft arrivals and departures a day rather than the one or two that it now handled each week. There were no plans for radar, no plans for anti-aircraft defences and there were no plans for fighter aircraft to protect the facility.

*

The very thing that threatened Broome's existence – its geographic location – suddenly made it very important in the first weeks of 1942. The tides of war were lapping ever closer to northern Australia as success followed success for the Japanese.

In Malaya, the Japanese landings on the northwest of the peninsula were a preamble to a measured advance to the southeast, through successive British defence lines towards the ultimate prize of Singapore. It was an advance characterised by a total domination of the air and by the use of dozens of small boats the British forces had failed to destroy as they retreated. The boats, packed with Japanese soldiers, would sail at night to landing places behind Allied lines. The troops would wade ashore to create havoc in the rear echelon areas. Australian defence planners could do nothing about the Japanese air dominance that emerged early in the fighting as they had no aircraft capable of matching the performance of the Japanese Zero fighter, but they were able to address the issue of the potential Japanese use of abandoned boats should the Japanese ever be so bold as to invade the Australian mainland.

In January 1942, Broome pearlers were informed that all their luggers would be purchased by the Australian government. A fair price would be paid for them, and any deemed unseaworthy would be destroyed. The remainder would be sailed south, to Fremantle most likely, where they would be put to work in supporting the war effort. Unspoken but implicit was the fact that removing all luggers from the northwest would also remove the possibility of them being captured and used by the Japanese. Eventually, 44 luggers were purchased at a cost of £80,000. A further sixteen luggers, found to be unseaworthy, were purchased for almost £9000, and burnt where they lay.

The task of crewing the remaining luggers and organising their despatch to Fremantle fell to RAN Reserve Lieutenant D.L. 'Beau' Davis, who flew into Broome from Melbourne on 9 February after being fully briefed at Defence headquarters. The middle-aged sailor was a good choice for the role. He had many years experience in the northwest and at one time had owned and operated a fleet of six pearling luggers out of Broome. When there was a neap tide on 17 February, Davis floated his luggers on Roebuck Bay, giving them, literally, a water test before fitting them out for the voyage south. He had no idea when that voyage would begin, however, because he was struggling to find crews for his little armada.

*

While Beau Davis was selecting and preparing the luggers to sail south, the war situation was steadily worsening. On

15 February, Singapore and the 90,000-plus Allied defenders surrendered to the Japanese. In the Philippines, American ground troops had been forced back onto the Bataan Peninsula and their own island fortress of Corregidor. Their army, air force and navy units had all retreated steadily to the south, first to the Netherlands East Indies (NEI), and then to Australia where they joined other American forces who had arrived there. A reinforcement route for the units that remained to face the Japanese in Java had been established along the old Qantas Empire Airways (QEA) flying boat route, via Timor and Bali into Java itself.

The NEI slowly but inexorably fell under Japanese control. Japanese forces attacked Borneo in December, then Sumatra, the Celebes (Sulawesi) and elsewhere across the archipelago. Regular air raids on Kupang in West Timor and its associated airfield at Penfui and the shooting down of a QEA flying boat, the *Corio,* effectively closed the air route through Timor.

The only alternative reinforcement route was a direct route between Australia and Java. The two closest points were the south coast of Java and the northwest coast of Australia. There were several possible departure points in Java – Bandung and Jogjakarta for land-based aircraft, and Tjilatjap for flying boats – but only one realistic destination in Australia.

That destination was Broome, and in a few short days, Broome went from being almost an afterthought, an alternative landing point for aircraft in times of inclement weather, to perhaps the most important port town in the western half of the continent.

A lot of work had to be carried out in a very short time. First was the airfield, which was simply too small for many of the aircraft it was expected to handle; an upgrade of its main runway was needed. The main contractor would be Bell Brothers, an earthworks company based in Perth. Co-owner Alec Bell travelled to Broome, his heavy equipment following him a few days later, and there he found a ready-made work-force awaiting him. It being the wet and the luggers being laid up, there were deckhands and support workers who now had nothing but time on their hands.

Most of the workers were Koepangers or Malays. Bell scooped up 180 of them. An iron aircraft hangar and a number of small huts were constructed at the airfield in quick time, while a lot of work went into extending and, where possible, strength-ening the runway. Maintaining the runway soon proved to be a never-ending task. While it coped with the lighter domestic aircraft that had been using it for a decade, the runway surface struggled with the heavier two- and four-engined aircraft that began to arrive in the second half of February. The twin-engined DC-3 Dakotas made depressions a couple of centimetres deep every time they landed; the big American B-17s (Flying Fortresses) and B-24s (Liberators) could gouge out 20 centi-metres or more during a rough landing. When the airfield got busy, which it soon did, Bell arranged for many of the 180 labourers' meals to be brought to them as they worked as main-taining the runways had become a full-time task.

The Japanese launched a massive air raid on Darwin on 19 February causing immense damage and substantial casual-ties there. That air raid destroyed the morale of most residents of Darwin, civil and military alike, because it showed them in harsh detail just how isolated and exposed they actually were. While disastrous for Darwinites, it did galvanise both civil and military authorities into further action. Shortly after news of that raid reached Melbourne, the War Cabinet meeting there issued its Minute Number 1916, which said,

> War Cabinet confirmed the order for compulsory evacuation of women and children from Broome and approved of the proposal for the use of civil aircraft for this purpose.

The actual evacuation was organised locally at Broome. The War Cabinet Minute applied only to European women and children and some of them had already been sent south to Perth by air. In Broome, two of the senior local officials, Inspector James Cowie and Beresford Bardwell, took immediate and decisive action. Cowie's police and Harry Macnee's VDC assisted the process and on 21 February more than 120 women and children departed for the south aboard the steamship *Koolinda*. One who refused evacuation was Biddy Bardwell, who was able to convince the relevant official – her husband – that her work at the Broome telephone exchange was vital to the town's operations. As there was no-one to replace her, Beresford agreed she could stay until someone else was trained to take over.

Broome's non-Europeans were not subject to the same order. The Japanese were already gone, held (under very lenient conditions) in the Broome gaol before being sent to internment camps in the south, their lovely club shut down. The Asians who remained – the Chinese, Malays and Koepangers – were by and large ignored. Most of them were not Australian citizens and many were not even Australian residents. They had shown, however, that they could cope with just about anything the northwest could throw at them and the majority had spent much of their lives in Broome. Even if it were possible to return them to their places of origin, most of those places were now either behind Japanese lines or sat directly in the Japanese line of advance. They were left to fend for themselves.

The Aboriginal and what was officially termed 'part-Aboriginal' population were subject to a different set of rules and regulations. Leprosy had been a scourge in the Aboriginal community and, because of this, a state law prohibited the movement of local Aborigines below the twentieth parallel of latitude. Local officials and the Native Affairs Department had factored this into their planning. Between 250 and 350 Aboriginal people, mainly women and children, were transported to the Beagle Bay Aboriginal mission, run by German monks from the Pallotine order, and located some 150 kilometres to the north of Broome.

The influx from Broome more than doubled the Beagle Bay population, and the Native Affairs Department made arrangements to assist the missionaries with building materials for the construction of new dwellings and with the promise of regular deliveries of additional rations to the mission.

Not all the Aboriginal and part-Aboriginal population were relocated to Beagle Bay. Those who had ongoing work in the town were allowed to make up their own minds about whether they would stay or go while others, sometimes described as 'indigent natives', were allowed to remain in their camps at Bones Well and Fishermen's Bend, just outside the town boundaries. The Native Affairs Department indicated that it would also supply both those camps with rations on a regular basis.

All of this was undertaken according to a prepared timetable. However, it was the wet, a season when timetables could become hit-or-miss affairs. A tropical cyclone, the third of the season, had swept through the area a couple of weeks earlier, and there had been heavy rains since. When those rains came, roads were impassable. Under the new timetable, the last truck would carry just a few remaining children from Broome to Beagle Bay – orphans from the newly built orphanage – and they would be accompanied by the one other white woman who had stayed behind, Sister Catherine Hayes. Sister Hayes and her charges were to leave Broome sometime during the morning of Tuesday, 3 March.

*

Qantas, through QEA, had responded almost immediately to Japan's explosive entry into the war. Singapore was the terminus of QEA operations to the west, and the company soon abandoned all its regular commercial flights to the island. In January, with the loss of Singapore looking more likely, Batavia (Jakarta), the capital of the NEI, located on the north coast of the island of Java, became the westernmost port for QEA flights, with Bali, Kupang in Timor and Darwin remaining the regular stops on that route. Disaster struck on 30 January when one of the QEA flying boats, the *Corio,* was shot down by Japanese fighters near Kupang on its mission from Darwin to Surabaya, killing thirteen of its eighteen passengers and crew, mostly Dutch women and children evacuees.

In the wake of that loss, the civil aviation department immediately instructed Qantas to bypass Kupang, and to organise an 'effective connection' from Java to the most convenient point of entry along the Western Australian coast. Qantas sent Lewis Ambrose, its senior QEA pilot, to Batavia to liaise with the relevant NEI authorities to determine which port to use.

In Batavia, NEI civil aviation authorities told Ambrose that the pace of the Japanese advance meant that both Batavia and Surabaya would soon be within range of land-based Japanese aircraft, and recommended the use of Tjilatjap (now Cilacap) on the southern side of Java. Ambrose agreed and organised for Malcolm Millar, a senior QEA representative in Singapore, plus some ground crew to be sent there. Millar was an ideal choice for the task. An experienced Qantas and QEA administrator, it had been Millar who established the Singapore base for QEA's operations, and who had, in the years since, built up a strong network of contacts throughout the region. Within a few days, the picturesque little town, a short distance upriver from the Indian Ocean, would become one of the busiest ports in the world.

With agreement on Tjilatjap, Broome's selection as QEA's Australian reception point was a mere formality. While Millar and his small staff set up at Tjilatjap, Qantas despatched one of its best men, Captain Lester Brain, to Broome to oversee the operations there. Again, it would be hard to find a more qualified person for the role. Brain was widely regarded as the best all-round pilot in both Qantas and QEA, and he had pioneered many of their domestic and international routes. A man of medium height and build, with a bright, open face, Brain's appearance sometimes belied the fierce energy which burned within. Brain coordinated the movement of ammunition and supplies to the NEI and the evacuation of personnel from there and, specifically, from Java. His task was a relatively simple one, or so it had seemed when it was presented to him. Lester Brain was to put together anything and everything necessary to anchor the Australian end of the QEA evacuation program at Broome, its Australian point of entry. He arrived in Broome on Saturday 21 February and immediately set to work. A week later, Brain would celebrate his 40th birthday; he hoped it would be a good one.

At the other end of the air route, Millar approached the Allied evacuation centre to apprise them of QEA's progress. He was not surprised to learn that the first batch of high-value evacuees had been identified and were standing by for departure on short notice. He was surprised, though, to learn that they were all female secretaries to high-ranking Allied officers.

*

Brain's orders from Qantas headquarters in Sydney and the Civil Aviation Department in Melbourne were that Brain and his staff would cooperate with the US Army wherever possible, but Brain would retain responsibility for the QEA flying boats. It was hardly an ideal situation, but it did mean that, in one area at least, Australian interests were being looked after by Australians.

Brain's QEA operations in Broome would eventually directly involve at least fifteen people from Qantas's air traffic, engineering and marine divisions, and at least one other manager. Many of those staff arrived on QEA flying boats from their original bases in Singapore, Batavia, Bali or Kupang. A fully furnished cottage was rented as a central point for QEA staff and operations, and outfitted to accommodate up to six QEA aircrew at a time. The remainder, if any, would stay in one of the town's hotels. To coordinate the ground operations, accommodation and catering, Brain had one of QEA's senior stewards, John Oram and a purser named Baron.

Brain also turned his attention to the complexities of the flying-boat operation on Roebuck Bay. Shortly after being requisitioned by the Royal Australian Navy (RAN), the coastal lugger, the *Nicol Bay,* and its captain, Harold Mathieson, were put to good use. The Norwegian-born Mathieson and his Fremantle-built lugger had spent most of the previous decade working up and down the North West coastline acting as a lighter for a Perth company. The tidal range in that part of Australia was extreme, and little ships like the *Nicol Bay* were needed to carry and deliver freight to places larger vessels were unable, or unwilling, to travel. Working primary out of Port Hedland, Mathieson and his locally-based crews had become a fixture in that part of Australia.

The *Nicol Bay* was instrumental in creating three flying-boat moorings at Brain's direction. Heavy anchors and heavy chains held the mooring floats in place so that aircraft could land on the water, taxi to the floats and tie up to them. Passengers, luggage and cargo would then be ferried to the jetty by small craft.

That was the theory. The moorings had to be placed in deep water because of the tidal range. Brain soon discovered that, at low tide, the seaward end of the jetty stood almost ten metres above the sand and mudbanks. To get to and from the moorings then involved a climb up or down the stairs at the end of the jetty, a walk of several hundred metres to deeper water and then a boat ride to wherever the aircraft was moored.

Passengers and crew would have to carry their own luggage for the whole distance. Even if the loading and unloading took place at high tide, there were complications.

To Brain's dismay, there was a distinct shortage of suitable boats in this port town. He could locate only a couple of rowboats, one small motor dinghy with an unreliable engine and the fleet of luggers waiting to be sailed to the south. After some enquiries, he was able to find and buy a motor launch and a motorised dinghy.

The *Nicol Bay* was ideal for refuelling the QEA flying boats, and with a stripped-down lugger in tow, could carry more than enough fuel for all flying boats it needed to service. If the tides were right, it could also ferry passengers and crew to and from the jetty. Brain's final plan was to minimise delays to the shuttle service. Each high tide was to be used to the full and, where possible, the flying boats would be refuelled either immediately after their arrival or just before departure.

The entire operation was in place by the night of 22–23 February, and it worked as well as Brain had hoped it would. After the experience with the *Corio* shoot-down, radio silence was enforced between Tjilatjap and Broome, with each base simply signalling aircraft departures and arrivals. Ambrose, who was familiar with the route, flew it as often as possible. On the outward leg from Broome, the flying boats carried such things as medical supplies and aircraft spares, while inbound flights from Tjilatjap carried up to 25 passengers, mostly Allied servicemen.

Just a couple of days into the service, Brain was informed that evacuation had taken precedence over reinforcement and resupply, so the big flying boats began flying to Java carrying nothing but their aircrew. On 27 February, Ambrose flew the *Coriolanus* into Broome and informed Brain that Allied headquarters in the NEI believed that a Japanese invasion of Java was imminent.

Brain was well aware of the forebodings. His diary entry for 26 February reveals that he was aware of just how precarious the situation in Java actually was, but also noted that there were political imperatives to keep the evacuation route open. He concluded his diary entry with: 'Millar agrees we will remain there and that we shall continue on a day to day basis.'

His diary entries around that time also reflected his growing pessimism. A practical man, Brain recognised that shutting down the evacuation operation too early would leave QEA, and Australia, open to criticism from the Americans who were still operating their own evacuation flights from Bandung. It was a decision he agonised over making, noting that: 'The position of Java is apparently hopeless and it is now a case of getting as many useful people out as possible.'

In the end, the decision was taken out of his hands. The next day, Millar in Tjilatjap received a radio message saying that two flying boats, the *Corinthian* and the *Circe*, had departed from for Broome. The *Corinthian* arrived safely on 27 February but no trace of the *Circe* or the twenty passengers and crew she carried were ever found. Later that day, Millar and his staff were told that civil aviation had suspended the QEA shuttle and recalled all aircraft to the west of Broome. The *Coriolanus*, which had taken off earlier for Tjilatjap, returned to Roebuck Bay.

Millar and his staff were directed to report to US Army authorities in Jogjakarta for their evacuation to Australia.

Shortly after 11 p.m. on 1 March, Millar and his team boarded a B-17 Flying Fortress at Jogjakarta airport for Broome. There, they found Brain, suffering from dengue fever, waiting for them. They also found the rest of the town waiting for something to happen, but not knowing what it was they awaited.

*

Australia's efforts to extricate its people from Java to Broome depended very much on the individual efforts of Lester Brain, Malcolm Millar and Lewis Ambrose and their small band of air and ground crews in Tjilatjap and Broome. Fortunately, they were supported by the people of Broome – those who had not been evacuated anyway, for Australia's military and civilian leadership could offer little beyond words of encouragement and formal directives. In many ways, this was in direct contrast to the American approach, which identified impediments to the desired outcome and then simply bulldozed them out of the way – mostly figuratively, but sometimes literally. For instance, they paid more for anything they wanted than the locals could afford. It might not have made them many friends, but it was effective.

The US Army wanted their air force servicemen evacuated; most were members of various USAAF squadrons who had been rushed to the NEI from Australia to shore up Allied resolve and resistance in Java. A few remnants of US forces from the Philippines did fall back onto the NEI; several Catalinas from PatWing 10 (Patrol Wing 10) had escaped to Ambon and, when they were bombed out of there by the Japanese, fell back again to Surabaya and then to Tjilatjap. The US personnel would eventually be concentrated in and evacuated from either Jogjakarta in East Java or Bandung in the west of the island. They were flown out in big four-engined bombers, the B-17s and the B-24s, which could fly to Broome without refuelling.

The final decision to evacuate the remaining 450-plus USAAF specialist flight and ground crew in Java was made by Lieutenant Colonel Eubank, commander of all the US forces there.

On 22 February, the United States Army Air Force (USAAF) Colonel Edward Perrin flew in to Broome to coordinate the American forces' transit through Broome's airfield. Perrin believed he was in command of this part of Australia because of an anomaly in Allied command arrangements. In an earlier attempt to coordinate Allied efforts against the Japanese, ABDA (American, British, Dutch, Australian) command had been established. Under its terms of reference, ABDA command held discussions with the governments concerned and then took nominal responsibility for a large slab of the Australian mainland – the area lying northwest of a line drawn from Onslow on the Western Australian coastline to the southeast corner of the Gulf of Carpentaria. Broome and Roebuck Bay fell clearly within that area.

After surveying the facilities, Perrin sought out Lester Brain to outline what he would take responsibility for. They were broad orders he carried, said Perrin, but they could be easily summarised: he was in charge of everything, and that included the loading and movement of all aircraft into and out of Broome. Brain said simply that he would seek some direction from senior officers in government about the best way to coordinate their various operations.

Perrin then sent out an urgent request for assistants. From Java came Lieutenant John Rouse and a captain named Schwanbeck, both B-17 pilots. Schwanbeck was appointed maintenance officer and given a crew of mechanics and technicians whose role was to ensure the aircraft were refuelled, serviced and sent on their way as quickly as possible.

Schwanbeck quickly learnt that turnaround time depended on a number of factors, some of which were well beyond his control. Fuel, for instance, had to be brought to the airfield from the dispersed fuel dumps by two old, civilian-registered trucks and then hand-pumped into the empty aircraft. The trucks' European drivers and their Aboriginal assistants seemed to speak a language that only they understood, and were only able to work at a single, constant pace – slow. A lack of servicing also caused frequent breakdowns and tyre failures on the aircraft. Schwanbeck and his men faced trying times.

John Rouse felt the same. He flew in from Java on 24 February and assumed a role as rationing officer. Rouse took over the now vacant Broome school, which he set up as a mess area, with cooking facilities in the playground behind the schoolhouse. He seconded some American-enlisted men to help him and, for the first couple of days at least, relied on the assistance of a couple of local volunteers and at least one Catholic nun.

The facilities Rouse established seem to have worked quite well for the first few days, but proved inadequate when significant numbers of evacuees began to pass through the town. He had extra staff and kitchen equipment flown up to Broome from Perth. Once he could look beyond the next meal to be served, Rouse decided to bury food caches behind the town in case of a Japanese landing. He marked the location of the caches on a Caltex road map he bought from a local shopkeeper.

The first American evacuees arrived in Broome on 25 February, and the following day two B-17s arrived, each carrying twelve evacuees. These successful flights were followed by more, then more, and within a week every US serviceman on their priority list had been evacuated from Java, through Broome and on to either Perth or Melbourne. The first aircraft from those southern cities flew into Broome on 26 February.

The Americans also evacuated other Allied military personnel and, in the case of QEA at least, civilian non-combatants were among the earlier evacuees despatched to Broome. The circumstances of the evacuation could be challenging. In the big B-17s and B-24s, passengers had to cram as far forward as they could for take-off – if there was too much weight towards the rear of the aircraft, the pilot simply couldn't get the tail off the ground. Battle stations were manned after take-off and the gunners remained in their turrets until the flight was halfway to Broome and presumably safe from Japanese fighters. Most flights left Java late at night and at Jogjakarta, American ground crews would create a flight path by tossing kerosene flares onto the sides of the runway from a moving car.

While its overall success cannot be discounted, the American operation was not without its own controversies, caused primarily by a lack of communication. From the beginning of its Broome operation, the USAAF believed that Allied agreements made elsewhere gave it the imprimatur to take command of all military assets in Broome. While this may have been clear to those who made the agreements, those who were on the ground, thousands of kilometres and several weeks away, were never given the same direction. The Americans assumed everyone knew they were in charge; the Australians (and Dutch, at times) assumed that the Americans were again being arrogant and overbearing. The lack of communication was in turn needlessly complicated by a lack of demarcation and a glaring absence of clear lines of authority and reporting. ABDA command was dissolved on 25 February, and when it was, the Americans simply stepped into the vacuum and assumed authority. Unfortunately, and in the words of one of the Americans present in Broome during those critical days, 'The US Army Air Force did not particularly mix with the Navy or the Australians or the Dutch or the civilians or anyone else.'

That observation was made by Second Lieutenant John Minahan, a 27-year-old bombardier with the 7th Bomb Group who flew into Broome from Java on 27 February. Minahan was ordered to remain in Broome by Perrin to assist with the evacuation operation. A keen diarist, Minahan opened his observations of Broome with, 'Our principal purpose was to save the combat force'. Everything else – Allies, foreign countries, civilians, cooperation – was subservient to this purpose, an approach that would come to grate with many people.

On the afternoon of Sunday, 1 March, Lieutenant Colonel Richard Legg flew into Broome to relieve Perrin as the US commanding officer. Those who knew Legg, whether as an equal in rank or as a junior, seem to have shared an opinion of him, and that was not particularly positive. A short man who seemed to try to project a larger, more aggressive version of himself to others, Legg was also prone to both hyperbole and self-aggrandizement. Generally, he was a man who generated neither respect nor confidence in other people. Legg had previously been with the 17th Pursuit Squadron in Java, and may even have spent time in transit at Broome before being sent there to take charge. Legg looked around the town, spoke to some people, and decided that he didn't really like Broome and its inhabitants. Broome was a small town in a large continent which was part of even larger war. It was a long way from the nerve centres of that war, and was therefore somewhere Legg preferred not to be. Legg's feelings were reciprocated almost immediately; most of the Australians who met Legg took an instant dislike to him.

*

Purely in terms of evacuation to and through Broome, until 1 March, the most affected by what was happening in the NEI – the Dutch colonists, civil and military – had been the least involved. For 300 years, the NEI had been administered by the Dutch and protected by Dutch arms. The longevity of the Dutch occupation may have encouraged feelings of invincibility among the Dutch colonists and military forces. If so, they were in for a rude awakening; rude, but slow. The first Japanese troops to invade the NEI did so at Miri, in Borneo, on 17 December 1942. After that, more landings forced the Dutch to fall back onto Java, the NEI heartland.

Even then, there was a belief that the NEI might survive if Java could hold out long enough. Two events shattered that illusion. The first was the naval Battle of the Java Sea, which began on 27 February and lasted, with subsidiary clashes, for two days. In that battle, the Japanese destroyed what was left of the Dutch Navy's NEI fleet, and so ended any faint hope the Dutch may have held over preventing Japanese control of all the sea lanes the way they now controlled the air.

The second was the invasion of Java at two points on the island's north coast on 1 March, landings that met with little more than token resistance. With the fall of the NEI now in sight, it was every man for himself. The Dutch rush to Broome had begun.

CHAPTER 2

The Flying Dutchmen

Two Douglas airliners stood on the runway warming up their motors. With the glimmer of shaded spotlights, military officers checked over the credentials of the passengers.

Jan Van Appeldoorn, *Departure Delayed*

The NEI colonial and military administrators knew as well as anyone that retaining control of their colony was becoming increasingly problematic by mid-February 1942. One of their original war plans had been to gradually withdraw to the central island of Java, destroying anything of value on the other islands as they withdrew. They would then hold on in Java until the industrial might and military strength of the United States could be brought to bear in the southwest Pacific. It was always a forlorn hope. By 15 February, with the surrender of Singapore, NEI planners put in place strategies to evacuate essential personnel to Australia, with a view to recapturing the NEI at some future date.

The nature of the NEI, with its thousands of islands separated by wide stretches of water, had ensured that the role of aircraft, especially flying boats, would always be important there. Fortunately, the Dutch in the NEI had one of the largest and best-equipped flying boat fleets in the world. At Morokrembangan, outside Surabaya, they also had one of the largest and best-equipped flying boat bases in the world.

Japanese control of the air made possible their control of the sea, so large-scale evacuations by boat to Australia were not possible. The evacuations had to be undertaken by air and at night, when flying conditions were relatively safe. As with the other Allies, lists of essential personnel were drawn up: at the top were senior bureaucrats and military personnel who had specialised skills or knowledge that would be necessary to continue the fight against the Japanese from Australia. In reality, the early evacuation flights carried mostly the wives and families of senior bureaucrats and army officers.

The Dutch, too, would originally follow the Batavia, Bali, Timor, Darwin route, but abandon it early for direct Indies flights between Java and Australia, with Broome as their point of entry.

The air evacuation would draw upon the three arms of aerial transportation available in the NEI, two military and one civilian. The military options were the local squadrons of the Royal Dutch Indies Air Force, the KNIL, and the Naval Air Force, the MLD (Marineluchtvaartdienst). The civilian support would come from the local affiliate the Royal Dutch Netherlands East Indies Airline (KNILM). Inevitably, as the

Japanese advanced, the evacuation program became correspondingly more desperate.

*

The KNIL had possessed an impressive inventory of aircraft before the outbreak of hostilities; its three bomber and two fighter groups each had three or four squadrons, but unfortunately those squadrons were equipped with aircraft that were already obsolete. In terms of aerial evacuation to Australia, there were no frontline army aircraft left to take part in it. There was, however, one KNIL air asset that could and would be used, the Depot Squadron, a base unit that had been used by the army as a transport squadron before the war. This unit had entered the war with its main fleet comprising nineteen L-18 Lockheed Lodestar aircraft, plus a number of smaller planes. The Depot Squadron had also accumulated some experience in passenger operations. Shortly after the Japanese struck, an Allied defence cooperation conference was held in Melbourne. The NEI delegation was flown there aboard Depot Squadron Lodestars from their base at Andir Airport on the outskirts of Bandung, the provincial capital of West Java. The Lodestars flew via Bali, Timor, Darwin, Cloncurry and Sydney.

One advantage the KNIL had was the quality of its pilots. At the top of that list was Flight Lieutenant Gus Winckel, the senior instructor at their Andir base. Winckel was a tall, 29-year-old with a bright, open face, thinning blond hair and a smile that could light up a room. He had made his first evacuation flight to Broome on 25 February, squeezing 25 passengers, a mixture of civilian and military personnel, into his L-18 Lockheed Lodestar, an aircraft which usually carried around eight passengers in comfort. It was an uneventful flight but there was a surprise for Winckel when he arrived at Broome. By now, he was more than aware of the capabilities of Japanese aircraft. Even if you ignored the range of the aircraft flown off Japanese aircraft carriers, the simple fact was that Broome was now within the range of their long-range reconnaissance aircraft and perhaps within the range of other types of Japanese aircraft as well. Winckel expected the town and airfield to be well protected yet, when he looked around at Broome, he could see no sign of any air defences or fighter aircraft.

After that first trip, Winckel flew almost every night from the beginning of the evacuation. If everything went well, he would time his flights from Andir to arrive in Broome sometime around 9 a.m. There, he would unload his passengers, refuel and perhaps rest before flying back to Java. That way, most of the flying within Japanese air fighter range was done in darkness. He knew that, sooner or later, the lack of sleep would catch up with him but, until it did, he was determined to keep going for as long as possible. For his flight out of Java on the night of 2–3 March, the second last he would ever make, Winckel had Sergeant C.C. van Tuijn as his flight engineer and Sergeant W.B. Maks as his wireless operator. There was no room on board for van Tuijn's wife and son, but the sergeant assured him he had organised another flight for them.

As usual, Winckel planned to touch down, unload, refuel and then be on his way again.

*

The first Depot Squadron Lodestar evacuation flights originated at Andir, and would stop at Malang in East Java for refuelling before flying south to Broome. As the pressure to evacuate increased, that route was abandoned, and direct Andir–Broome flights commenced. To enable their aircraft to fly the distance, three Lodestars were fitted with extra 400-litre fuel tanks which allowed them to make the nearly nine-hour flight. When the tanks were successfully tested in-flight, the auxiliary tanks were also fitted to other Lodestars.

The Lodestars were also stripped back to their basics for the evacuation flights. Passengers' seats and most of the interior fittings were removed from the cabin, and the rear windows were taken out to allow for machine guns to be fired through them. Each aircraft carried two 7.7 millimetre machine guns for defence. No luggage was permitted and passengers were expected to sit on the floor of the aircraft.

At Andir, passengers had their travel documents checked by armed soldiers before they were allowed to board the aircraft. While that aircraft was being loaded, other soldiers would fill buckets with petrol-soaked cotton waste that they would then place at regular intervals along either side of the runway. When the aircraft was ready to depart, these makeshift runway lights would be lit.

On their outward flights in late February, the Lodestars always carried civil servants and/or NEI military personnel who were needed in Australia. Those evacuation flights were halted for the night of 28 February–1 March because of the Battle of the Java Sea, a battle which ended any faint hopes the Dutch may have held about successfully resisting the Japanese advance. When the flights resumed the following night, it was in accordance with the senior Dutch military officer in the NEI, Admiral Conrad Helfrich's directive to evacuate everything of value to Australia. That night and the next, the Lodestars carried primarily the wives and families of KNIL flight crew. Four Lodestars departed Andir shortly after dusk on the night of 1–2 March. As well as family members and some essential personnel, those aircraft carried gold, currency and banknotes, as well as stock and share certificates plus a large amount of foreign currency. The NEI Treasury and the major bank in the colony – the Javasche Bank – were sending out as much of their reserves as possible. By 2 March, most of those reserves had been sent to Australia. In between the four departures, Gus Winckel returned from his most recent flight to Broome, ready for yet another.

*

At the beginning of the war, the largest fleet of aircraft in the NEI belonged to the Dutch Naval Air Force and comprised both multi-engined flying boats and single-engined float-planes. The latter were not suitable for use in air evacuations. The flying boat fleet consisted of two types of aircraft. The first was the German-manufactured Dornier Do 24, a three-engined flying boat that would be used in both peacetime and war as a long-range reconnaissance and naval support aircraft. The first of these new Dorniers, numbered X-1 to X-3, were shipped directly to the NEI in 1937 and were based at the MLD's main seaplane base at Morokrembangan near Surabaya on the north coast of Java. Besides its crew of seven, the Dorniers were also designed to carry up to six passengers, albeit in fairly primitive conditions

The second aircraft type was the PBY Catalina, produced by Consolidated Aircraft in the United States. Both before and after the outbreak of hostilities, the Catalinas were used in more varied roles than the Dorniers. Known as Y-boats because all their designations had the prefix 'Y', they, too, were used for aerial reconnaissance, but also as bombers, for mine-laying, and for providing air cover for Dutch shipping. Though the Catalinas were considered to be rather slow, both they and the Dorniers were especially suited to the long-distance flights over the sea that the evacuations would entail. When the Japanese struck in December, the MLD had 73 modern flying boats, 37 Dornier Do 24s and 36 PBY Catalinas.

*

From the beginning of the war, it was almost as if the Japanese had deliberately singled out the MLD for attention. The big Dutch flying boats were in action from the moment Japanese troops waded ashore at Miri in Borneo. The action was all very one-sided though – the flying boats' relative lack of speed, manoeuvrability and armament meant that they were sitting ducks if caught in the open by Japanese fighters. The MLD lost eight craft in December, with others destroyed or damaged while moored at their bases.

Those bases had been spread across the NEI, but as the Japanese advanced from the north and west, the bases were destroyed and abandoned, their aircraft ordered to fly back to the Javanese heartland where they were dispersed among the rivers and lakes of East Java. From those hidden bases, they continued their reconnaissance and combat missions into January and February, flying to attack targets as far away as Kuching in Borneo.

It was an uphill battle. Frontline combat exposed the aircraft's limitations and vulnerabilities, and their role was increasingly confined to simple reconnaissance and air-sea rescue. At times, even these seemed to be beyond their capabilities: aircraft broke down and the crew started showing signs of exhaustion and battle fatigue.

The MLD had been methodically driven out of its forward bases, and in January it lost another five flying boats. In February, that number would rise to one a day. By the eleventh of the month, the MLD had virtually ceased all offensive operations and, when land-based Japanese aircraft moved within range of Java, it ceased daylight operations as well. Between 8 and 25 February, nine major Japanese air raids destroyed their main Morokrembangan base. The commanding officer further dispersed his people and their aircraft, knowing that both were now running out of time and space. The Japanese would not, could not, be stopped.

*

The MLD flying boats were not involved in the air evacuations until very late in the process. With the destruction of what remained of the Dutch Navy in the Battle of the Java Sea, its new commander, Admiral Conrad Helfrich, specifically directed all naval assets to escape to either Australia or Ceylon (Sri Lanka) if they could. Because of the dispersal of the MLD flying boats, they could not be injected directly into the ongoing shuttle service operating between Tjilatjap and Broome. This meant that the evacuees they carried on the nights of 1–2 and 2–3 March were overwhelmingly MLD personnel and their families, many of whom were small children because they were the closest, physically, to the dispersed aircraft. No records were kept of who actually boarded the flying boats for evacuation to Broome. The overwhelming majority were either MLD aircrew who no longer had an aircraft to fly, or the families of MLD aircrew. It seems possible that some parents gave their children to friends and asked them to take the children to Australia while the parents remained in Java.

The flying boats departed Java at night, stealthily leaving their secret hiding places in Lake Grati, Lengkong, Teloengagoeng, Mendil and the Brantas River. For many of the aircraft, Broome was at the very end of their range, given their passenger loads. Several removed some or all of their armaments to lighten the load, jettisoning anything that was not imperative to their flying in order to take on more evacuees. Of the two aircraft types, the Catalinas had a longer range but flew at a slower speed than the Dorniers, and could take up to fourteen hours to reach Broome. The Dorniers would take between eight and ten hours, but required refuelling in-flight. Except for the crew members on both vessels, there were no passenger seats; the evacuees either sat on wooden floors or propped themselves against the aircraft's walls. They would be uncomfortable, but they were on their way to safety.

Only two MLD aircraft flew out on the night of 1–2 March. One of them was the Dornier X-23, carrying a young flight sergeant named Rudi Idzerda who would act as navigator on this flight. The X-23 eventually made it to Broome via Port Hedland. Another was the Dornier X-36. In the darkness, the X-36 missed Broome and Roebuck Bay, and eventually landed on the sea near the Anna Plains Station to the south of Broome. There, it was stranded in the mud when the tide receded and was subsequently burnt by its crew to prevent it falling into the hands of the Japanese. The following night, the MLD's four remaining Catalinas and four remaining Dorniers flew out of Java towards Broome. Aboard were 80 MLD servicemen and 81 civilians.

*

With the loss of what remained of the Netherlands East Indies naval forces main military resources in the Battle of the Java Sea, it became a case of ordering those who could get out of the NEI to proceed with evacuation as quickly as they could. Those who found themselves trapped in the western reaches of the archipelago tried to make their way to either Ceylon (Sri Lanka) or India. Those in the central and eastern regions had but one possible destination, and that was Australia. Crammed aboard the flying boats and passenger aircraft, they trusted their lives to the skill of the pilots and navigators, many of whom had little or no experience with long range flights. The stories of the passenger and crew manifests, and the circumstances of the take-off and flight were all different, but the outcome for those who headed south to Australia would be the same.

Four of the MLD's Catalina Y-boats made the flight on the night of 2–3 March 1942. The pilot of the Y-59 Catalina was Lieutenant F.J. Wissel and two flight engineers were corporals Henk Weehuizen and E.G. van Spreeuw. The radio operator was the seventeen-year-old Frits van Hulssen. Wissel's co-pilot was Sergeant Bart van Emmerik; among the evacuees they carried was Emmerik's wife, Fredericka, and the couple's baby son, Bernhard.

The Y-67 Catalina carried the families of two of the Dutch Navy's most senior officers in the NEI – Admiral Karel Doorman and Captain Eugene Lacomble – respectively the fleet commander and flagship captain of the Allied fleet that had been destroyed in the Battle of the Java Sea just two days earlier. Both had died when Doorman's flagship, the *De Ruyter*, was sunk. Doorman's wife, Isabella, and their six-year-old son, Theo, were aboard the Y-67, still coming to terms with their bereavement. The Doormans had been forced to flee their home with little more than the clothes on their backs. Also aboard were Eugene Lacomble's widow and twelve-year-old son, Robert. The aircraft would be directed by Sergeant Navigator Henri Juta. Also aboard were Juta's wife, Lucie, and 32 other evacuees.

The Y-70, flown by Lieutenant Commander A.J. de Bruijn, carried 26 passengers and crew, all MLD officers or their families. Among them were Captain Pieter Hendrikse, the acting commanding officer of the MLD, travelling with his wife, Jenny; also aboard were Sergeant Major J.H. Lokman, his wife and five children, and Albert van Vliet, the flight engineer. It was the first time van Vliet had flown on the aircraft. His usual flying boat had been destroyed and he was simply told to join the Y-70 as the manifest was being drawn up. Commander de Bruijn's wife and two children were also aboard.

The Dornier flying boats had similar passenger and crew manifests and made similar flights, mostly without incident. The X-20 was flown by Wing Commander Bastiaan Sjerp, one of the MLD's senior pilots, whose wife, Alida, and small son, David, were aboard. At Miri, on the day the Japanese invaded, Sjerp had attacked and sunk a Japanese destroyer, the *Shinonome*, which blew open and disappeared after one of the X-20's bombs dropped straight down a funnel.

A contrast, in rank at least, was the X-1, flown by 25-year-old Flight Sergeant Henk Hasselo. An experienced and somewhat hard-bitten airman by this stage, Hasselo had seen and learned a lot since he joined the MLD as a teenager in the years before the war. Aboard Hasselo's aircraft was another flight sergeant, J. van Persie, whose wife, mother-in-law and brother-in-law were with them. One of the Dornier's flight engineers, Jan Piers, was also flying with his wife, Cor, and two of their sons, Cornelis and Frans. Their oldest son remained behind; he was in the NEI Army, fighting the Japanese somewhere in Java.

Among the passengers who flew in the main fuselage of the aircraft were the Koens family. Simon Koens was an aircraft maintenance engineer who had worked for the MLD at their main base at Morokrembangan. Flying with Simon were his wife, Sara, their thirteen-year-old son, Pieter, and their ten-year-old daughter, Elly. When the Japanese invaded Java the Koens abandoned their home in Surabaya and hid in a nearby sugar plantation.

The X-1 had been flying operational missions, bombing, reconnaissance and escort, primarily targeting Japanese shipping in the early days. Both aircraft and crew were beginning to feel and show the strain. They took off from a river near Mendil at 11 p.m. on what Hasselo expected to be a flight lasting at least eight hours. The weather promised to be clear and calm all the way. Hasselo took this as a positive omen because this would be his first flight to Australia, and all that he really knew about Broome was that it was an emergency stopover for QEA flying boats seeking to avoid tropical storms.

Like all the Dorniers and the Catalinas, the X-1 had been built to carry a crew of six or seven, depending on the circumstances, plus whatever armaments and equipment each specific mission dictated. The pilot's compartment was at the front of the aircraft, with the forward gun turret in front of it. Behind the pilot's compartment was the work space for the navigator and the radio operator. Behind that was the crew rest area, containing two bunks and facilities for storing and preparing food and beverages. In the fuselage behind was a single toilet and a wooden walkway that extended down the fuselage to the rear hatch and rear gun turret. Unlike many of the other aircraft, Hasselo had left the front and rear machine guns in place in case they were needed.

For most of those aboard the X-1, the flight to Australia was anything but pleasant. Not only was the aircraft crowded, noisy and difficult to fly because of the load it carried, there was only one toilet aboard for all the women and children as well as the aircrew and other MLD officers and men. The toilet soon overflowed and, mingled with the petrol fumes during the in-flight refuelling, created an almost unbearable flight environment. It was increasingly cold, and the children aboard were particularly upset by the noise and the cramped conditions. Just to rub it in, there was nothing to eat or drink beyond whatever they had brought with them, and for most, that was little beyond some fruit.

Sometime after 5 a.m., the sky to the east began to lighten. Within an hour, the sun was above the horizon and within another hour they were approaching a rugged-looking coastline with an arid hinterland – Australia. Soon afterwards, they were skimming low over a bay coloured an iridescent turquoise and then, with barely a bump, they were down. Hasselo taxied to a clear area among a dozen or more other flying boats, turned off the engines and ordered the anchor dropped.

They had arrived in Broome.

*

During that night of 2–3 March, four aircraft took off from Andir Airport at Bandung. The first was Gus Winckel's KNIL Lodestar, which departed around midnight. It was followed half an hour later by one of the KNILM DC-3s, carrying the registration number PK-ALV. Just over half an hour later, a second DC-3, PK-AFV called the *Pelikaan (Pelican)* piloted by the Russian-born Ivan Smirnoff, flew off into the dark, while the fourth, another KNIL Lodestar, left around 2 a.m. All four aircraft carried a mixture of passengers, with some evacuating aircrew squashed in.

If there had been enough light, those passengers would have looked out at a scene of devastation at Andir Airport. From the first days of the war, the Japanese had identified Andir – and Bandung – as keys to the Dutch defence plans. For several weeks now, Andir had been bombed regularly, day and night. Wrecked hangars and wrecked aircraft, some of them still burning, littered the margins of the main runway, which was itself pockmarked by hastily filled-in bomb craters. As it was, those huddled aboard the aircraft could hear the heavy crump of anti-aircraft artillery somewhere off in the distance and, every now and then, the ripping noise of machine guns firing at some real or imagined enemy in the skies. Apart from the shaded torches of the soldiers controlling the evacuation process, no lights of any kind were permitted until that final moment when, with the engines run up and straining, two lines of temporary flares would be lit and an aircraft would roar down the runway between them before disappearing into the night.

Ivan Smirnoff had not been a happy man for much of the evening. The Russian was a larger than life figure. His close friends had given Ivan the nickname 'The Turc' because of his size – over 190 cm tall, 100 kilograms and just large all over – his swarthy appearance, and his sometimes mysterious and mercurial ways. He was also an extremely talented pilot, he had been Russia's second highest scoring fighter pilot during World War I, and he had also served in the RAF. It was no accident that he met and married one of Europe's leading actresses in the post-war period; he just had that kind of character and presence. He had also survived many close encounters with death because he had developed a number of life-preserving attributes. One of those better attributes, his patience, was sorely tested the night of 2–3 March. He had been ready to depart Andir Airport for Broome shortly after dusk: his aircraft had been refuelled, crew and passengers were aboard in readiness for the long flight ahead. Instead of being the night's first departure, Smirnoff's aircraft was ordered to sit and wait on the tarmac for something – and whatever that something was, it remained a secret no-one shared with him. And so he sat and waited while first a Lodestar and then another KNILM DC-3 took off ahead of him.

Smirnoff was one of the most experienced pilots on the Bandung–Broome route; he had been one of the first to fly it. All KNILM pilots had been inducted into the Dutch Air Force reserve, liable to be transferred to military duties should the situation demand it. The Japanese invasion was just such a situation and, after being called back to active service, one of his earliest missions had been to evacuate his wife, Margot, and the wives of several other senior KNILM pilots and officials to Australia. That time, he had flown to Sydney via Broome, Alice Springs and Charleville. Since then, it had been just regular trips between Bandung and Broome. He carried passengers on every outward trip but, until recently, he had also brought war material back to Java on his return flights. On the afternoon of 24 February, for example, he had flown back from Broome with an urgently needed cargo of weapons, weapons' parts, ammunition and spare parts for aircraft. Now it was just passengers on the outward flight and get back as soon as you can.

Other things had changed as well. The bright metal surfaces of the KNILM's DC-3s had all been painted a camouflage green and most of the interior seating and fittings had been removed to save weight. Rules and regulations had also been changed to reflect the changing circumstances. On Smirnoff's early evacuation flights, the passengers were allowed to bring luggage aboard. Margot Smirnoff had even managed to take most of her husband's spare clothes and uniforms with her to Sydney. Because of the luggage being taken, Smirnoff and the other KNILM pilots had refused to carry more than seven passengers a trip. Now, however, personal luggage was banned and the DC-3s carried as many passengers as their pilots thought they could safely carry.

Smirnoff had made many of these flights now, and had the

attitude that the next might be his last. Java might fall, his aircraft might become unserviceable, he might be jumped by Japanese fighters – anything could happen. Twenty-five years of flying in peacetime and war had at least taught him that. On his flights between Bandung and Broome, Smirnoff flew with no weather forecasts and no radio compass. He also flew without engaging the automatic pilot, his experience telling him that, should he find himself in an emergency situation, his reflexes and reactions would be a lot faster than a mechanical device.

The *Pelikaan* was Smirnoff's regular aircraft. His crew were also regulars. The second pilot was 'Neef', Johan Hoffman, another experienced KNILM pilot, and their radio operator was Johan Muller, known to the others as 'Jo'. The passenger list was also typical of the last few evacuation flights Smirnoff had made – a mixture of servicemen, KNILM officials and the relatives of civilian or military aircrew.

There were five other pilots aboard the *Pelikaan*, all being flown to Australia because there were now far more pilots in the NEI than there were aircraft available for them to fly. Two of those pilots, flight sergeants Heinrich Gerrits and Dick Brinkman, were MLD aviators and were flying light because they had lost just about everything they owned when they had to abandon their base just ahead of advancing Japanese forces. Both expected to be posted to an operational squadron that was in the process of being formed in Brisbane upon their arrival.

The other three were all army pilots from the KNIL, sent to attend a flight school in Adelaide. They were flight lieutenants Daan Hendriksz and Pieter Cramerus, and Flight

Sergeant Leon Vanderburg. Cramerus was the oldest of the three and a true NEI native. He had been born in Sumatra in 1916 after his Dutch parents had moved to the NEI to seek their fortune in the rubber industry. After Cramerus' father had died there, Pieter and his mother had returned to Holland before Pieter was sent to school in Switzerland. Upon graduation, Cramerus returned to Holland to enrol in medical school.

With war looming, Cramerus left university and joined the Royal Dutch Air Force. Once he completed his training, he was posted to a KNIL squadron in the NEI, flying Glenn Martin bombers. The aircraft were no match for the Japanese fighters they came up against. Cramerus' aircraft was shot down over Java, but he survived the crash and made his way back to Bandung on foot. There he became one of a small group of pilots selected for evacuation to Australia for further flight training.

Hendriksz had just learnt that his seventeen-year-old wife, Jacqueline, was pregnant with the couple's first child. Because the three KNIL pilots were reporting for duty in Australia, the regulations were relaxed for them and they were each allowed to travel with some luggage, personal equipment, personal arms and a parachute each. Smirnoff didn't begrudge them that, although he did doubt whether anyone aboard knew how to bale out of a passenger aircraft.

There were also two KNILM officials aboard, Hendrik van Romondt and J.F.M. Blaauw. Van Romondt was a technician and 'Joop' Blaauw an apprentice mechanic, both skilled tradesmen who would be needed to help rebuild the airline when peace returned. The other two passengers were civilians,

28-year-old Maria van Tuijn and her eighteen-month-old son, Johannes. Maria's husband, Sergeant C.C. van Tuijn, was the radio operator aboard Gus Winckel's Lodestar. In the stripped back interior of the DC-3, only one seat had been left intact. Known as the 'captain's seat', it was close to the bulkhead behind the flight deck and was used by the pilots to rest. The seat was given to Maria and Johannes van Tuijn, who were strapped in tightly.

By 1 a.m., Ivan Smirnoff decided that he had waited long enough. If he was forced to delay his departure from Andir Airport much longer, he doubted whether he would be beyond Japanese fighter range by dawn. He was about to give the take-off signal to Hoffman and Muller when he caught sight of someone running across the tarmac towards the *Pelikaan*. Moments later the airport manager, a man named Wisse, burst into the cockpit, almost out of breath.

Between deep breaths, Wisse thrust a package into Smirnoff's hands. Slightly larger than a cigar box, it was tightly bound with brown paper, which was taped and covered with official seals. It was addressed to 'Commonwealth Bank, Melbourne', but there were no documents or written instructions with it.

When he regained his breath, Wisse shouted to Smirnoff to take good care of the package because it was quite valuable. He added that it would be collected by someone from an Australian bank at the other end. With that, Wisse disappeared back into the night and Smirnoff threw the package into the aluminium box below the dashboard that was used as a document storage locker. He then gave the take-off signal, received clearance from the control tower and taxied out onto the runway with its temporary flare path. A few minutes later, when the undercarriage had retracted, Smirnoff glanced down at his watch: it was 1.15 a.m., local time.

Once airborne, the *Pelikaan* circled and climbed steadily to clear the mountains around Bandung before setting course for Broome. In the main cabin of the stripped back DC-3, passengers either squatted or lay on the wooden floor, trying to snatch some sleep. Those with parachutes pushed and prodded them into shapes that approximated beds or pillows. Soon, nothing could be heard but the steady drone of the engines.

*

Early the next morning, the president of the Javasche Bank in Bandung sent a telegram to Jan van Holst Pellekan, the Dutch Trade Commissioner to Australia based in Melbourne. The telegram informed Pellekan that the package containing the diamonds had been safely despatched. The diamonds were the property of the N.V. de Concurrent jewellery store in Bandung and had originally been placed in a safety deposit box in the Javasche Bank. There were hundreds of diamonds in the package valued at around £30,000 ($30 million today). Now that he knew they were on their way, Pellekan could make arrangements to collect the diamonds when they arrived.

Three days later, Bandung fell to Japanese forces.

CHAPTER 3

Ground Zero

The atmosphere of expectancy at Broome was heightened considerably on 2 March 1942 when a Japanese reconnaissance aircraft appeared over the town at about 3 o'clock in the afternoon. The plane flew at approximately 9000 feet, made three circuits of the bay and then departed.

RAAF Official Report, August 1942

Broome, 2 March, noon–midnight

In Broome, it seemed to many people that it was just a matter of time before the whole rickety apparatus of the evacuation from Java came crashing down. Things were just too busy, there was too much to do, there were too many people and still the planes kept coming and going, coming and going. If there was something to hang on to, it was the realisation that the process was finite, that there were only so many people to be evacuated and so many aircraft in which to evacuate them. An end would come – it could even be in sight – but until it did, there would be no respite.

New people had taken over the town. The three hotels were full all day and night; it didn't seem to matter what time it was, men could be found drinking in the bars, fast asleep in the crowded bedrooms or just trying to grab some rest in the corners of the verandahs and the shade of the trees. People simply walked into empty houses – there were plenty of them – found the best bed and fell asleep. They curled up in the darkened seats of the open-air theatre, in the corners of the briefing hut at the airfield or in the control tower. At times, it must have seemed like the old days of bustling Broome, the Port of Pearls.

The American bombardier John Minahan would later recall, 'We were completely disorganised. People were coming in and being billeted and moving out, but there was no particular procedure.' Minahan was one of those responsible for organising the evacuation, charged with ensuring that it all worked, that the invisible road from Bandung and Jogjakarta to Melbourne and Perth via Broome remained open for as long as it was needed. From the outside, it looked at least as though someone knew what they were doing, that it was a smooth operation, another example of the 'can do' attitude Australians were coming to associate with Americans. The school they had taken over for a mess was preparing dozens, hundreds of meals a day, and Rationing Officer John Rouse could proudly write in his diary on 2 March, 'The mess is functioning smoothly and serving good food – the first American food we have had in several months.'

It was by and for the Americans though; the locals who had eagerly volunteered when it was opened were now gone, replaced by young American servicemen conscripted for K.P. (kitchen patrol).

To those outside the inner circle of senior American officers, there seemed to be little thought given to structuring what was happening. While the Dutch evacuation flights would follow a similar pattern of early morning arrivals from Java and early to mid-afternoon return flights, American aircraft arrived in an almost constant stream. Besides their overnight evacuation flights from Bandung and Jogjakarta, there were American shuttle flights to and from Melbourne and Perth, carrying evacuees and bringing in supplies, including the vital 100-octane petrol which the multi-engined aircraft needed, to support the American operations in Broome. Any benefits to others were more by accident than design.

As well as Rouse's successful catering operation, Perrin established and Legg maintained an American health service at the Mechanics' Institute Hall. Evacuees, and Americans based in Broome, could receive treatment from US service doctors there. A number of the evacuees who arrived were either wounded or ill, while some of the locally based staff, like many who lived in Broome, were beginning to suffer from dengue fever by the end of February. The Broome Hospital and Dr Jolly, its only doctor, do not seem to have been used at all by US authorities who preferred their own doctors and their own facilities.

To relieve some of the strain on the town's infrastructure, an air service between Broome and Port Hedland was introduced, mainly to accommodate those who could not be housed or fed in Broome. There was a general agreement that women and children, the sick and the wounded, would be given priority on the shuttle flights from Broome to the southern cities, and others would have to wait for their turn. There does not appear to have been any discrimination either on the basis of the origin of the aircraft flying the shuttles to Port Hedland, while those in real and urgent need for substantial medical assistance were flown down to Perth, irrespective of whether the aircraft that flew them was Australian, American or Dutch.

Most of the ongoing activity in Broome was now linked to the air bridges that passed through the town. Bell Brothers' labourers worked constantly to maintain the runway during what was now a round-the-clock operation. Trucks went to and from the gravel pit and the fuel dumps set up around the town, with activity reaching a crescendo on 2 March. That evening, Rouse wrote in his diary that:

> This place looks like La Guardia Field at its busiest. The entire small airdrome [sic] is covered with ships. Men are sleeping on the floors, porches or any other shelter they can find.

The figures quoted about the scale of the air evacuation are all best guesses as no meaningful records were kept, but it is likely that there were 57 aircraft arrivals and departures that day in Broome.

*

The strain was also felt on the waters of the bay. Just as the air traffic using the airfield increased significantly over the period from 27 February to 2 March, so, too, did the air traffic using Roebuck Bay. The evacuation shuttle service operated by the QEA flying boats had been joined by the arrival and departure of other flying boats. On 2 March, an American naval float-plane, American Catalinas, an RAAF flying boat and the first Dutch Dorniers and Catalinas would all arrive.

On land, refuelling aircraft was hard work, as the entire process involved the physical labour of hand-pumping the fuel. On Roebuck Bay, there were additional complications, the least of which were the fact that both aircraft and refuelling vessel bobbed up and down on the waves in an area famous for its tidal range. Harold Mathieson and his crew on the *Nicol Bay* became very adept at refuelling flying boats, and could have one of the larger craft refuelled and ready to go again in around an hour.

There were limitations, though. The one-hour refuelling cycle was dependent on it being daylight with no significant tidal activity, and with everyone and everything working according to the plan, preconditions that were not always met. The *Nicol Bay* could carry around 200 drums of fuel, each containing 44 gallons (200 litres), and its tethered lugger perhaps another hundred. This would theoretically be enough to refuel at least six flying boats in ideal conditions; with restocking the fuel supplies from the jetty, this would occupy one tidal cycle. It didn't work out that way, but at least it was a theoretical target to aim at.

Parts of the system worked very well. The little steam train that ran through the town and out to the end of the long jetty proved ideal for the refuelling operation. The driver, only ever described as a pleasant and helpful little old man, would collect the fuel drums from a dump and drive them out to the end of the jetty where they would be lowered onto the *Nicol Bay* and its lugger. After that, it became a bit problematic. Under the hastily put together agreement covering this part of the war zone, the Americans – in particular the USAAF – were responsible for the evacuation of Allied men and equipment from the NEI. For the Dutch, the evacuation of military and civilian personnel had become a case of getting out however they could with whoever they could. For Lester Brain and QEA, it was a matter of trying to work with several masters at the same time. As the American forces left in Java were ground-based USAAF units or infantry and artillery, land-based aircraft were used in their evacuation efforts. In contrast, the Dutch and QEA relied on amphibious aircraft, flying boats; this led to a bifurcation in control and command between Broome airfield and Roebuck Bay, each of which had its own 'sort' of evacuation effort. While the airfield was basically an American operation, Roebuck Bay, to begin with, was primarily a Qantas operation with some civil aviation and RAAF input. When there were just one or two flights a day, it worked. More, especially if they were not Australian aircraft involved, could be a recipe for a clash of cultures at the very least.

Human factors also had an impact on the Roebuck Bay operations in a way they didn't for the land-based aircraft. Because there was no obvious operational centre, control tower or the like associated with the flying boat operations on Roebuck Bay, there seems to have been an assumption that things would just happen, that aircraft would be refuelled and that someone would come out to ferry passengers and crew into Broome where they would be looked after. If the aircraft was a QEA flying boat, Lester Brain and his staff would certainly endeavour to do just that, but nothing permanent was put in place for aircraft that were not part of the QEA operation. Other crews were expected to make their own arrangements, but few were aware of the fact. Later, Harold Mathieson would say, 'If the pilots did not come and ask for juice, I didn't know whether they wanted any and there was no central authority ashore to advise me of their needs.' The American dominance of the evacuation process was starting to cause problems.

Human nature also played its part. Many of the passengers and crew who flew into Broome aboard the flying boats knew nothing at all about Roebuck Bay. When they saw the seabed exposed at low tide, they did not know if it was safe to walk on or if they would be stuck in the mud or even swallowed up by quicksand. If they did set out to reach that distant jetty, there was deep water to negotiate before the mud- and sandbanks, and a long walk in the hot sun. For older evacuees and those with small children, it was challenging, and many evacuees preferred to remain on the aircraft until transport could be organised for them.

By the afternoon of 2 March, the people of Broome had just about had enough. The aircrews may well have been those closest to breaking point. They would fly in, find something to eat and drink while their aircraft was being refuelled and either loaded or unloaded, then find a corner to grab some rest before flying out again. There was reportedly one pilot who had been on duty for 84 hours without a break.

As concerning was the general air of tension that pervaded

Broome. There was an understanding that Java was almost lost, as Singapore, Malaya, Ambon and Timor had been lost. When Java fell, the only thing between Broome and the closest Japanese forces would be a stretch of the Indian Ocean. The more nervous residents had already made preparations to leave at the first signs of trouble. Many of them, including some of the servicemen in town were, however, labouring under something of a misunderstanding. They were aware that the Americans had assumed responsibility for air movements into and out of the town, plus some of the catering and accommodation requirements for evacuees and aircrew.

But they also assumed the Americans had also taken over responsibility for the town's air defence.

*

The other keen diarist in Broome, Lester Brain, started his diary entry for 2 March with the statement, 'I shall not be surprised if all this activity brings on an enemy raid'.

When Brain had taken up his position just ten days earlier, the expectation had been that there would be one, perhaps two, QEA flights a day with up to a dozen Allied aircraft using either the airfield or Roebuck Bay. The volume passing through Broome was several times that figure, and Brain was convinced that the Japanese were aware of Broome's role in the evacuation of Allied forces from Java. Even if they had no direct evidence, Brain knew that the massive increase in radio traffic from Broome would not have gone unnoticed. He wondered what the Japanese made of it and what, if anything, they were going to do about it.

*

Around 3 o'clock that afternoon, Norm Keys, a civilian employee of a regional carrier MacRobertson Miller Airlines (MMA), heard aircraft engines high above him in the sky. The aircraft made quite a distinctive sound, one that was unfamiliar to him, and when he finally spotted it, he estimated that it was at a height of around 10,000 feet (3200 metres). It was a very large, four-engined flying boat, a type of aircraft he had never seen before. The flying boat was the only aircraft in the sky, and Keys wasn't sure what to make of it. At first, he thought it may have been an Allied aircraft, perhaps one of those Dutch flying boats, waiting to land, but now he was not so sure. It made three lazy circuits over Broome and Roebuck Bay before turning north and slowly disappearing in that direction.

At around the same time, two maintenance engineers from Broome's power station had wandered out to look at the flying boats sitting on Roebuck Bay from the aptly named Lookout Point. They were enjoying the weather; it was near the end of the rainy season and except for some puffy cumulus clouds over near the horizon it was clear. The boats were rocking gently on the blue waters of the bay, and all around them was a sense of peace and tranquillity, a stark contrast to the fighting going on over the seas to the north. The men's reverie was broken by the sound of an aircraft quite high above them. It flew a circular route for about three minutes then headed away to the north. Back at the powerhouse, one of the engineers later recalled, there was some talk that the craft may have been Japanese but, 'no-one bothered much – too busy with their own affairs, trying to figure out what to do next'.

Others at the airfield, aircrews and evacuees alike, had recognised the plane as soon as it had appeared, and several of them had also seen one of them at much closer range. It was a Kawanishi flying boat, an enormous long-range reconnaissance and bomber aircraft known to the Allies as a Mavis. They were a common sight during the fighting in the NEI, and one had been shot down by American fighters just two weeks earlier while shadowing an Allied convoy travelling from Darwin to Timor. Those who spotted the Mavis were uncertain about what its appearance might mean.

Shortly after the Mavis disappeared, a KNILM DC-3 flew in from the northwest and landed without ceremony. One of the passengers who disembarked was a young RAAF pilot named Herb Plenty and, when told about the recent overflight by the Mavis said he thought he knew what it meant and asked to see the airport controller. The American officer that Plenty spoke to was never identified, but whoever it was heard from the young flight lieutenant that he had experienced such reconnaissance flights in Malaya and the islands of the NEI since he first went into combat against the Japanese on the very first day of the Pacific War. The Mavis, Plenty believed, was verifying and photographing potential targets, and Broome could therefore expect a Japanese attack, probably as early as the next morning. He added that he expected it would be a low-level bombing or strafing attack.

Plenty was thanked for his concern and his information, but the officer he spoke to suggested that Broome should still be beyond the range of all Japanese land-based aircraft. Herb Plenty was never able to identify the officer with whom he spoke. The dismissive response suggests it was most likely Richard Legg, who believed he knew everything about everything!

*

Lester Brain had also seen the Mavis overhead, which strengthened his conviction that some form of enemy action was imminent. When the earlier search for the QEA flying boat *Circe* – presumed to have been shot down between Java and Broome – revealed nothing, Brain had reorganised the flying schedules so that there would never be more than one QEA flying boat in Broome at any single time.

Later that afternoon Brain learned that the coastal steamer *Koolama*, the sister ship to the *Koolinda*, had been bombed and disabled off Cape Londonderry, well to the north of Broome and about halfway between Broome and Darwin. The QEA flying boat *Camilla* was diverted to the area and picked up 25 passengers from the damaged vessel. Brain contacted the captain of the *Camilla*, a pilot named Sims, and instructed him to overnight with his passengers at Wyndham or Derby. Under no circumstances was Sims to return to Broome with the *Camilla* before 11 o'clock the next morning.

*

Later again that day, six large US aircraft flew in from Melbourne to collect evacuees. Five of them took on board a full complement of passengers, refuelled and took off again for Melbourne. The sixth was a B-24 Liberator and was the personal aircraft of General George Brett, the second-in-command of all American forces in Australia and was flown, as usual, by Captain Jack Berry. It had arrived a little later than the other aircraft and Berry opted to remain in Broome overnight and fly back to Melbourne the following day. If only Berry had known the consequences of his decision to stay.

*

Herb Plenty was right. The photographs taken by the Mavis would have shown three flying boats moored in Roebuck Bay and half a dozen or so aircraft parked alongside the main runway at the airfield. Most of those aircraft were multi-engined, long-range USAAF bombers. The overall number had increased significantly by the time the sun set that night.

The photos would have also shown thirty-year-old American Jack Lamade's little Seagull aircraft which had returned to Roebuck Bay again; for two weeks Lamade had been trying to find someone to actually direct his activities. Originally, he and his observer, Tubbs, had been ordered off their vessel, the USS *Houston*, as that cruiser prepared for battle and on at least two occasions they had almost succeeded in rejoining the *Houston*, but combinations of missed communications and enemy action had prevented the reunion. The *Houston* was sunk, along with HMAS *Perth*, in the Battle of Sunda Strait a week earlier, and Lamade, his observer and his little spotter plane had since flown south to Port Hedland, for no result, and north to Wyndham, with the same outcome. Lamade had determined to now fly to Perth via the US refuelling facility at Exmouth. He thought that just about anything would be better than waiting for the war to catch up with him at Broome.

Lamade's aircraft, at anchor in Roebuck Bay, was joined there overnight by three MLD Dorniers, the X-3, X-23 and X-28, all now in the process of seeking directions for their future movements plus fuel for wherever those movements might be.

Lieutenant Colonel Richard Legg and his staff had also rethought their earlier position. The overnight reconnaissance and the weight of opinion supporting Herb Plenty's position carried the day. By the morning, there were several other experienced pilots in Broome all saying the same thing – get out! When aircrew enquired about the possibility of a Japanese attack, they were now told that all aircraft would be despatched before 10 a.m. because that was the earliest time that Japanese land-based aircraft could arrive from their bases in the NEI. When the three Dornier pilots requested clearance to leave as soon as their aircraft had been refuelled, permission was refused and they were instructed to attend a final briefing to be held at the Continental Hotel the following morning. They therefore decided to familiarise themselves with this Continental Hotel, and walked out into the gathering gloom.

*

Penfui Airfield, Kupang, 2–3 March

While Broome waited, the Japanese readied themselves for a strike. When the Japanese forces, including paratroops, had attacked Kupang in Dutch West Timor on 19 February, they had landed behind and well away from the prepared defensive lines occupied by Australian and Dutch colonial troops. After several days of heavy fighting, the Australian and Dutch forces had surrendered and the Japanese went on to occupy all of Dutch West Timor. The object of their invasion had not been to destroy the Allied forces there, that was a bonus, but to seize what those forces had been put in place to protect – the deep water harbour at Kupang and the all-weather airfield at Penfui, just on the outskirts of Kupang. Once captured, both were repaired and quickly brought into use to support the Japanese war effort.

Within days of their capture by the Japanese, Kupang Harbour and Penfui airfield had become naval air bases for the 3rd Naval Air Squadron of the Imperial Japanese Navy (IJN). The commander of that unit was a distinguished naval aviator named Colonel Takeo Shibata, and he was soon at work. Shibata was aware that Penfui had been used as a key transit point on the route between Java and Australia, at first for reinforcing Allied forces fighting in Java, but more recently in the evacuation of key personnel to Australia. He was also aware of the significant increase in radio traffic coming from the small town of Broome – and understood that the two were probably connected.

On 2 March, he sent a Kawanishi Mavis from Kupang Bay on a reconnaissance mission to the south with specific instructions to observe and photograph all activity on and around Broome's small airfield. The Mavis made landfall around 100 kilometres to the south of Broome, but soon corrected itself and overflew Broome and Roebuck Bay at 3200 metres, making three photographic runs over the port town. It was evening when the Mavis touched down again at Kupang. Shibata was waiting to debrief the aircrew and examine the photographs taken.

After doing so, Shibata ordered an air strike for the following day. He had seen there were at least eight multi-engined aircraft at the airfield and three flying boats on the bay and he wanted them all destroyed.

In Takeo Shibata, the IJN had the ideal man for such a job. During the 1930s, he had been the chief naval test pilot, and in that capacity had been instrumental in developing the long-range capabilities of the Mitsubishi Zero. With the outbreak of the Pacific War, he had the opportunity to put some of the theories he had developed into practice. Shibata had surprised the Americans in the Philippines with some long-range Zero raids launched from Formosa (Taiwan). The raid on Broome, however, would be the longest Japanese fighter mission yet attempted in the war.

Shibata decided that this would be a purely military mission, and the town of Broome would not itself be attacked. He planned the technical details and briefed his pilots accordingly. Nine Zeros, under the command of Lieutenant Zenjiro Miyano, would carry out the raid. They would be accompanied by a 'Babs' aircraft, a two-seater reconnaissance and observation plane whose primary role would be to direct the fighters onto targets and to photograph the results of the raid.

The Zeros flying the raid were serviced overnight. To enable them to make the round trip to Broome, a 320-litre, teardrop-shaped tank was fitted to the belly of each aircraft. Weight was also a consideration in the aircraft's effective range, so the ammunition loaded aboard the planes was limited. Each Zero would carry 60 rounds of 20 mm cannon ammunition and 500 rounds of 7.7 mm machine-gun ammunition for the two machine guns, and two cannons with which each aircraft was armed. The machine-gun ammunition would also comprise incendiary bullets, specially produced cartridges containing chemicals designed to ignite the fuel Shibata believed the Allied aircraft would be carrying.

The round-trip from Penfui to Broome would cover 1600 kilometres and time over the targets would be limited, so Shibata made sure his pilots received a comprehensive and detailed briefing. He had worked hard before the war to devise navigational techniques for single fighter pilots, using only visual navigation techniques to chart courses, and these, too, would be tested. On this raid, Ashmore Reef – a large collection of reefs, sandbars and cays – would provide an excellent visual check of their position when they were halfway between Penfui and Broome.

Shibata had complete faith in the pilots flying the mission. The flight leader was Lieutenant Zenjiro Miyano, a 26-year-old who had flown combat missions in both China and the Philippines, and had secured combat victories against the Americans. His senior pilot was 28-year-old Warrant Officer Osamu Kudo, the squadron's ace pilot with seven aerial victories in combat over China and the Philippines. The pilots agreed tactics at their early-morning meeting on 3 March. Miyano and two others would fly top cover for the raid, in case of Allied fighters. The other two flights of three aircraft each would first sweep the bay and then attack the airfield in formation. They would spend ten minutes over the target and destroy every Allied aircraft there.

Shortly after 7 a.m., Miyano led his squadron into the air. They formed up over Kupang before turning south and heading out over the Indian Ocean. Two hours and twenty minutes later, Miyano spotted Broome.

*

Broome, 3 March, midnight–dawn, the night before the attack

Meanwhile, the hours after sunset had been very busy out on Roebuck Bay. The captains of the MLD Dorniers found the

Nicol Bay captain Harold Mathieson and organised for their aircraft to be refuelled. Mathieson, Charlie D'Antoine, his senior deckhand, and their crew had seen to this. Refuelling at night was a challenge but, apart from taking longer than usual, it had progressed smoothly. Lester Brain had also seen Mathieson and had arranged for the *Corinna* to be refuelled in the morning so it would be ready to depart as soon as the incoming tide brought in enough water. Mathieson chugged across to the jetty where he supervised the loading of fuel drums aboard the *Nicol Bay* and the lugger – 180 and 100 bright red drums respectively – and then sailed back to the edge of the deep-water channel and anchored there. They would all sleep aboard that night and begin refuelling again at first light and when the tides were right.

Other flying boats packed with evacuees began to arrive in the early hours of the morning. Among them were two American Catalinas from PatWing 10, both carrying their full complement of ten crew and up to 30 evacuees. One craft had been damaged during a recent operation, and was close to being scuttled before its crew and ground staff got it back in the air again. With its starboard engine loose in its frame, and with 30 evacuees and 250 kilograms of vital equipment packed on board, it took off from Tjilatjap on a ten-hour, twenty-minute flight to Broome where it made an ungainly but successful landing. After a bit of rest for those aboard and a full load of fuel, the PatWing 10 Catalinas were scheduled to continue their flight to Melbourne the following day.

Two RAF Catalinas, designated FV-N and FV-W, also flew in from Tjilatjap. Both were from No. 205 Squadron, originally based in Singapore, and had been gradually falling back ahead of the Japanese advance. Before departing Tjilatjap, they had taken on board a number of evacuees, mainly RAF technicians and aircrews with no aircraft. There was also a civilian, a single Dutch woman who had rowed a small boat out to FV-W, introduced herself as Mrs Schneider and begged to be taken with them. Upon arrival at Broome most of the Catalinas' crews opted to remain aboard their craft. The lateness of the FV-W's arrival meant that its crew and passenger Schneider remained aboard.

Not long before dawn, the four MLD Catalinas arrived in sequence, and shortly afterwards the final two Dorniers, the X-1 and the X-20, also touched down on Roebuck Bay, bringing to fifteen the total number of flying boats plus Jack Lamade's little floatplane. Daylight revealed there were several problems with this: there were only three permanent moorings for those sixteen aircraft, and two had already been taken by the big Short Empire flying boats, the QEA's *Corinna* and the RAAF's A18–10, itself a QEA Short Empire flying boat which had been requisitioned by the RAAF.

The others had to rely on their anchors to hold them, which had been problematic at the turning of the tide shortly before dawn. One of the PatWing 10 Catalinas had dragged its anchor and drifted on the tide into the *Corinna*. Fortunately there was only minor damage but the incident did illustrate what could happen if a tropical storm blew in or if more aircraft arrived before those already there had departed. At low tide, the space available to the flying boats was limited. At around 6.15 a.m. Lamade's floatplane and several of the Dorniers were actually resting on the sand and mud and would remain there until around 10 a.m., when there should be enough water below their hulls for them to manoeuvre into the deeper channels for refuelling and take-off. The flying boats were increasingly clustered into an area less than two kilometres long and one kilometre wide because so many had come in on the low tide.

By 9.15 a.m. Roebuck Bay was a hive of activity. Out on the water, Mathieson and his crew had been toiling under an increasingly vicious sun for more than two hours and had just tied up ahead of the *Corinna* and were preparing to refuel the QEA aircraft. Mathieson estimated that the tide was about halfway in, almost deep enough for some of the refuelled aircraft to take off. It would also soon be deep enough for the passengers and crew of the recently arrived Dutch boats to go ashore if they wanted to. He could see many of them sitting or lying in the sun, stretching or walking along the sponsons and mainplanes of the Dorniers and Catalinas.

There were only a couple of tenders capable of carrying more than half a dozen people, but they could perhaps use the launch the American seaplane tender, USS *Childs*, had left behind when it passed through, en route to Exmouth Gulf, a few days earlier. He noted an American aircraft on the water and assumed it would assist the others.

Sam Male, a long-term Broome resident and partner in the Streeter & Male store, was standing at the back of the store, looking across Roebuck Bay and at the crowd gathered at the end of the jetty. He guessed that there were up to 150 people there, crew and passengers from the flying boats waiting for one of the little boats to take them out to their aircraft for departure to the south. Among them were Lewis Ambrose and his 25 passengers from the *Corinna* waiting for the Qantas launch. Brain had set up an account for his crews at Male's store, and Male had come to know the pilots and their movements in and out of town quite well. Male also knew that a lot of those out on the jetty were Broome locals who had gone out there to have a look. 'Stickybeaks', Biddy Bardwell would call them, but the sight of fifteen flying boats taking off from Roebuck Bay promised to be a sight not to be missed.

Others watched from different vantage points. In one direction, and not all that far away, Rudi Idzerda, despatched with a wireless operator by the X-23's captain to both scout the area and to find out about refuelling, sat on a sand dune between the town and the long jetty, looking out at the same scene. They had just arrived after paddling and dragging a dinghy from the Dornier to the main beach just below the small town. Around 100 metres in the other direction, another long-time Broome resident, a Koepanger known as 'Old Adam', had made his way down to the foreshore between the Roebuck Hotel and a smaller jetty known as Streeter's Jetty to watch the display from there.

Some of the pilots and aircrew had spent the night ashore, and had met in the Continental Hotel bar for a last drink before they departed.

*

It had also been a busy night at the airfield. Earlier in the afternoon of the previous day, one of the American B-24s had flown out on an emergency flight to Jogjakarta. No-one really knew why it had gone – or if they did know, they were not saying – or what it would find there or when it would return. It was a special B-24, a cargo variant of the Liberator bomber and it carried neither machine guns nor self-sealing fuel tanks.

In Edson Kester and William Ragsdale, though, it did have two of the more experienced pilots in the USAAF.

There had been a bit of a scare at around 2 a.m. A large aircraft flew low over the airfield. Thinking that it was an evacuation flight, those in the control tower turned the tower's lights on and off quickly to indicate that it was safe to land. They also used a signal lamp to verify the identity of the aircraft, but were unable to read the reply flashed back. Just as the realisation that it might be a Japanese aircraft sank in so, too, did the realisation that, for a few seconds at least, someone else in Broome had been shining lights up to the aircraft as it flew overhead. Those in or near the control tower had seen a light, possibly a torch, pointed upwards and turned on and off several times. It appeared to have come from somewhere in the town, perhaps even from the jetty beyond.

Several armed two-man patrols were sent off to investigate, and returned with the news that the mysterious light was a torch shone by one of the on-duty operators at the radio station. Hearing an aircraft sweeping low overhead, he had rushed outside and shone his torch on the radio mast. It was almost 50 metres high and he wanted to prevent a pilot, possibly unfamiliar with the area, from crashing into it. Another Japanese aircraft was supposed to have flown low over the town and Roebuck Bay around 5 a.m., but this was most likely one of the Allied Catalinas coming in to land.

Normal airfield activity commenced again shortly before dawn. Just as the sky was light enough for people to see what they were doing, the KNILM DC-3 that had arrived the previous afternoon took off for Melbourne, Herb Plenty and the crew happy to be getting away from Broome. Shortly after 7 a.m.,

Edson Kester and William Ragsdale's B-24, named somewhat whimsically *Arabian Knight*, touched down and taxied to the parking area at the edge of the runway where it would be refuelled. Their flight to Jogjakarta had been wasted. They had arrived over Jogjakarta without any problems. Once there though, the prearranged safety signal of a huge bonfire was not sighted, so they simply turned around and flew back to Broome.

While Kester's *Arabian Knight* was being refuelled and checked for airworthiness, one of the American loadmasters was putting together a passenger manifest for it, one that would eventually see twenty passengers and crew board the aircraft. For the flight to Perth, the loadmaster selected several servicemen who had been badly wounded during the fighting in Java, and who were now stretcher cases requiring medical treatment in Perth. Some were in a serious condition, and so a doctor was selected to fly south with them. That doctor was a flight surgeon with the 7th Bombardment group, a 34-year-old captain named Charles Stafford. Before his evacuation from Jogjakarta, Stafford had done sterling work in the military hospital there and several of those who were to travel were already his patients. The rest of the passengers were enlisted men from the 17th Pursuit Squadron.

Kester and Ragsdale were ready to depart just after 9 a.m. They collected their charts and radio codes from the briefing room, ran their pre-flight checks and tested their engines. Then they sat just off the end of the runway waiting for clearance to take off from the control tower. They had to wait longer than they would have liked.

As they sat there, a KNILM DC-3 flew past and landed, throwing up a cloud of dust. It was painted a dull camouflage green with its white registration letters PK-ALV standing out clearly against that background. Then they had to wait some more. Eventually another dull green aircraft came in and landed just in front of them. It was smaller than the DC-3 and Kester recognised it as a military aircraft, a KNIL Lodestar. As it was slowing down and turning off the runway to park near the refuelling point, other aircraft prepared for their own departures after Kester had cleared the runway. A RAAF Hudson had run up its engines earlier, but was now idling and sitting back some 50 metres behind Kester. Further back again, another B-24 looked like it was almost ready to commence loading.

When the Lodestar cleared the runway, Kester again asked for clearance to take off. This time, it was given. He pushed the throttles forward, the engines roared and the big aircraft started to move slowly down the runway.

Meanwhile, there had been something of an argument in the Hudson behind Kester's craft. The plane had been fully fuelled and was loaded with bombs for a proposed hit-and-run raid on a Japanese-held island to the north. For the moment though, they were not going anywhere. The Hudson would be flown by a senior officer, Wing Commander Ivor James 'Claude' Lightfoot, who moments earlier had been embarrassed to find that he had left his flight maps and radio codes in the briefing hut. With some diffidence, Lightfoot asked his co-pilot, an American on exchange with the RAAF named Jim Harkin, to run across to the hut to retrieve the documents. Harkin's drawled answer could be translated and summarised as, 'Your maps, your problem.' Lightfoot unstrapped himself and exited both the flight deck and the aircraft.

Towards the other end of the runway, lieutenants John Rouse and John Minahan sat in a jeep parked alongside one of the B-17s. They were discussing how the air evacuations from Java would soon be coming to an end, and how lucky they had been to get through their Broome experience without any need for air defence.

The Lodestar that Kester had waited for was flown by Gus Winckel. Winckel noted the B-24 waiting to take off as he landed and taxied past it on his way to the refuelling point. He parked as close to that point as he thought practical, leaving his aircraft diagonal to the runway, knowing that the Americans always insisted that their aircraft be parked perpendicular to the runway, with their noses facing it. He did not intend to stay long enough to have to argue the point with them. Winckel turned off the engines, climbed out and walked the 50 metres across to the fuel dump and refuelling point. He recognised one of the men there, Jock de Castella, and asked de Castella about having his Lodestar refuelled quickly. He stopped talking mid-sentence and looked out towards the entrance to Roebuck Bay, where he spotted nine single-engined aircraft flying in an almost perfect formation.

'Jock,' he asked, 'are there any RAAF squadrons flying manoeuvres here today?'

De Castella said there were none that he was aware of, adding that if there were, he would know.

'In that case, we may be in a bit of trouble,' said Winckel. 'They are Zeros and they are coming here.'

And with that, he sprinted towards the Lodestar.

CHAPTER 4

The first strike: the attack on Roebuck Bay

> We had just gone ashore when we heard the drone of aircraft engines high up in the sky. We looked up and saw a perfect formation of nine fighters, which first went into line astern followed by a dive, one by one . . . Then all hell broke loose with a deafening din.
>
> Rudi Idzerda, *Adventures of a Flying Dutchman*

The first to spot the Zeros were those at the airfield. Some were specifically keeping an eye out for aircraft, others were those whose lives depended on constantly scanning the skies for aircraft, and still others were those whose eyesight or hearing were better than average and therefore saw or heard things well before others. When the noise of engines and the little spots in the sky were near and clear enough, it became obvious that a squadron of single-engined aircraft were flying down the coast from the north. They were flying at perhaps 5000 feet (1524 metres), in three V formations of three aircraft each, and as they flew parallel to Cable Beach and a kilometre from shore, they changed formation into a line astern pattern and dropped down to 1000 feet (300 metres).

A large sweeping turn to port brought them to the entrance to Roebuck Bay, and Zenjiro Miyano could not believe what lay ahead. Instead of the three flying boats he had been expecting to see, at least a dozen lay spread out on the water before him. Miyano immediately adjusted his plans and snapped out his orders. He would take his wingmen Sergeant Takashi and Private Zenipei Matsumoto up with him to protect the other two flights, as originally planned. Those other flights would both attack the flying boats. After one sweep, Osamu Kudo and his wingmen would break off the attack and continue across to the airfield to destroy any aircraft they found there. The second flight would then join that attack when all the flying boats had been destroyed. Miyano climbed, his wingmen following. Kudo led the others into a shallow dive, engines screaming as they did. Just before they selected their individual targets, the Zeros dropped their belly tanks, armed their weapons and concentrated on the enemy aircraft now filling their gun sights.

*

The crescendo of the engines instantly attracted attention right across Broome. In her kitchen at home, Biddy Bardwell heard the noise and at first thought it was another flying boat coming in to land, but then realised there were too many engines and they seemed to be heading right for her. Looking up and across the bay, she saw what she thought was about eight bright silver aircraft streaking across the bay at high speed. Her next thought were that they may have been escort aircraft for the flying boats already there, but as soon as she had formulated that thought, realised just how ridiculous it was. The engine noises continued, rising and falling, but now she could also hear another noise, something that she first took to be a car backfiring. Almost immediately, she saw smoke rising above the bay. The backfiring was now clearly gunfire, and as Biddy tried to understand what was happening, her house girl, a delightful young Aboriginal woman named Gladys, rushed inside and reported to her.

'War's here, missus,' she said. 'Planes with suns on wings.'

'Wait till I get my glasses,' Biddy replied, and when she had, they both went outside and ran for cover.

Broome's Mobil Oil agent, Ken Archer, was in his office in town when his Malay assistant rushed inside to tell Archer that a large formation of Allied aircraft was flying into Broome. Intrigued, in part because Mobil supplied fuel to just about everyone in town and he had not expected a large number of planes, Archer followed his assistant out into the street. He had a clear view over Roebuck Bay and could see that the aircraft were a bright silver colour with large red circles on their wings and fuselage. He knew what they were and he knew what was about to happen. He rushed back inside to warn as many people as possible.

Lester Brain was in his room at the Continental Hotel, writing one of his regular letters to Hudson Fysh, the head of Qantas, bringing him up-to-date with what was happening with the QEA flying boats. He must have been deep in thought as it seems he did not hear the aircraft engines: 'Am interrupted by the unmistakeable sound of machine guns and pop outside the hotel . . .' he recorded in his diary. Despite feeling incredibly weak from his latest bout of dengue fever, Brain ran across the road to a spot overlooking Roebuck Bay. He knew at once what was happening and what would inevitably follow.

Others scattered around the bay also had a clear view of the attack as it unfolded. The Koepanger, Old Adam, was seated at the point where the first Zeros pulled up into a climb before circling around to launch another attack. One of the Japanese planes pulled into a steep banking climb near where Old Adam sat and, as it did so, its belly tank dropped away. Old Adam believed it was a very large bomb that seemed to be coming directly at him. With no time to run and nowhere to hide, he thought his time was up. The tank crashed into the ground ten metres in front of him, the impact knocking him over. When he realised that he was still alive, Old Adam scurried back into town.

Not far away, Inspector James Duff Cowie also heard the scream of engines and the chattering of machine-gun fire. Cowie had been ill: his dengue fever was worrying him, he had a sore throat and had been having chest pains in recent weeks. His request for a transfer on health grounds had been approved, but he would remain in Broome until his replacement arrived. He had hoped that his last few weeks in the town would be quiet and uneventful, but it was not to be. In a hurry, he pulled on his uniform and walked across to one of the sandhills overlooking Roebuck Bay to see for himself what was happening.

Out at the end of the jetty, Lewis Ambrose stood with the 25 passengers he would soon be flying to Sydney aboard the QEA flying boat *Corinna*. He knew his aircraft was being refuelled and he was just waiting for the tide to come in far enough for him to shepherd his charges into a launch and out to his aircraft; the flight would be easy after all they had been through recently. When he heard the sound of approaching engines Ambrose, too, assumed it was Allied aircraft preparing to land at the airfield. He spotted the planes as soon as they flew into Roebuck Bay and recognised them for what they were. Not far from where Ambrose and his passengers stood were 50 full drums of aviation fuel. Radiating a calmness he didn't really feel, Ambrose proceeded to lead his charges down the stairs at the end of the jetty to shelter underneath. The tide had not yet come in; they barely got their feet wet.

Rudi Idzerda also had an uninterrupted view of events as they unfolded. When he first spotted the aircraft, his initial reaction was one of admiration for the precision flying he was witnessing. He watched an almost perfect formation of nine fighter aircraft flying in line astern, when one flight of three planes soared up in a climb as the others, one by one and in order, went into shallow dives. He was about to turn to his wireless operator to comment on what modern aircraft the Australians had when he realised they were in fact Japanese aircraft and he was witnessing a classic fighter ground attack. Then all hell broke loose with a deafening din.

Jack Lamade should have had the closest, if not the best, view of the attack, but he was too busy concentrating on getting his Seagull up off the water. He thought his take-off had been good – very good in fact – and almost flawless. Throttle forward, slowly picking up speed, bouncing up and down, and even a little bit sideways, but finally breaking free of the water's grip and lifting up into the sky. He knew there was a crowd on the jetty and they were all watching him. He also knew that there were other pilots in that crowd, so he thought he might make a low pass over them before turning south for Port Hedland as a farewell wave. As he swung around to line up the end of the jetty, a succession of silver shapes swept past, like barracuda. There were flashes at their gunports and Japanese markings on their wings and Lamade realised he was in real trouble.

The two RAAF pilots who had landed their flying boat, the A18–10 on Roebuck Bay the previous day, Keith Caldwell and Freddy Durham, had spent a frustrating eighteen hours trying to find timber planks for the extra drums of fuel they had placed aboard for the long range mission they were to undertake when they flew out of Broome. The drums were just sitting amidships in their aircraft, and needed to be battened down for the flight, hence the need for timber. They had begged and pleaded with all the authorities in Broome, mostly to no avail, but they had finally succeeded in their quest that morning and were heading from the town to the port, hanging onto the side of the truck carrying their precious planks as it bounced along the road. They knew the sooner they had the planks stowed aboard, the sooner they could depart and so were in a hurry to get back to the jetty and out to the A18–10. Their crew had christened it, 'Our Wonder Boat', for reasons that now escaped everyone, but it was a home of sorts and they were a family of sorts, and they just wanted to be back there now. The two pilots hung on to the truck as it drove through town to the jetty. As they got closer, Caldwell saw something in the sky out to his right. He shouted across to Freddy Durham, 'Fighters,' and then added, 'Zeros!'

The driver saw them, too, and pulled off the road near a ten-metre high bluff that overlooked the long jetty out to the right with the flying boat anchorage in Roebuck Bay spread out before them. The three men jumped down from the truck and ran to the edge of the bluff where they flattened themselves on the ground. From where he lay, Caldwell had a panoramic view of the events as they unfolded on the stretch of water below him. Ironically, the first flying boat to be attacked was his own, the A18–10.

*

The aircrew aboard the A18–10 had absolutely no idea of what was about to happen. They sat together in what they called the spar compartment, nursing the hangovers they had worked so hard on the previous evening and sipping either coffee or cocoa, and generally reflecting on the poor shape of the world. The first they knew that something was amiss was when several things happened all at once. There was a series of loud noises. One, clearly recognisable, was the sound of several aircraft engines at full throttle, a sound that seemed to be coming closer very rapidly. The second was a sound akin to someone with a huge stick running it along a corrugated iron fence. Together they were loud enough to drown out the men's grumbling.

For some reason, they assumed the aircraft were American, perhaps showing off as they were sometimes prone to do.

Jack Cummings looked out at the planes swooping down, and said out loud, 'Those bloody silly Yanks!'

Nineteen-year-old gunner/armourer Sergeant Doug Dick thought the same thing, calling out that the Americans were always looking to put on a show.

From the front of the plane, Cummings still looked at the first plane he had seen.

'I watched him. I watched him turn around and start to come back at about 1000 feet and I saw him put his nose down. I knew then it was a Jap, so I tried to hide behind a tin hat.'

Doug Dick looked through one porthole and saw a number of single-engined aircraft flying straight at them, coming in very low and very fast. Wireless operator Frank Russell also looked out and saw the nearest aircraft drop what he first thought was a large silver bomb that hit the water barely ten metres from where he watched. Others saw that a line of small holes had appeared in the fuselage and across the bulkheads. Realising that their aircraft was under attack, the men all sprang into action.

Dick saw a second aircraft diving towards them, firing as it went into a shallow dive. He jumped into the next compartment where the aircraft's weapons were kept. Among them were two World War I vintage machine guns, one a Browning and the other a Lewis, which were to be placed on special gun mounts installed alongside two of the aircraft's upper hatches. Unless the aircraft was on an operational flight, the machine guns were to be kept stowed away securely, as they were now. Just the day before, Dick had carefully cleaned the guns and he now called out to Russell to give him a hand. Mounting the guns was a two-man operation, and Dick needed someone to pass them up to him, as the gunners stood on shelves set into the wall of the fuselage. Russell hurried to give him a hand.

One of the aircraft's mechanics was Corporal Andrew Ireland and, when the rest of the crew jumped to their feet, he rushed forward to the flight deck to get the rubber dinghy that was stowed there. As he was pulling it from its stowage, another Zero swept in. After a brief burst from its machine guns, it opened fire with its cannons, the first shots blowing the left wing off the A18–10 and spilling gallons of fuel onto the water. Back towards the rear of the aircraft, both Dick and Russell felt the impact of the cannon shells, saw the wing break off, and realised two old machine guns were not going to save their aircraft now.

Abandoning their efforts to mount and fire those guns, they looked to find and launch a dinghy, a task given some urgency when Russell revealed to Dick that he had never learned to swim. When doing his housekeeping the previous day, Dick had hammered a spike into the cradle in which the dinghy sat to stop it bouncing around during take-off and landing. As he looked around for something to pry the dinghy loose with, Dick felt and heard a large explosion from the front of the aircraft. When he looked back, he saw that Russell had dived out through an open hatch and was now splashing about in the water.

Andrew Ireland had found the forward dinghy and was standing in an open hatchway, trying to force it through, when the third Zero's attack blew the wing off. He was still trying to force it through when there was a massive explosion. That explosion scorched his face and chest, and blew both he and the dinghy through the hatch and into the water. Ireland inflated the dinghy, climbed aboard and set out to find the rest of the crew. He must have been in pain, but he didn't notice it until after the adrenaline wore off many minutes later.

The other four crew members who had remained in the spar compartment took to the water when the A18–10's wing was shot off. The explosion that blew Ireland and his dinghy through the forward hatch was one of the main fuel tanks blowing up. Ireland did not have to paddle far to find the rest of the crew – Russell and Dick were all in the water and drifting away from their doomed aircraft. As he paddled towards them, the six drums of fuel that had needed support planks and had thus caused all their problems exploded with an almighty bang. The explosion split the aircraft in two, and it sank immediately. The A18–10 crew, now without an aircraft of their own, sat back in the dinghy and looked at the destruction now being wrought on others.

*

The Japanese's second target was the other Short Empire flying boat, Lewis Ambrose's QEA craft, the *Corinna.* Attached to the *Corinna* was the *Nicol Bay*, from which Harold Mathieson had seen the Zeros move into their attack formation and begin their dives towards the aircraft on the water. Refuelling had just commenced, but Mathieson didn't hesitate. He called across to C.F. Jenkins, the engineer on the *Corinna*'s wing, telling him to take cover. He chopped through the rope tethering the *Nicol Bay* to the flying boat and opened up his boat's throttle, slowly separating the two craft. Mathieson was acutely aware of his fuel load, and guessed he was barely fifteen metres from the *Corinna* when he heard machine-gun bullets and cannon shells strike home.

Engineer Jenkins was a little slower to react, but realising the danger, dropped the fuel line and dived headlong into the water. He kicked out hard, swimming to put as much distance as possible between himself and the *Corinna*. He could hear the impact of machine-gun bullets striking the water above and behind him. When he resurfaced, Jenkins turned around and saw that the *Corinna* was already well alight. He swam across and climbed up into an empty dinghy floating past.

In the meantime, senior deckhand Charlie D'Antoine was unaware of the catastrophe that was developing around him. While Mathieson and one of the deckhands facilitated the refuelling of the *Corinna,* Charlie was aboard with two other deckhands, checking that all the supplies were aboard and stowed correctly and generally giving the aircraft a look-over and a clean-up before the crew and passengers arrived. He was just finishing up his work inside the *Corinna* when the sound of screaming engines and rattle of machine guns hit. His two companions almost flew out of the hatch and into the dinghy, which they started paddling furiously away from the *Corinna.*

Charlie was one deck and some distance away from the hatch and the dinghy the others jumped into. He went up onto the flight deck and from there, he saw another flight of Zeros swooping down to attack. He had no doubt as to which aircraft they would be firing upon, and he had no doubt that if he was still there when they did, he would die. It was a time for action and not a time for panic, so Charlie calmly tried to open the escape hatch, but it was locked so he forced one of the windows open and climbed through it. He balanced himself for a second and then pushed off, diving as deep as he could and swimming away underwater. When he surfaced, the

Corinna was burning from stem to stern and there was no sign of his erstwhile companions.

From the relative safety of the space beneath the long jetty, Lewis Ambrose watched in horror as the A18–10 exploded. Within seconds, his own *Corinna* was reduced to a burning hulk. The speed of the attack amazed him. Flames and smoke were beginning to obscure the other flying boats, but he could still see, hear and feel the explosions as cannon shells and machine-gun bullets struck and exploded fuel tanks. The Zeros would dive down, fire, and then pull up for a go-around before their next attack. It was terrible to watch, thought Ambrose, and he couldn't imagine what it would be like to be in the middle of it all.

*

After the initial attack, the fate of those out on Roebuck Bay was very much a roll of the dice. As fuel tanks exploded and burning petrol spilt across the surface of the water, black smoke billowed up, obscuring some of the remaining flying boats, for a few seconds at least. Survival was a matter of whether you were one of those briefly protected by the smoke.

In the mayhem, both of the American PatWing 10 Catalinas were destroyed, but no American lives were lost as their crews were ashore.

The two RAF Catalinas of 205 Squadron were not as fortunate. One of them, FV-N, was hit early and hit hard in the attack. Six of the crew and service evacuees aboard were killed in the first sweep and the plane was set on fire. Those who survived the initial onslaught took to the water without even a dinghy to cling to. One of them was the Catalina's co-pilot, Mohan Singh.

Singh was not a swimmer, and was supported in the water by other survivors until he found a large piece of floating debris to hang on to. The others swam off to seek assistance, but Singh was never seen again. The other survivors, six or seven men, were picked up by rescuers, except for a man named Pozzi, a flight sergeant who managed to swim all the way to shore even though one of his arms had been broken by shrapnel.

Those aboard the other RAF Catalina, FV-W, fared better. They were not in the first group of aircraft attacked, and when they saw what was happening there was an immediate scramble to try to get to battle stations. Leading aircraftman Jimmy Bowden found his way to his gun turret blocked by Mrs Schneider, the Dutch woman they had taken aboard at Tjilatjap. She had been forward when the attack commenced, and Hugh Garnell, the aircraft's pilot, pushed her to the floor and protected her body with his own. A bullet killed him, and another struck Schneider, a glancing blow to the back. She recovered herself and then tried to find a way out of the aircraft. As Bowden thought about his next move, how to get around or past the shaking woman, three of his crew mates simply grabbed the woman and unceremoniously bundled her through an open hatchway and let her fall into the water.

Bowden was now able to reach the turret but as he settled into his seat bullets smashed into the hull and he was struck in the face by shrapnel. The Zeros swept overhead, and as Bowden prepared to cock the machine guns he realised his aircraft was on fire. He climbed out of his turret and went aft, towards the main hatch. Bowden couldn't swim, so he stopped to search for a life-vest or something to hang on to in the water. He could find nothing and kept searching. But not for long – like Mrs Schneider, Bowden was carried to the hatch and thrown into the water. When he resurfaced, his aircraft was a blazing wreck.

*

The Dutch Catalinas fared no better than their American and British counterparts, and their passengers and crews would fare far worse. Aboard the Y-67, six-year old Theo Doorman had not been especially impressed with his first view of Australia; the view was through one of the flying boat's portholes and consisted of water, mudflats and sand, with some scrubby land beyond. He did not particularly want to leave the aircraft to get a closer view, especially as his mother had brought along some of his favourite toys. While the others were leaving the cabin to go outside and climb around the plane, Theo was more than happy to play with his toys on the floor of the aircraft between the two blister turrets.

Henri Juta, the Y-67's sergeant navigator, was just relieved that the trip was over and he could relax. After they had landed and everything had been locked down and loaded away, he helped his wife through a hatch and up onto the main plane in the open space and fresh air. Beside them, Robert Lacomble was also stretching out in the sun. A bit further away, the fiancée of another MLD pilot, a sergeant named Van Der Plas, was enjoying the freedom from confinement.

It was Juta who looked up at the sound of engines and who spotted the aircraft going into a shallow dive as they entered Roebuck Bay.

When he saw the flashes at their gunports, Juta didn't hesitate. He stood up and shouted out a warning at the top of his voice. Those on the wing around him seemed paralysed, watching the approaching aircraft without making a move. Juta did what he then thought necessary, pushing Van Der Plas's fiancée and Lacomble off the wing and into the water and then grabbing his wife and jumping in with her. He was only underwater for a few seconds, but when he surfaced, his whole world had changed. The Y-67 had been hit hard by the attacking Zeros and was already alight, and the people who had remained inside were all trying to get out. His wife and Robert Lacomble had drifted away, while Van Der Plas's fiancée had somehow climbed up onto a spar that was attached to one of the floats.

As he watched, she screamed, 'I'm hit!' and blood poured from her face into the water below. He looked away, and saw that his wife was drifting even further away on the current. She called out to him, and he swam to her, placing an arm around her and supporting her in the water.

Inside the Catalina, Theo Doorman had been engrossed in the game he was playing with his toys when he heard a strange *clack-clack-clack* noise and something hot grazed his knee. His mother suddenly appeared and pushed him underneath a bunk, protecting him with her body. The clacking stopped as an aircraft passed over the top of the flying boat, which young Theo suddenly realised was on fire. His mother took him by the arm and pulled him forwards toward the flight deck. They passed Leonie Lacomble – Robert's mother – lying on the floor in obvious pain. Theo thought he heard Leonie tell his mother to keep going, as she couldn't swim anyway. Theo and his mother made it to the flight deck where there was an open hatch near the starboard pilot's seat. They climbed through that and dropped into the water where they were immediately separated by the powerful current.

Supporting his wife, Juta looked across at the burning Y-67. He saw Theo Doorman and his mother drop from the hatch and disappear towards the other side of the aircraft. As he looked, other aircrew and evacuees also jumped into the water as the Catalina was reduced to a burning and sinking hulk. He saw Van Der Plas swim across to his fiancée, who was drifting away with the tide, but Juta suspected that she was already dead. Another Zero swept down towards them, and Juta dragged his wife under the water until he thought it must have flown past.

When he broke the surface this time, Juta saw other sights he knew he would never forget. As he watched, a man jumped into the water from the large hatch in the fuselage, a small child in his arms. They disappeared under the water, but then popped up again. From twenty metres away, the man looked across at Juta and called out, 'Please help me, I cannot swim.' Before Juta could react, they again disappeared beneath the waves; this time, they did not reappear.

By now, the forward section of the Catalina was well alight and starting to sink. Juta saw another woman, Leonie Lacomble, appear at the rear hatch, obviously injured and struggling to get out of the doomed aircraft. It seemed to Juta that her clothes had somehow become entangled in the machine guns that were stowed nearby. Her efforts were becoming increasingly desperate and she was screaming at the top of her voice when the Catalina broke in half and the back half slid quietly beneath the water taking her with it.

Juta felt exhausted and close to giving up. He realised that his flying boots were still on, and kicked them off. For good measure, he also tore his shirt off. Still supporting his wife, he began to swim slowly and carefully towards some clear water beyond.

Not all that far away, Theo Doorman had decided to do the same thing. After he had dropped into the water and was separated from his mother, Theo had had some frightening moments. The wing of the Catalina had been on fire as the tide carried him beneath it, and he had been scared that it might fall on him. He held his breath and put his face underwater. When he looked up again, he was well past the danger. His parents had always said he was a good swimmer. He would now swim to shore. He was pretty certain that his mother would be waiting for him there.

*

The Y-59 was also packed with crew and evacuees when it arrived, and many on board had moved outside to escape the claustrophobic conditions inside the fuselage. Unlike the Y-67, no-one on the Y-59 was able to shout a warning before the bullets and cannon shells smashed into the aircraft and those both inside and out.

Albert van Tour was an MLD sergeant, a radio operator who escaped Java on the Y-59 with his wife, Sophie, and their twelve-year-old daughter, Catherina. The van Tours were inside the Catalina when the Zeros struck, and in the opening fusillade, either a bullet or a shell splinter struck Catherina. Van Tour immediately grabbed a life-jacket and helped his wife put it on before pushing her through an open hatch and into the water. Once he was sure that she was safe, he wrapped Catherina in his arms and jumped into the water himself.

Already several metres away, Sophie watched as Albert and their daughter jumped into the water. They disappeared for a second or so, and then bobbed back up to the surface. They disappeared a second time and Sophie waited for them to bob up again. They never reappeared.

Also inside the aircraft when it was attacked were its co-pilot, Sergeant Bart van Emmerik, and his wife, Fredericka, and six-month-old, Bernhard. Recognising the attack for what it was, van Emmerik used his own body to shield his wife and son. He was struck several times in the back by either shrapnel or bullets and died in his wife's arms. Fredericka herself was badly wounded in one arm, and in the panicked rush to get out of the aircraft, lost her son in the crush.

As she drifted away from the now burning aircraft, Fredericka spotted Leendert Brandenburg, the Y-59's flight mechanic, clinging to the plane's starboard anchor rope. Brandenburg was shouting for help – he was either wounded or he couldn't swim – but those shouts suddenly turned to screams as the fuel tank in the wing above him exploded and he was covered in burning petrol. Fredericka drifted further and further away from the plane, now a funeral pyre for her husband and son. Somewhere within the flames Leendert Brandenburg's wife and five-year-old son also perished.

Willie Josina Maria van Aggelen was a little girl, not yet ten years of age. She did not know what was happening around her. One minute, she was sitting quietly inside the aircraft with her parents, Johannes and Josina – he a sergeant pilot and she a loving mother – and the next moment there was screaming and shouting, pushing and shoving, and she was in the water. She looked around for her mother and father, but would never see them again. Just as she thought she might drown, another man in an MLD aircrew uniform scooped her up and laid her across his shoulders. He spoke softly to her, and Willie knew she would live.

Frits van Hulssen, the Y-59's radio operator, saw many scenes like this, and more. He would never, ever be able to shut out what he had witnessed and was on the edge of despair, floating by himself and watching people die when a small child, frightened and alone, drifted past. He grabbed her, told her everything would be all right, and trod water while he waited for the rescue he was now certain would come.

*

For those aboard the Y-70, the attack also began with little or no warning. When Lieutenant Commander A.J. de Bruijn realised what was happening, the aircraft's captain, ordered one of the crewmen to launch the plane's dinghy to evacuate passengers and crew from the Catalina. De Bruijn's order was carried out, but the crewman neglected to tether the dinghy to the plane and it drifted off on the tide. De Bruijn was a good swimmer, and he simply dived in to recover the dinghy. As he swam, the Y-70 exploded behind him from the barrage of bullets and cannon shells.

Only those outside or near exits, like crewman Albert van Vliet, the flight engineer, survived the attack. Many of the others, crowded together, died when the bullets struck home and the aircraft exploded. Among those to die were four children from the one family, the Lokmans, aged nine, six, three and one, while their parents and two other siblings survived. The bodies of Jeanette, Jan, Johannes and Hendrik Lokman were never recovered.

A middle-aged couple, Pieter and Marie Schraver, also perished, as did Anna Kuijn and her six-year-old daughter, Elizabeth.

The MLD's commander, Captain Pieter Hendrikse and his wife, Jenny, both died. He was a good swimmer, but she had never learned to swim. When their bodies were later recovered, they were locked in an embrace, as if unwilling to be apart from each other, even in death.

*

The MLD Dornier X-boats were as scattered as widely on Roebuck Bay as the Catalinas had been, and tragically it made no difference to their fate either.

When the X-1 reached Broome, Flight Sergeant Henk Hasselo was like all the other passengers and crew aboard the flying boat, relieved that the long and difficult flight was over. The passengers were disappointed that the state of the tide meant that they would probably have at least another couple of hours on the boat. All hatches and doors were opened, even the hatches on the machine-gun turrets, for fresh air to circulate through the aircraft. Passengers were allowed, even encouraged, to climb out onto the sponsons and up onto the main plane.

It was one of those passengers, a woman standing far out towards the wingtip, who first saw the approaching aircraft and pointed them out to others, commenting on just how fast the Australian planes flew. Hasselo was standing in the hatchway in the middle of the Dornier when he heard her call out, and recognised the aircraft as Japanese and their flying as presaging an attack on the X-1. They would not do so unmolested, Hasselo thought. About half the passengers and crew were still inside the Dornier and Hasselo realised that trying to fight his way through them would eat up precious time. Instead, he hauled himself up onto the top of the fuselage and ran back along it to the rear turret, where he lowered himself down into the gunner's seat. He checked the ammunition, flicked the safety catch off and cocked both guns. Then he looked up.

The Koens family – Simon, Sara, Pieter and Elly – were all outside when the Zeros attacked the X-1. Simon and Pieter were out towards one wing tip with Sara and Elly closer in towards the fuselage some distance away. Some instinct made Pieter move and, when he did, a diving Zero sprayed bullets across the wing, missing Pieter but killing a boy he had been standing next to. Simon Koens jumped off the wing and into the water, calling Pieter to follow him.

When Pieter had also jumped in, Simon called out to his wife and daughter to jump in as well. Sara leapt in immediately, but Elly took her shoes and socks off first, before she was thrown into the water by an explosion. The incoming tide immediately caused the family to drift apart but all four Koens could swim and were eventually able to reunite. To save energy, they alternated between floating and swimming across the current towards the distant shore, with one of them always watching out for patches of burning oil. At one point, Elly swam into the tentacles of a stinging jellyfish, but the family remained together, confident that if they continued to do so, they would all survive.

Jan Piers, another aircraft engineer at the MLD's Morokrembangan base, had also escaped with his family aboard the X-1. Piers had jumped into the water from a sponson at the same time as Simon Koens, but his wife and two sons had not followed. As the Koens drifted away, they could see the tragedy that was unfolding for the Piers family. Cor Piers screamed at her husband, 'I can't swim! I can't swim!' Piers was not a strong swimmer either, and made no progress as he attempted to swim against the current. Distressingly, none of the Koens were in a position to assist.

Eventually Cornelis, at fifteen years the older of the two boys, worked up the courage to jump from the strut to which he had been clinging. Just as he jumped, he was struck by a bullet. His body went straight under and did not return to the surface. Another burst of fire struck the sponson, killing Cor Piers and seven-year-old Frans instantly. Elly Koens witnessed the incident from twenty metres away and the images would stay with her for the rest of her life.

In the aircraft's rear turret, Hasselo was only vaguely aware of what was going on behind him. With his machine guns armed and aimed, he took a moment to see how the Zeros were operating before he commenced firing at them. They were easy to see, their bright silver wings and fuselage with large red circles stood out against the pale blue sky. Their attacks followed a clear pattern, with each Zero having an individual target. Their fire was concentrated on the forward sections of the flying boats, particularly the fuel tanks in the wings and sponsons. Hasselo could also see the streaks of smoke the incendiary bullets left and imagined that he could almost see the slower-moving cannon shells.

He swivelled and fired, swivelled and fired, moving the guns up and down and from side to side as the various targets flitted across his gun sights. He used up one box of ammunition, and became a target when his turret was struck by a burst of machine-gun fire. A bullet splinter hit him in the side; it was red-hot and actually cauterised the wound it had caused. The hydraulics of the turret were also affected, and Hasselo found that while he could still raise and lower the guns, he was now unable to swivel the turret. Possibly in the very same attack, the starboard sponson was destroyed and the X-1 began to sink towards that side. Hasselo realised he had done all that he realistically could. The gun turret was now inoperable and, looking back down the fuselage, he could see that parts of the aircraft were on fire while the body of the aircraft was also starting to fill with water. He climbed back out of the turret, removed his flying boots and stepped off into the water. As the current picked him up, he thought that he was pretty certain that he'd hit at least one of the Zeros. It was a thought that gave him some satisfaction, for he was a soldier and he had fulfilled his soldier's duty. He also thought it might be little recompense for what he suspected he would find in the waters around him.

*

Aboard the X-20 its captain, Bastiaan Sjerp, was determined to do everything he could to save his family, who had flown out from Java with him. In the short time before the Dornier was attacked, he told his wife Alida what they must do to survive. His wife could not swim and he knew she would struggle by herself, let alone if she was also responsible for David, the couple's sixteen-month-old son. Before the X-20 was struck, Sjerp organised a life-jacket for her and detailed one of his crew to stay with her at all times in the water. He strapped David to his own chest and lowered himself into the water as a Zero swooped down. Sjerp's plan worked; all his family would survive that day.

The Blommert family would not be as lucky: 39-year-old Sergeant Johannes Blommert was trying to organise his nine-year-old daughter, Catherina, when the X-20 was attacked. He was struck and killed by machine-gun bullets in the opening seconds of the attack and little Catherina was knocked over and pinned to the floor in the panicked rush that followed. Fortunately, one of the crewmen picked her up and threw her out as far as he could into the water. Catherina couldn't swim, but she did not have to worry. As she bobbed back up to the surface, another man grabbed her and supported her in the water. She could see that he had been wounded, but he smiled at her and told her they would be safe now.

At first the X-23 seemed to escape the attention of the Japanese. It had been anchored some distance from the main concentration of flying boats and, although the wind was very light, the smoke from some of the burning fuel had partially obscured it for a short while. The crew aboard knew that any respite would only be temporary and took the opportunity to get away from the aircraft while able to do so. Sure enough, the smoke cleared, the X-23 was spotted and in short order was reduced to a fiery hulk.

From some distance away on the beach, Rudi Idzerda watched his aircraft go up in flames. He had resigned himself to the fact that there was absolutely nothing he could do – yet – about the carnage taking place in front of him, and so he was able to watch it with a degree of detachment. He mentally noted some points for future reference. The Japanese were certainly good shots; in attack, they used a minimum of ammunition, firing in short bursts, yet appeared to have destroyed every flying boat on Roebuck Bay. He also noted that the Catalinas seemed to burn more fiercely than the Dorniers and wondered whether that could be because the Americans used more magnesium in their aluminium alloys than the Europeans.

The attack on the flying boats was over now and the Zeros were swooping and buzzing down over the airfield. Idzerda stood and indicated to the radio operator that they should go back to their dinghy and return to the flying boat moorings out in the bay. He knew there would be work for them to do there.

*

In the middle of the maelstrom, the *Nicol Bay*'s lugger drifted towards one of the burning flying boats. It had drifted since the beginning of the attack, when it was cast off from the larger boat, which allowed its crew to see the worst of the attack from close up. What they saw would never be forgotten. It was as though they had entered a new and frightening world which appeared out of nowhere on the usually peaceful waters of Roebuck Bay. It was a world of loud colours and louder noises – the red flashes at the gunports of the fighter aircraft as they swooped down and the rat-a-tat-tat of machine gun and pom-pom-pom of cannon fire. The red and yellow blasts of exploding fuel tanks in the aircraft around them, a splash of bright colour followed by a deeper, concussive boom. The plumes of smoke that suddenly appeared then drifted away on the light breeze. The splashes and the screams and yells as people jumped or were thrown or blown into the water.

Worst of all were the rising and falling screams of those in mortal peril alongside the wails of those who had lost someone or were about to die themselves. The sights that accompanied the sounds just didn't bear thinking about, although they would never be forgotten. Blackened corpses floating in the water, bodies smashed into pieces by bullet and shell and, worst of all, the vision of women and children trapped inside the burning aircraft, clawing at the windows and turrets in a vain effort to escape in the seconds before that aircraft exploded in a ball of fire.

The occupants of the *Nichol Bay* looked again, and there was nothing to see.

*

Out on Roebuck Bay, the incoming tide was flowing with increasing strength, separating crews as it did families and virtually ensuring that anyone who could not swim would struggle to survive. The fuel that had poured out of the shattered aircraft soon ignited and some parts of the bay became small lakes of fire. To Lewis Ambrose, it formed a 'blazing scum' that bobbed and moved but that couldn't cover up the fact that, while some people were dying, other people out there were trying to save as many lives as they could.

One of the rescuers was Harold Mathieson. His fear that the bright red fuel drums on the *Nicol Bay* would attract the Zeros had been unfounded. Their pilots had certainly given him a close look over. Several had flown past at masthead height, their cockpits open and their goggles pushed back on their foreheads. But they probably saw him as outside their orders, which were to destroy all aircraft they found and to leave everything else alone. Mathieson believed he could almost read the expressions on their faces. He also believed that if he'd had a rifle, he could have shot all of them. Mathieson navigated between the patches of burning fuel and rescuing anyone who survived the inferno that Roebuck Bay had become.

Those further away were better placed to observe the simplicity and ferocity of the Japanese attack, and to assess just how all-consuming and horrible the results of that attack were. The aircraft on Roebuck Bay really had been sitting ducks, and in selecting and destroying them one by one, the Zeros had left nothing to chance. They flew in hard and fast – one observer likened them to wasps. Their gunnery was concentrated and accurate, and their formation flying exemplary. On his bluff above the bay, Keith Caldwell could not admire what he saw, even if he could recognise the efficiency and proficiency of the Japanese pilots. When it was over, and every flying boat had either been sunk or was sinking, Caldwell glanced down at his watch. It was just seven minutes since the attack began.

The efficiency and discipline on display in front of Caldwell and the others on and around Roebuck Bay did not end when the last of the flying boats caught fire. Warrant Officer Kudo's section had begun its attack on the airfield, and the second section now attacked the land-based aircraft as they had attacked the flying boats. This time, though, they would not enjoy unalloyed success.

CHAPTER 5

The second strike: Broome airfield

> As the fighters turned towards us we hightailed it into the scrub.
>
> John Minahan

From the cockpit of his Seagull, Jack Lamade recognised the silver aircraft that flashed past him as Japanese Zeros and knew that, unless every saint in heaven was on his side, he may soon be up there with them. Any idea he had about a flashy fly-past over the jetty was now long gone; his whole focus was now on just surviving the encounter. He opened up the throttle and turned south, staying as low as he could, hoping that the Japanese might think he was not worth pursuing.

It was a forlorn hope. The Japanese were under orders to destroy every aircraft they found in Broome and, while Lamade's little Seagull was sometimes the butt of other pilots' jokes, it was a US Navy aircraft, a legitimate target – and it had been spotted by Warrant Officer Osamu Kudo.

After he led his section in their initial attacks on the flying boats, Kudo banked around and led them after the small American floatplane he had seen flying low over the water. The Zero's top speed was more than double that of the Seagull, and he soon caught up with Lamade. His first burst of machine-gun fire missed the floatplane, which was now weaving from side to side. A second burst also missed, but as he slowed onto the tail of the Seagull to make certain of the kill, Kudo suddenly opened the throttle and made a steep turn back towards Broome. Someone, perhaps the observer aircraft or maybe even Zenjiro Miyano, had spotted a large four-engined aircraft taking off from Broome airfield. Kudo was instructed to leave the small floatplane and return to attack the airfield before any aircraft there could escape.

Lamade could hardly believe he was still alive and seemingly safe, for the moment at least. He stayed low, kept weaving and offered a little thank you to whomever or whatever had saved him.

*

On the tarmac, Gus Winckel pleaded with Jock de Castilla to sound the air-raid alarm and to urge everyone at the airfield to take cover. Winckel thought that he might have a minute, perhaps two, before the Zeros arrived and determined to make the best possible use of that time. He ran back to his Lodestar, calling out to van Tuijn to get the passengers out, now. As they tumbled out of the aircraft's rear door, Winckel pointed to some concrete pipes twenty metres away, well back from the edge of the runway. He told his passengers to shelter there. When the Lodestar was empty, he climbed inside and removed one of the Colt machine guns from its mounting in the rear window. He dragged a box containing 400 rounds of ammunition out on to the runway. There, in knee-high grass, he fed a belt of ammunition into the machine gun, pulled back the cocking lever and rested the barrel on his forearm. Away to his right, out over the bay, a flight of Zeros had just lined themselves up with the runway.

*

Not far from where Gus Winckel had parked his Lodestar, the two American lieutenants, John Rouse and John Minahan, realised that the aircraft they were watching in formation over Roebuck Bay were actually Japanese Zeros. Their business with the flying boats finished, the Zeros were obviously targeting the airfield next. Neither man hesitated; they jumped into a nearby jeep and drove up and down the flight line, calling out to the flight and ground crews gathered at each aircraft to seek shelter because Japanese aircraft were on the way. It took no more than a minute for them to shout out their warnings, and they stopped again at the B-17 where they had started. Looking back, they could see American servicemen running towards and jumping into the slit trenches that had been dug along the edges of the runway. They could also see the first flight of Zeros making a shallow dive from over the town towards where the aircraft were parked. For a moment, the idea of manning gun turrets aboard the B-17 was raised, but then scrapped. Instead, the men ran away from the B-17 into the grass that stood almost a metre high on the verges. There were no trenches there, but if they lay flat and didn't move, no-one would know they were there.

*

Claude Lightfoot had begun the 300-metre walk back to his Hudson, its engines still ticking over, his satchel containing the all-important maps and radio codes. He had paused to watch a B-24 trundle down the runway and came to a complete halt when an American jeep drove up with the two officers in it saying that the Japs were coming. Looking up, he saw the Zeros and realised that he would never make it back to his aircraft in time. Instead, he turned and ran for the nearest slit trench.

Aboard Lightfoot's Hudson, the crew had noted Winckel's sprint to his plane, its sudden evacuation and the equally sudden appearance of unknown aircraft over Roebuck Bay. Jim Harkin proposed taking off, following the B-24 that was now gathering speed as it taxied down the runway, out over the Indian Ocean and out of harm's way. Harry Simpson, the wireless operator, vetoed the idea and, in Lightfoot's absence, ordered that the engines be shut down. The tail gunner Chuck Owens said that he was prepared to engage the incoming aircraft but would need power to be maintained to his turret to do so. Simpson was adamant the engines be shut down, and the aircraft evacuated. It happened as he ordered, and the three men ran and dived into the long grass just as the leading Zero opened fire.

At the edge of the long grass, Winckel's brain was racing, calculating rates and angles of fire, deflection allowances, speed and height of target and the rest. He understood that his Lodestar was a target and that it would soon be destroyed. His final calculations were completed just as Osamu Kudo's Zero screamed low down the length of the runway, firing at the aircraft lined up before him. Two hundred metres further back was his wingman, with a second wingman a similar distance back.

Winckel rested the barrel of the machine gun across his left forearm, holding it tight in his cupped left hand, and braced his feet against the ground. He knew that the Zeros would be flying too low, too fast and too close for him to have any chance to track them and to actually fire at a particular aircraft. Instead, he would aim and fire at a particular point, a spot he believed the attacking aircraft would fly through as they carried out a low-level strafe. He picked the spot carefully and, when he believed the first Zero was approaching, squeezed the trigger. As the first plane went past in a blur, he eased off for a second, squeezed again, paused, then fired again as the third Zero sped past. When he stopped, he had fired off almost all the ammunition in the box. Winckel had been taught that the correct way to fire a machine gun was in short bursts of half a dozen rounds. He had purposely ignored that training, instead firing three very long bursts, using up hundreds of bullets in doing so.

This profligate way of firing had two results almost immediately. The first was that the gun barrel grew very hot very quickly. Winckel's left hand and forearm were burnt badly, almost to the bone in places, although Winckel – fuelled by adrenaline – did not notice the burns until well after he had ceased firing. The second was that Winckel's plan actually produced results. The first two Zeros had flown through his field of fire and both had been hit by several bullets. For the second aircraft, the damage was superficial – a few bullets through non-essential parts of the fuselage and tail.

For Kudo, the damage was far more serious, with at least one bullet nicking a fuel line. Kudo probably did not even notice that his aircraft had been hit. As he pulled up from his strafing run along the airfield, he switched his concentration to the big B-24 that had taken off a minute or two earlier and was now struggling to gain height over the ocean.

*

In the B-24, *Arabian Knight*, Edson Kester and Bill Ragsdale were only five kilometres off the coast and 150 metres above the water when the Zeroes struck. When the all-clear to take off was given, they immediately taxied down the runway, past the KNIL Lodestar that had just landed, past the two American officers standing at the tail of a B-17 and then, off the ground and into the air, the engines straining under the load. They crossed Cable Beach and, with the pilot still straining, gradually gained height. It was then that the Japanese attacked.

Kudo and his wingmen easily caught up with the B-24, but throttled back before launching their attack. It appeared that the big bomber was unarmed, so Kudo decided on a beam attack, sweeping down from the side and aiming his machine guns at the plane's fuel tanks. After his attack, Kudo banked away and watched as his wingmen repeated what he had done.

He believed he saw fingers of flame from the bomber's fuselage and it was definitely starting to trail some smoke.

One of the 21 American servicemen aboard the B-24 was Sergeant Melvin Donoho, an armourer with the 17th Pursuit Squadron, from Covington, Oklahoma. Donoho was not wounded in the opening attack, nor was Willard Beatty, another sergeant mechanic from the same squadron. Both had been added to the flight quite late in the process of compiling the manifest. Donoho was sitting in what would have been the bomb bay after take-off, lulled by the sound of the engines, when another sound, something 'funny', intruded on his thoughts. At the same time, a series of sparks jumped from one side of the fuselage to the other. The spattering sound continued and Donoho suddenly understood that what he was seeing and hearing was an attack by an aircraft using incendiary bullets.

Somewhere forward, a fire had started and those in that part of the aircraft were beginning to move. Crouching as low as he could, Donoho climbed up onto the aircraft's central catwalk to get a better understanding of what was going on. Other passengers were using the catwalk to move towards the tail to avoid being burnt, but suddenly the overhead tank caught fire and the rear of the plane was covered in a sheet of flame.

It's all over, he thought, and Donoho lay down, waiting for the inevitable.

The *Arabian Knight* was now a mass of flames and Kester and Ragsdale, even if they were still alive, had lost all control over the craft. The B-24 dipped, then crashed into the sea perhaps ten kilometres off Cable Beach. The impact killed several of those aboard, broke the aircraft in two and threw Donoho and Beatty well clear of the wreck. The rear section of the aircraft sank from sight immediately but the front section remained afloat. As he bobbed in the water, Donoho had a clear view into that section. He saw the doctor, Charles Stafford, working frantically to free the stretcher cases who were trapped there. The next moment, the entire section disappeared beneath the waves. No-one escaped.

Floating among the debris and dead bodies, Donoho and Beatty found each other. They agreed that their only chance of survival was to stay together until they were found by the rescue craft they were certain would be sent out to search for them. At worst, they could swim for the yellow sand beach that was visible as they rose and fell with the waves.

They had survived an aircraft crash with only superficial injuries; they would survive this as well.

*

Osamu Kudo probably realised he was in trouble when he attempted a climbing turn after attacking the B-24. The fuel line nicked by Gus Winckel's bullets finally burst, and the thin plume of smoke his Zero had been trailing became a fireball that engulfed the engine and the cockpit in an instant. The Zero pulled up into a steep climb, stalled, and dropped into the sea like a stone, hitting with an enormous impact. When the water at the point of impact settled, there was no sign of either Kudo or his aircraft. In a few seconds, there was no sign of anything but the waves heading forever east.

*

Back at the airfield, the two Lockheed aircraft, Gus Winckel's Lodestar and Claude Lightfoot's Hudson, were among the first to be destroyed. With the *Arabian Knight* shot down off the coast, Kudo's two wingmen returned to attack the airfield, and were soon joined by the three Zeros that had concentrated on the flying boats in Roebuck Bay.

Lightfoot's Hudson, abandoned on the edge of the runway, was an obvious first-choice target. Its three crew had run across to the long grass to seek safety. Frustrated by their relative powerlessness in the face of the Zeros, Harkin, Owens and Simpson all drew their service revolvers and blazed away at the Zeros as they flashed past. They had no success but their actions gave them a clear view of the planes and their pilots. Flying just fifteen metres above the ground and with their cockpits open, each pilot was clearly visible. They also had a clear view of the end of their aircraft. Set on fire by the incendiary bullets, the Hudson's fuel tanks and bomb load exploded in a tremendous fireball.

The three men were not the only ones shooting at the Zeros as they sped by. From firing positions in the trenches dug near the hangar, Harry Macnee and several members of the Broome VDC also took potshots at the Japanese aircraft, their lack of obvious success in no way discouraging their determination to put on a good show in front of the Americans.

Back near the refuelling point, Winckel did not have enough ammunition to launch another assault on the Zeros and his burnt hand and arm were starting to hurt. He crouched behind a concrete pipe, watching as the Japanese planes continued their attacks.

While Winckel was attending to his wounds, a young Dutch woman holding a baby tightly to her bosom stood and walked through the grass towards the Lodestar, stopping before she reached it. Perhaps she had left something aboard the plane, or perhaps she was just disoriented, discombobulated by the gunfire and explosions all around her. Jock de Castilla, crouching in a slit trench near the fuel dump, spotted her and didn't hesitate. He leapt out of the trench and ran across to the woman, pulling her towards him as a Zero started a strafing run. He used his body to shield her, expecting to be hit any minute as the bullets struck the ground.

Then the Zero was past. They were still alive. He led the woman across to his trench and helped her and her child in before dropping down alongside them.

Behind them, Winckel's Lodestar had been struck and was starting to smoke. Although its fuel tanks were nearly empty, it suddenly exploded with such force that pieces of debris were scattered over a radius of twenty metres.

What followed was almost an exhibition of modern combat. One official report would later describe how:

> The pilots appeared to be enjoying themselves as though it were a display at a pageant. They flew where they liked and as low as they liked, even touching the bushes with their wing-tips. Hedge-hopping an aircraft and putting a burst into the next and so on.

With five aircraft involved in the attack, the job was done quickly and with the same efficiency the pilots had displayed over Roebuck Bay. In line, they would dive down to the airfield, firing short bursts at the grounded aircraft in sequence. Two passes, no more than three, and all the damage was done.

When the Zeros had finished, every Allied aircraft at Broome had been destroyed. Fifteen flying boats had been sunk on Roebuck Bay, and seven aircraft destroyed at the airfield. Two of them were B-17s and one a B-24, General Brett's plane that Jack Berry had opted to keep overnight in Broome. As well, two Lockheed Hudsons, one of them Claude Lightfoot's, had been blown up, along with Gus Winckel's Lodestar and the KNILM DC-3, PK-ALV, which had touched down shortly before the attack. Edson Kester's *Arabian Knight* had been shot down shortly after it took off, bringing to eight the total number of land-based aircraft and 23 overall in Broome.

Surprisingly, miraculously, there were no casualties at the airfield. Eighteen Americans died when Kester's aircraft was shot down, but Winckel's burns were the most serious injury suffered at the airfield. There would have been more had the Japanese pilots not been such accurate shots. On several occasions, people who were in the direct line of fire escaped injury when the bullets and shells either started or finished just before or past them. With limited ammunition, the Japanese pilots tried to make certain that every bullet, every cannon shell struck where it was supposed to strike.

Twenty minutes after they were first spotted out over the Indian Ocean, the Zeros again flew into a V formation, although not before five of them made a low-level sweep over the airfield, waggling their wings as they did so. At around 5000 feet (1524 metres), and with the Babs still above them, they formed up behind Miyuno and headed north.

*

Broome Inspector of Aborigines, Laurie O'Neill was caught up in the fury of the Japanese attack as he tried to evacuate the last of the Broome Aborigines to Beagle Bay. Still shaken by what had happened, O'Neill later wrote of his experience to the head of the Native Affairs department in Perth, describing how:

> Mr. Knight and myself were taken quite unawares in the street . . . when the planes appeared. Unfortunately we were not near an air raid shelter and had to see it out crouched under bushes between the aerodrome and the wireless station . . . we had the unpleasant experience of hearing machine gun bullets whistling around us the whole time the raid was in progress.

Despite the fury of the attack on the airfield, there were no casualties among those hiding in the long grass on either side of the perimeter fences.

*

What the Japanese left behind them resembled a series of small battlefields, on the land and in the waters of Roebuck Bay and off Cable Beach. The Americans in charge at the airfield sent jeeps off in all directions, recalling personnel from the homes, hotels and schoolhouse where they had been billeted with orders to attend urgent meetings. Some were also sent to the long jetty to see if the Americans aboard the PatWing 10 Catalinas required assistance. The BDA component of ABDA, the British, Dutch and Australians, were very much left to their own devices. Many of them, civilian and military alike, started to drift down to Roebuck Bay dreading what they might find there.

CHAPTER 6

The Last Flight of the *Pelikaan*

Smirnoff put up the greatest show of flying anybody in the world will ever see.

Pieter Cramerus

It had been a long and uneventful flight and the Australian coastline had come into sight, but Ivan Smirnoff was not yet ready to relax. They had been flying in bright sunlight for two-and-a-half hours now, and Smirnoff had seen no other craft in the sky or on the sea since departing Andir more than eight hours ago. It had been a simple flight, a case of just following a compass bearing and trusting that nothing would go wrong with the aircraft. The Australian coastline was where he expected it to be and had appeared when he had expected to see it, so his flight calculations had proved accurate too. From what he could see below, Smirnoff thought that they were probably around 100 kilometres to the north of Broome, and he told his co-pilot and radio operator, Neef Hoffman and Jo Muller, so. He also asked Hoffman to keep an eye out for the town and Muller to see if they could pick up anything on the radio. It was around 9.45 a.m. and he guessed they would be on the ground in half an hour or so.

Smirnoff estimated the *Pelikaan*'s position to be 80 kilometres north of Broome when Muller said that, after several attempts, he had managed to get through to the control tower at Broome, but he wasn't really certain what to make of what the tower had said. The radio operator at Broome usually broadcast a regular call sign to direct incoming craft, followed by confirmation and clearance to land. That morning, Muller had been unable to pick up either of these. When he had spoken to the radio operator, the only response was a curt, 'The airstrip is OK for the time being.' As the three men pondered just what this might mean, one of them spotted something on the horizon, around the spot where Smirnoff expected Broome to be. In that instant, they all recognised they were looking at black smoke, and quite a lot of it. Then Smirnoff spotted three small black shapes – aircraft – speeding towards them from that direction.

*

Zenjiro Miyano urged his men to remain vigilant as they flew away from the qualified success that Broome had been. Success, certainly, with every enemy aircraft on the water and at the airfield destroyed, but a success that was qualified by the loss of the squadron's most successful pilot, Osamu Kudo.

When another enemy aircraft was spotted flying towards Broome just minutes after they had left, Miyano forgot about what had been and concentrated on what was. Five of his Zeros had been the attacking force while he, Takashi and Matsumoto had flown top cover. Those five had already used up a lot of fuel and could not engage in further combat if they wanted to make it back to Penfui. He ordered them to fly back, directed his wingmen into their attack positions behind and to his side, then climbed up in readiness to attack.

*

Smirnoff was shocked to see Japanese Zeros operating this far south. He didn't dwell on the thought, but put the *Pelikaan* into a shallow dive as the Zeros disappeared above and behind him. If he wondered where they had gone, he did not wonder for long. Without warning, the attack came in from the port-side. Bullets smashed into the port wing, the fuselage and the cockpit.

Smirnoff half-turned and screamed into the cabin behind him, 'Down! Down everybody, on the floor. Hold on tight!'

A second attack immediately followed the first, and as the bullets and cannon shells struck the aircraft, Smirnoff reeled back as he, too, was hit. He shook off the pain, and pushed hard on the control column and the rudders at the same time.

The Japanese attack caused mayhem in the main cabin. Leon Vanderburg had been drinking coffee from a thermos when Hoffman, the second pilot, was called forward to the flight deck to look at the smoke rising in the distance. Vanderburg was waiting for Hoffman's return when machine-guns bullets rattled on the aircraft's skin, followed by

Smirnoff's shouted warning and the crash of cannon shells striking the *Pelikaan*. In an instant, the lining of the main cabin was shredded and the small window above the radio operator's desk was shattered.

Someone, probably Hoffman called out, 'Lie down, Japs,' and they all looked for whatever cover they could find.

The attacks seemed to come without any break, from all directions, but mainly from above and behind, and there was nothing anyone in the cabin could do. Vanderburg crawled forward, towards one of the reserve fuel tanks, which he knew were empty but which he hoped would offer some sort of protection. Others used parachutes, valises, anything they thought might provide some sort of cover.

Sometime early in the attack a number of those inside the *Pelikaan* were hit. Marie van Tuijn was struck by two bullets, one in the back and another in her left leg, almost severing it above the knee. Baby Johannes was also shot in the foot, possibly by one of the bullets that struck his mother. Daan Hendriksz was hit as well, and collapsed, unconscious, to the floor.

On the flight deck, the second attack also struck hard. Smirnoff was hit four times, twice in his left arm, once in the right and once in the left hip. The windscreen on that side of the plane was shattered and Smirnoff could see that the port engine had also been struck. Despite the pain and the blood loss, Smirnoff was not prepared to accept what seemed inevitable and drew upon everything he had ever learned as a pilot, in peace and in war. He threw the *Pelikaan* into a series of violent corkscrew manoeuvres, trying to time them for the exact moment when the attacking Zero would open fire. He changed speed and he changed direction on a seemingly random basis. If the Japanese thought he would make a run for Broome, he confused them by turning inland before doubling back between attacks. He did this against the sounds of increasing panic back in the main cabin.

Maria and Johannes van Tuijn were both screaming, she in mortal agony and he in pain and shock. Maria was too badly wounded to be able to do anything for little Johannes so, when there was a short period of relative calm, Vanderburg moved across to take the baby from her. As he did so, another burst of gunfire hit the plane and Vanderburg felt a hot, stinging pain in his left leg, hand and side. Behind him, he heard Pieter Cramerus cry out in pain as shrapnel hit him in the shoulder and scalp. Almost immediately, the cabin filled with acrid smoke and the engine noise changed.

When he saw flames starting to emerge from the cowling around the *Pelikaan*'s port engine, Smirnoff knew that the end was near. If the fire spread to a fuel tank, the subsequent explosion would destroy the aircraft mid-flight. If that did not occur, the fire could so weaken the aircraft's structure that the wing would simply fall off. Neither alternative was acceptable or avoidable as long as they remained in the air, so Smirnoff put the aircraft into a tight spiral as he looked for a suitable place to put the *Pelikaan* down. Spotting what appeared to be a long and relatively smooth beach, he pulled out of the spiral and roared in, close to the spot where the waves were reaching up onto the sand, putting the aircraft's belly down as close to the water's edge as possible. As the *Pelikaan* slowed, Smirnoff booted the rudder, causing the plane to slew to the left, into the water. The nose swung into the waves, which also splashed into the port engine, extinguishing the fire there. The other pilots aboard believed it to be one of the greatest displays of airmanship they could imagine.

Just as the *Pelikaan* slid to a stop, one of the Zeros dived down and fired a long burst at the stationary aircraft. The attack caused no additional injuries but prompted Smirnoff to crawl back into the smoky main cabin and call the others to him. They would all probably die if they remained in the aircraft, he told them, and he had not been able to spot any other shelter as he put the *Pelikaan* down.

He paused as another Zero flew in on a strafing run, and then continued, saying that the safest place for them would be behind the aircraft, in the shallow water, up alongside the hull. To get there, they would have to time their exits into the water and around the aircraft's tail to the few seconds between the various Zeros' attacking runs. Hendriksz and Maria and Johannes van Tuijn would have to take their chances inside the aircraft as attempting to carry them – both adults were by now unconscious – would slow the others down and leave them vulnerable during an attack.

Those who had not been wounded went first, dropping into the shallows and running around behind the *Pelikaan* before flopping down into the shallows near where the starboard wing met the fuselage. When it was the young mechanic Joop Blaauw's turn, something went horribly wrong. The timing was all out and as Blaauw dropped down into the water from the rear passenger door, an attacking Zero opened fire. Several bullets struck him in both knees and he dropped straight down, screaming in pain and unable to move. In the break between attacks that followed, one of the others jumped down, lifted

Blaauw up by the shoulders and dragged him around to the protected side of the aircraft.

The attack that wounded Blaauw was one of the last made by the Zeros. Miyano was well aware of their fuel situation and it was still a long way back to Penfui. The last Zero simply dived down, fired and then climbed up to join his companions. They formed a V, turned north and flew out of sight.

*

When he was quite certain that the Zeros were gone and would not be returning, Smirnoff resumed command and began to issue directions. Only five of those who had been aboard the *Pelikaan* had escaped without injury: the two KNIL pilots Heinrich Gerrits and Dick Brinkman, his two aircrew Hoffman and Muller, and the KNILM man, Hendrik van Romondt. As a first task, he instructed them to move the badly wounded – Hendriksz, Maria and Johannes van Tuijn and Blaauw – out of the *Pelikaan* and out of the water, and to take them up the beach and make them as comfortable as possible. He and the other lightly wounded would collect the first-aid kit, emergency rations and reserve water and meet the others on the beach.

Hendriksz could not be helped: he was obviously badly injured with little hope of recovery, and was in a deep coma, well beyond pain. Blaauw was conscious and in agony, and going into shock. One knee was completely destroyed, held together only by sinew and skin. The other was almost as bad. A bullet had smashed directly into it and, even if it could be repaired, Smirnoff doubted that Blaauw would ever walk again. He asked one of the others to make a tourniquet to control the bleeding and another to make splints for both legs from driftwood. He then took a vial of morphia from the first-aid kit and gave Blaauw a large dose. The mechanic lapsed into a deep sleep.

Maria van Tuijn was unconscious, but would groan and toss from time to time. Both her wounds also looked serious and Smirnoff doubted whether she could survive them. Little Johannes was whimpering and appeared to be going into shock. His foot wound looked quite bad and he also had an injured wrist. Smirnoff thought they could not do much more than dress the wounds and hope for the best.

The survivors then had a quick look around where they had landed. They did not know it, but they were on the shores of Carnot Bay, some 80 kilometres to the north of Broome and one of the most isolated spots in the northwest. What they saw was a long and very wide beach, typical of the beaches in the area, with several hundred metres between the peak high and low tides. On the landward side of the beach were low sandhills with a few sparse bushes scattered across them. Further inland was what seemed to be an endless plain, covered with low bushes with an occasional tree standing out. There was no sign of human habitation, and no source of fresh water.

It was obvious they would have to rely on what they had with them for survival until they were rescued. Smirnoff issued further directions. A couple of the fit men were sent back to the aircraft to collect the parachutes and blankets, plus anything else they thought would be useful in the makeshift campsite they were to establish in the sand dunes. The parachutes were fashioned to provide some shelter for the van Tuijns, Hendriksz and Blaauw.

Muller was sent with them to remove the radio and to find something they could use as an aerial. Muller's radio was undamaged. He set it up under another parachute shelter and began sending out SOS signals, giving the *Pelikaan*'s call sign. He told Smirnoff he would continue to do so until the radio's battery went dead, which he didn't believe would take too long at all.

He also told Smirnoff that the *Pelikaan* was still smouldering inside. He believed a couple of blankets and perhaps some insulation were slowly burning somewhere in the main cabin; when he had passed through there had been quite a lot of thick, acrid smoke. He added that the seawater might soon put it out though – when he left the aircraft waves were breaking over both wings, and through the open rear door. It was not yet high tide and the main cabin might be flooded when it was.

Van Romondt was the biggest and strongest of the unwounded survivors and Smirnoff called him over and asked him to return one more time to the *Pelikaan* to collect all the items that had been stowed in the aircraft's 'safe'. Smirnoff particularly wanted the *Pelikaan*'s logbook, but he asked van Romondt to also collect a bundle of official letters for Dutch and Australian authorities, and the package he had been given just before take-off, describing its dimensions and wrapping.

Van Romondt had something of a struggle to get back aboard the aircraft. The tide had come in a long way and the waves were now breaking against the side that faced the ocean. The open door was on that side, and he had to half-walk, half-swim to get around to it, and was knocked off his feet several times as he did so. Water was washing around in the rear part of the main cabin but something somewhere was still burning, as a lot of smoke remained inside the aircraft. He could not avoid breathing in some of it and soon found himself feeling nauseated. In the cockpit, he found the container Smirnoff had described – it could hardly be called a safe, he thought – retrieved its contents and quickly made his way back to the rear door.

As he lowered himself into the water, a wave struck him from an unexpected angle, knocking him over and snatching the cigar-box package out of his hands and into the water, where it disappeared to the churning thrash of white water below the door. He thought about searching for it but Smirnoff did not seem to think it was especially important, so van Romondt splashed through the water to their camp.

Smirnoff was not too concerned about the missing package – he had more pressing matters to address. While he had no doubt that a rescue party would be formed to search for them, he could not be certain how long it would take for the alarm to be raised. The cryptic message from the Broome control tower, the black smoke rising in the distance and the fact that the Zeros had been flying from Broome all suggested to him that they had been caught up in the aftermath of a Japanese raid on Broome. The results of that raid could well determine how long it would be before a search-and-rescue mission could be mounted.

Smirnoff made an inventory of what they had and then drew up a mental list of what they would need to survive the day, perhaps two, it would probably take for the rescuers to reach them.

CHAPTER 7

Roebuck Bay

When the Japs have finished there will be nothing left afloat to rescue the survivors.

Lester Brain

The agony on Roebuck Bay did not end when the Zeros flew off to attack the airfield. All their departure really meant was that there would be no more deaths from machine-gun fire and cannon shells; it did not mean that there would be no more deaths. The main threats to life and limb were the fires that still burnt across the bay and on the waters of the bay itself. Those fires would eventually burn themselves out. The 'blazing scum' drifted on tide and current and could be avoided by those who were reasonable swimmers. Unfortunately, many of those in the water were poor or non-swimmers, while some had been driven beyond reason by what they had seen and experienced in the preceding ten minutes.

The tide was strong and the tide was inexorable. It carried all before it: bodies and body parts, patches of aviation fuel both alight and inert, empty life-jackets and dinghies, and those who had somehow survived the shooting and the panic and the fires. The tide carried them deeper into Roebuck Bay, towards Dampier Creek and the mangroves that fringed the bay in so many places. It carried them towards what should have been safety – shallow water and the possibility of walking onto dry land. They were not to know that, though, because none of those who had flown into Broome in the past few hours knew anything about the tides and currents of Roebuck Bay. What they did know was that there was a long jetty out into the water and, beyond that jetty, a small town. They knew, too, that they were being carried away from both jetty and town and so they fought the tide. The lucky ones would make it by swimming at an angle to the tide and resting frequently. The others would perish.

*

Once he understood that the Zeros had no interest in attacking the *Nicol Bay*, Harold Mathieson tried to ignore what was happening in the air above him and to concentrate on what was happening on the water around him. He was short-handed as Charlie D'Antoine and two other deckhands had been aboard the *Corinna* when he severed the connections, but he had Robin Hunter, another local Aborigine and one other deckhand to help him. Mathieson concentrated on keeping his boat away from danger and Hunter concentrated on spotting bodies in the water. The dead were left in the water as there was nothing anyone could do for them now. Anyone found alive was hauled aboard. When he had rescued as many people as his craft could hold, Mathieson made for the jetty and then returned to search for more. He trusted himself to judge when there would be little chance of finding further survivors.

Mathieson was not alone in his rescue efforts on the bay. Qantas engineer Jenkins may have been alive because of Mathieson's warning, but he was not yet ready to leave the bay. Swimming strongly, he managed to reach a dinghy that he believed had been cut loose from the *Nicol Bay*'s refuelling lugger. It had oars and Jenkins could row, so he moved backwards and forwards between the remains of the flying boats and across the tide rescuing people. Whenever he came across someone in the water, Jenkins stopped to help them into the dinghy. Some were wounded, but others unharmed and these people he asked to help him by either rowing or seeing to those who were hurt. When he thought the dinghy was at capacity, he started the long row to the jetty.

The RAAF crew of the A18–10 also stayed on the water. Andrew Ireland was by himself in his five-man dinghy. He pulled four Dutch aircrew and a wounded Dutch woman aboard before turning and paddling for shore.

The rest of the crew were also in an inflatable rubber dinghy and they, too, rescued as many people as they could before returning to the jetty. Fearing that the Japanese aircraft would attack the bright yellow dinghy, the men had slipped over the side whenever a Zero had dived in their direction. But the Zeros were gone now and when they spotted a small group struggling to stay afloat in the current they paddled straight over to them. It was a mixed group of Dutch passengers from one of the Dorniers that had been destroyed and consisted mainly of women and children. The airmen lifted and pulled them aboard the dinghy. When there was no more room inside, a number of airmen volunteered to go into the water and hang onto the lifelines; Frank Russell and Jack Cummings were the first to volunteer.

Once in the water, the young men's thoughts turned, predictably, to sharks and the stories they had heard about the man-eaters of Roebuck Bay. They agreed that such giant sharks would have detected the presence of blood in the water – at the moment, there was certainly no shortage of that. No sharks appeared, but it soon became clear that having fifteen men, women and children in and attached to a five-man dinghy was an issue also. Many of those clinging to the dinghy's lifelines were in an obvious state of deep shock, and others were wounded. If things remained as they were, there was a chance that none of them would survive. The dinghy was dead in the water, almost impossible to move, and certainly incapable of being propelled towards the jetty. Russell and Cummings felt that they were holding it back. They spotted the *Nicol Bay* quite close by and saw that it, too, was plucking survivors out of the water. They decided to swim across to see if they could be of any assistance there.

Once aboard Mathieson's ketch, the young airmen did all they could to assist the skipper and his crew. It was a confronting experience. They pulled a young Dutch woman out of the water and assisted her across the deck to a place of shelter. Russell heard her retching and turned to see her convulsing and vomiting large amounts of seawater. She was clutching something very tightly to herself, and Russell assumed it was an old and favourite rag doll. Peering more closely, he realised it was actually the tiny lifeless body of a baby. Together, Russell and Cummings convinced the young woman to release the baby. They found it had a single bullet wound to the chest.

The women and the children that they hauled aboard had the greatest impact on the young Australian airmen. Russell would later write that:

> . . . some of the wounded, many of them kids, whom we picked up were in a terrible condition. I shall always recall one girl of around my own age, with half the flesh ripped off an arm and a bullet in a kidney, who swam to us. She sat in the boat and was obviously in a bad way, but somehow managed to smile.

When he felt they could not fit any more on board, Mathieson again took the *Nicol Bay* across to the jetty – there was enough water in the bay for that now – and organised for those on the jetty to assist in unloading the dead and wounded, as well as the emotionally shattered survivors.

*

In the relatively short time it took to motor across to the jetty, some of the more seriously wounded aboard the *Nicol Bay* passed away. They, too, were carried up the wooden steps to the end of the jetty where quite a crowd had gathered. As the injured were being offered assistance and the bodies of the dead laid out, Mathieson climbed to the top of the stairs and called out to the crowd. He was going back out onto the bay, he said, as he thought there were more survivors out there. He asked for volunteers to assist him.

At first, Mathieson's plea was met with a stony silence. Then a man dressed in an RAF uniform came forward through the crowd and turned around to face them. He spoke loudly, saying that he was a veteran of the war and that people should not be congregating on the jetty. He had considerable experience in situations like this, he continued, and that experience told him that a bombing raid would certainly follow the attack made by the fighters.

Turning now to Mathieson – who had watched the performance in amazement – the English officer said that he should not go out again. To do so would be to court disaster. The grumbling in the crowd told Mathieson that the situation could turn ugly very quickly, so he simply stepped forward to show that he, and not the Englishman, was the responsible officer present, and again called for volunteers. That seemed to defuse things, so he simply stepped forward to show that he, and not the Englishman was the responsible officer present, and again called for volunteers. and three men stepped forward to offer assistance. One of them was the injured Andrew Ireland of the A18–10, and he had just delivered his own dinghy-full of survivors to safety.

As the Englishman melted back into the crowd, Mathieson led his new volunteers down the stairs and across to his boat to resume his search for survivors. No Japanese bombers were sighted that day.

*

Soon after the *Nicol Bay* headed back out to look for more survivors, the A18–10's packed rubber dinghy reached the jetty where it was met by a small crowd that included Keith Caldwell and Freddy Durham, who had made their way down to the jetty from their vantage point on the bluff above Roebuck Bay. While both were very relieved to find that their crew had survived relatively unscathed, the two pilots had also seen the full extent of the calamity and wanted to assist those who were still out there in the water, fighting for their lives. The rubber dinghy was too small, but they had spotted a wooden rowboat. They made their way across to it, dragged it to the edge of a deep-water channel, jumped in and started rowing. Ahead of them were drifting palls of smoke and they could occasionally hear yells and screams in the distance.

The same imperative that drove Keith Caldwell and Freddy Durham also drove Lester Brain. When he was certain that the Zeros had departed, Brain staggered from the Continental Hotel and down and across the beach and onto the sand and mud of the seabed. A large, clinker-built rowboat was sitting there and he knew that if he could get it into the deeper water, he would be able to do something, anything, to help those whose lives were in peril. Dengue fever had weakened him considerably though, and the rowboat barely moved as he pushed as hard as he could. Help arrived in the form of senior QEA representative Malcolm Millar, who had seen Brain make his way to the boat and understood what he was trying to do.

Together, they pushed the boat to one of the deep water leads and then rowed out to what remained of the flying-boat anchorage. They were closer to the heart of that anchorage than those who started out from the jetty, and, as Brain later wrote in his diary:

> After getting about half a mile out we could see heads bobbing in the water and hear shouts for help. On coming up we found seven Dutchmen, two of them supporting a young Dutch woman who was in a state of collapse.

The woman was exhausted and deeply distressed but was unable or unwilling to talk. Nearby, another Dutch serviceman was cradling the young woman's baby as he trod water. As they were helping this little group into the boat, another Dutch aviator drifted by, lying on his back and with a young boy strapped to his chest. Bastiaan and David Sjerp had survived.

Given the woman's condition, Brain decided to return to the beach to drop off those they had rescued before going out again to search for more survivors. As they turned the boat towards shore, another group drifted towards them. Among them was an eight-year-old boy who insisted on swimming and supporting himself. By now, there was only enough room in the rowboat for the Dutch woman and her baby, the Sjerps and three of the more exhausted swimmers. The rest had to hang on as well as they could as Brain and Millar rowed back to shallow water. They were tired because of illness, and sick at heart because of what they had already seen, but there was still work to do and neither Malcolm Millar nor Lester Brain would give up before the job was done. Then the boat was turned around and the two men rowed out again.

Others also set out on rescue missions on their own initiative. Maurie Carseldine was the coxswain of a motor launch owned by the Shell Oil Company. With another Shell employee named Munro, he tied a dinghy to the launch and set out to ferry those he rescued across to the *Nicol Bay*. Another launch put to good use was the one left behind by the USS *Childs* a week earlier. It was intended for the US forces but its coxswain took it straight out to rescue survivors in the water.

Rudi Idzerda had watched it all happen from the beach, amazed at the efficiency of the Japanese attack and shocked by what he could see left behind in its wake. He knew the aircrews were comprised of young and fit men; soldiers who, if they weren't injured, would be able to save themselves and either swim or paddle to safety. There would certainly be some injured though, and Idzerda knew that he and the wireless operator should do whatever they could to be of assistance. They pushed their dinghy out to deep water and paddled. They could hear the shouts and screams of the wounded and realised that there were women and children somewhere out there ahead of them. Idzerda would never forget what happened next. Spotting a round, black head bobbing up and down in the water, he dived in to assist what he thought was a Javanese who had escaped with the Dutch, possibly a house servant or a native soldier. It was neither. It was a Dutch woman, so badly burned that she had lost all her hair and her skin was scorched and blackened. She was still alive, though, but carried the body of a dead baby gripped tightly under one. Crying and sobbing, she told Idzerda that she had another child somewhere, but she had lost them.

Idzerda and the other Dutchman very, very carefully helped the woman into their dinghy, and removed her baby from her grasp. Then they turned and slowly headed back towards the beach.

*

Out on the killing ground that the boat anchorage had become, individual survival was more often than not determined by whether or not the survivors could swim and whether they were alone or in a group. It also depended on what assistance was close at hand.

Charlie D'Antoine found himself in the thick of things. He had not been particularly worried when he dived into the water as he was a good swimmer and he knew the tides of Roebuck Bay very well. His only concerns were the Zeros above and the sharks below, but he also knew that there was not a lot that he could do about either. He watched the Zeros going about their work, flying so low that he could see the individual pilots quite clearly in their open cockpits. When they were gone, he heard a woman cry out to him as he was swimming towards the distant beach. He stopped, and saw a Dutch woman struggling in the water just a few metres away.

D'Antoine swam across to her, stopping just short of where she was splashing. She didn't speak English and he didn't speak Dutch, so he indicated that she should hang on to him as he swam slowly through the water. They moved off. A launch, either the American or the Shell launch, appeared alongside and D'Antoine helped the woman aboard, following her into the boat. Once aboard, she hugged D'Antoine tightly, refusing to let go, and talking rapidly in Dutch.

When he was able to disentangle himself, D'Antoine could hear other voices calling out. He indicated to the woman that he needed to go back into the water. This time, it was a young girl calling out; she and her mother were struggling to stay afloat. D'Antoine repeated what he had done earlier with the woman and helped them aboard the launch. Someone on the launch asked D'Antoine if he would like to swim to shore to collect a dinghy for himself but he said, no, there were still others out there he could save. D'Antoine kept swimming until he had done all that he could possibly do. Then he went with the other survivors to the jetty.

*

The experiences of those who made it into the water were as varied, as confronting and as horrible as their earlier experiences during the attack aboard the flying boats had been. Some, a fortunate few, were swept clear of the burning boats as soon as they entered the water. Their survival would ultimately depend on their ability to keep their heads above water. Others had their fate determined by seemingly chance events; whether the current carried them into or away from patches of burning fuel. There were those who tragically gave in to hopelessness, and drowned, and then others who were simply determined to do everything in their power to survive.

The Koens were one of the few families to remain intact through the experience. Only Simon sustained some shrapnel wounds, although Elly believed a shark had swum to the surface very close to where she and her family were floating. The Koens were picked up by one of the rescue boats and taken back to the jetty where they landed wearing everything they now owned.

Henri Juta and his wife also survived, and would carry with them things they had seen and heard for the rest of their lives.

After Juta half-assisted and half-dragged his wife away from the burning Y-67, they drifted with the tide until Juta regained his composure. An empty water bottle floated past. Juta grabbed it and gave it to his wife to use as a flotation device. He took off his boots and socks and told his wife that their best chance of survival lay in swimming to shore. He held her by her hair and head and began to swim for shore, using long and economical strokes.

At one point, Juta saw another survivor clinging to one of the discarded belly tanks dropped by the Zeros. As Juta and his wife drew closer, the tank filled with water and sank, followed down almost immediately by the man who had been clinging to it. At another point, he heard a woman screaming and spotted a man and woman trapped in a pool of blazing fuel. The woman's hair was on fire. Juta looked away until the screaming stopped. After perhaps half an hour or more in the water, Juta's bare foot brushed something he convinced himself was a shark. By then, he had also convinced himself that his end was near, but the contact with the shark and the sound of an approaching engine made him snap out of his fugue.

A launch pulled up alongside the Jutas and they were hauled aboard by an American, first his wife and then Juta. Towards the front of the boat, a young Dutch woman was resting with her back against the side of the boat. One arm seemed almost completely smashed below the elbow by machine-gun bullets. In the middle of the deck was a rubber dinghy, with pools of blood at its bottom. The American explained that the girl was the first survivor he had rescued. Juta surmised that her parents had placed a tourniquet high up on the girl's arm before placing her in the dinghy. He also surmised that her parents were now dead.

The American took a knife from his belt, a can from a carton near his feet and used the knife to punch holes in the top of the can, which he passed to Juta's wife, apologising that fruit juice was all he had. He then restarted the engine, and the little group went looking for more survivors.

The launch moved slowly through the water and Juta heard many calls for help. He and the American worked together, pulling people into the boat, working in tandem and to a system. At times, they were unsure if the person they hauled aboard was still alive or not, and then decided that it didn't really matter anyway. Among those they lifted aboard were men and women with their faces completely burnt and others with no obvious marks on them. It seemed to take no time at all for the launch to fill with those scooped out of the water. To make more space, Juta dropped the dinghy over the side and tethered it to the launch. It was not fully inflated, but floated well and he thought they could fit two or three more people in it.

Again, the launch became overcrowded and a crewman from one of the RAF Catalinas and Juta volunteered to move to the dinghy. It took the overcrowded launch and dinghy almost twenty minutes to return to the jetty.

When the launch arrived at the wooden stairs at the end of the jetty, Juta and his RAF colleague were first out and assisted the wounded. Juta's second trip involved carrying a lifeless young woman, dressed in black trousers, a blue blouse and a blue scarf. She seemed to merely be asleep, in a coma perhaps, and with the help of another girl, Juta carried her up the stairs before gently lowering her onto the flatbed carriage of the steam railway. He turned her onto her stomach and lifted her blouse up to enable him to loosen any tightly fitting underclothes she might have been wearing.

There, between her shoulder blades, he found two neat bullet holes just above the young woman's heart.

Of all the things Juta had seen and would see that day, this upset him the most. He stood up and looked at the sky and the sea, the little town and the endless plain beyond, and thought, what a senseless world we lived in.

*

Henk Hasselo swam away from the doomed X-1, and decided that he would try to swim to the distant shore rather than stay where he was and wait. He had not gone far when he came across a nine-year-old boy who said simply, 'I'll die. I can't swim any more.'

Hasselo told the boy that he must keep going and slapped his face when he thought the boy was about to go into hysterics. The rough treatment worked, and Hasselo and the boy continued to swim together slowly towards the beach.

At one point, the boy stopped swimming and started to slip beneath the water, but Hasselo was able to grab him and pull him back to the surface before he disappeared. As he supported the boy in the water they were joined by another Dutchman, Jan van Persie, Hasselo's co-pilot from the X-1. Together, the two men supported the boy between them in the water and slowly progressed towards the shore. Their stops became more frequent and lasted longer and both Hasselo and van Persie began to think that all three of them may not make it.

As they trod water, a voice called out to them, 'You fella's want to stay there or what?' It was Robin Hunter aboard the *Nicol Bay*. Within minutes, all three were aboard the boat.

The longer their time in the water the further the tide would take the survivors, who were soon spread out over a large area. Those rescued were often plucked individually from the water as groups of people dispersed. Sophie Blommert and the wounded man who had helped her in the water drifted well away from all the others. The man stayed with Blommert, talking to her and calming her down when she grew fearful. When she finally felt that she was going to survive it all, the man simply let go of her, slipped beneath the waves and was gone. Just as Blommert thought she was certainly going to drown, she was plucked from the water and pulled into a rubber dinghy by a young man wearing an RAAF uniform.

Jimmy Bowden, the non-swimming RAF gunner from the Catalina FV-W, also thought he would drown if he was left alone, and knew he was fortunate to have companions with him. In the water, two of his crewmates supported Bowden and showed him how to stay afloat. While he could not swim, Bowden found that he could at least propel himself through the water, albeit very slowly. Fortunately he did not have to do that for very long as he, too, was soon picked up by the *Nicol Bay*.

When he was able to, Bowden lent a hand in the rescues, and almost wished that he hadn't. The first person he helped to pull aboard was a beautiful young girl floating on her back. It wasn't until they had brought her board that Bowden and the others realised she was dead. A short time later, three children drifted past the boat. They were all holding onto each other, but they were floating face down and not moving.

Frits van Hulssen, the Y-59's seventeen-year-old radio operator, rescued a small boy he found drifting among some wreckage from one of the planes, and trod water with him for just a few minutes before they were picked up by one of the launches. Theo Doorman and Rob Lacomble found each other in the water and stayed together until they were picked up by the US Navy launch. Doorman's mother drifted some distance away and spent well over an hour in the water, carried along on the tide. Close to exhaustion and fearing that she would soon drown, she was rescued just as she was preparing herself for death.

A number of survivors actually declined to be rescued by the *Nicol Bay*, seeing the drums of fuel on board, and knowing if the boat was attacked all aboard would die a terrible death. They opted to either wait for another boat, or to attempt to swim to either the beach or the jetty.

Jan Piers' wife and sons had been killed in front of him. He tried to swim to the spot where they had disappeared beneath the water, but it was now a sea of fire and he was physically restrained from doing so by two other MLD airmen who had been aboard the X-1. The two men stayed with Piers and swam with him in the direction of the town beach. Once on dry land, Piers broke down completely.

An American named Frank Kurtz who had flown in on one of the PatWing 10 Catalinas was on the same beach when he saw another Dutchman, possibly Jan van der Plas, struggle ashore, towing a woman by the hair. The lower part of the woman's face had been shot away and she was obviously dead. The man was crying.

The last survivors to swim to shore were a husband and wife who had swum well over a kilometre, battling the tide most of the way. When they reached the shallow water, they both stood up, put down the small children they had each been carrying under one arm, and walked together up onto the beach.

*

The initial, almost instinctive responses to the unfolding tragedy on Roebuck Bay by people like Lester Brain, Rudi Idzerda and Harold Mathieson were soon complemented by a more organised response.

Out towards the end of the jetty, Lewis Ambrose had just seen his flying boat, the *Corinna*, go up in flames. By age and experience, Ambrose was probably the senior officer on the jetty, and he spoke to his passengers and aircrew, telling them to take cover if the Japanese aircraft returned. Otherwise, they were to assist in any way they could. Then he led them back up the stairs and onto the jetty.

There, Ambrose began to organise the 70 or more people who had remained either on or under the jetty during the attack. The steam train was now brought down to the end of the jetty with its two empty flatbed carriages. John Oram, the senior QEA steward who had been organising the logistics to support the company's Broome operations, had accompanied Lewis Ambrose and his passengers and crew to the jetty that morning. At Ambrose's request, he now organised the little steam train to carry both dead and wounded back off the jetty. Others were sent into town to alert Dr Jolly of the significant numbers of casualties coming ashore and to assist at the hospital if they were needed there. Ambrose also organised other staff into a reception party to assist when the first casualties were brought ashore.

Al Armbruster, another of 30 US servicemen who had flown into Broome aboard the P-7, one of the two PatWing 10 Catalinas destroyed by the Japanese, was one of many who sheltered under the jetty during the raid. He joined one of the small groups pushing boats into the deeper water to search for survivors. On their first trip, his boat found several survivors and returned them to the jetty, where they were passed on to one of the reception parties.

Fewer survivors were found on subsequent trips, and later they recovered bodies rather than survivors. These, too, were taken back to the jetty, which was a hive of activity.

Some Broome residents were now assisting in the operations. Dr Jolly was also at the jetty treating people, when he realised the scale of the disaster and saw that he needed to return to the hospital. There, he worked with volunteers to prepare for the arrival of mass casualties, and also arranged to take over a nearby house for the overflow as it appeared likely the small hospital would be overwhelmed by the numbers.

The *Nicol Bay* was approaching the jetty just as Armbruster's little boat was heading across the water to look for more survivors. From the time Harold Mathieson had first pulled up alongside the jetty, there had been a steady stream of small craft travelling the kilometre from the end of the jetty out to the heart of the flying boat anchorage. The American's boat was the last of them.

The men, women and children recovered from the water were a mix of the fit, wounded and close to death. All were suffering varying degrees of trauma. Some had the obviously physical trauma of the wounded and dying. Less obvious, but still hinted at in the haunted faces and empty eyes, was the trauma of having your world snatched from you at the very time when you thought you may just survive the war. The fit were brought together and escorted off the jetty and into town, generally to one of the hotels in the first instance. Those whose wounds and injuries required medical assistance were also taken into town, either on foot, or aboard the steam train, and were then escorted to the hospital. The corpses were laid side by side on the jetty.

The disposal of the dead and the needs of the living were priorities. As more and more bodies were brought to the jetty, it became clear that they would need to be buried, that leaving them where they lay was just too upsetting to the survivors and rescuers. Someone, perhaps Ambrose, sent a message across to Colonel Legg, requesting some servicemen to help bury the bodies of those killed on Roebuck Bay. Legg's reply, delivered through John Rouse, was that the Dutch would have to assume responsibility for burying their own dead. The Americans were too busy at the airfield to spare any men.

More aircraft were expected to fly in from Perth; they would need to be refuelled and loaded with evacuees as quickly as possible in case the Japanese returned. Colonel Legg did, however, provide some surplus flying suits so that any naked bodies could be clothed for burial.

Al Armbruster was one of the volunteers who helped to place the bodies on the flatbed carriages of the little train, a task he would later compare to stacking cord wood. It was confronting and heartbreaking. Confronting because some of the dead were so badly burnt that their age could only be estimated by the size of the body and it was often impossible to tell if the body was that of a man or a woman. Others had literally been shattered by machine-gun bullets and cannon shells. If that was not enough, devastatingly, most of the bodies were women and children. Thirty bodies were carefully placed on the carriages and taken to an open space alongside the original Pioneer's Cemetery overlooking the foreshore, not far from the base of the jetty.

Many of those who were there later commented on a strange ennui, an apathy among the Dutch survivors, who seemed to not want to do anything but be left alone to make sense of what had happened. When asked if they would help with the burials, not one Dutchman volunteered to assist, so the task was undertaken primarily by members of the Broome VDC and civilian volunteers, John Oram included. One large mass grave was dug and the 30 bodies were laid in it. Two more bodies were brought in as the large grave was being filled, and individual graves were dug for them. One cross was erected for each of the dead.

The 32 bodies in the little makeshift cemetery would be joined by others in the days that followed as more dead washed up on the shores of Roebuck Bay or were disinterred from where they had been buried and reinterred with the other victims. Several stories were told of a Dutchman who was never identified, but who was probably Jan Piers, finding the bodies of his wife and child washed up on a sandy beach. Distraught, he dug a grave with his bare hands and buried them where he had found them. He marked the grave with pieces of debris from the aircraft that had also washed up on the beach.

Other stories surround an old Malay man who found the body of a young girl, probably about twelve years of age, washed into the mangroves near Fishermen's Bend in Dampier Creek. The little girl appeared to be at peace, resting rather than dead. The man carried the body back to a small plot alongside his home, where he dug a grave and buried the girl in it. To prevent the sand from falling on her face, he placed an old door over her body, and marked the grave with both a cross and with a border of old bottles. When authorities learned of this, the girl's body was removed and reinterred in what was now known as the 'Dutch Cemetery'.

*

Legg cared little about the dead, but he was prepared to offer assistance to the wounded. The hospital, and the house that served as its annex, were soon overcrowded and Dr Jolly was being run off his feet. A USAAF doctor, probably a flight surgeon named Dimmock, was sent across to assist him, and a decision was taken to evacuate the wounded to Port Hedland, where there was a small but well-equipped hospital, as soon as possible. For most, that turned out to be later that afternoon. The doctors were also assisted by a number of labourers from the airfield and by some US aircrew who were waiting to be flown out.

Henk Hasselo's experience was typical of many. Because he was wounded, with a bullet splinter lodged in his body, he was escorted to the hospital and then taken a short distance to the annex an ordinary house which had simply been requisitioned by Dr Jolly. There he was given a bed in one of the bedrooms. Another wounded Dutchman was placed in another bed in the same room. That Dutchman was unconscious and died soon after he was admitted. During the afternoon, Hasselo was driven to the airfield, put aboard Jimmy Woods' MMA Electra, which had arrived on a scheduled flight shortly after the Japanese aircraft flew away, and flown to Port Hedland. Dr Jolly accompanied the flight and helped admit Hasselo to hospital there.

The number of wounded and the evacuees strained all the resources available in Broome. The Americans, in particular, struggled to communicate with the Dutch survivors. None of the Americans there spoke either Dutch or Javanese, which appeared to be the only two languages the evacuees and the understood. The Americans were frustrated by the lack of documentation and identification among the evacuees and the language barrier just added to their frustration. While it was possible to communicate using sign language with the adults, the children, and in particular the smaller children, quickly became a problem. Several of them appeared to be unaccompanied and were easily scared. Eventually someone discovered a young woman who spoke some English; she and another young Dutch woman took over responsibility for the small tots and children.

Further assistance also arrived. Just a couple of hours after the raid, an RAAF doctor, Flight Lieutenant Hamilton Smith, flew into Broome from Perth, his aircraft taxiing past the still-smoking wreckage on the side of the runway. He had little time to assimilate just what he had seen though as Smith was taken directly to the Broome Hospital and annex where he found the two doctors, the Australian Jolly and the American Dimmock, working on the wounded. He joined in straightaway, noting as he did so the high proportion of the dead to the wounded, and estimating the total death toll to have been around 53, with most of those killed being Dutch evacuees.

Jolly and Dimmock were evacuated to Port Hedland later that afternoon to be with their patients. Hamilton Smith remained in Broome. He had just two patients left in his care. One was a Dutchman who had sustained multiple bullet wounds to his upper abdomen; he died later that evening. Smith's second patient was a young Dutch woman who had a kidney injury and a gunshot wound to the knee. She was given a blood transfusion and her condition was stabilised before she was evacuated to Perth aboard a B-17 the following evening.

*

Long after the attack was over, Charlie D'Antoine remained out on the water, working on one of the launches, helping to recover bodies from the sea. Because he knew Roebuck Bay, he knew where the tides would most probably carry the survivors and the bodies of the poor souls who had perished. They worked until it was almost too dark to see, and then they returned to the jetty.

D'Antoine was as tired as he could ever remember being in his life. When he finally walked home to his little house at the rear of the Sun Theatre, the darkened streets were deserted. His mother, brother and sisters had taken a few personal items and simply walked out, leaving the house much as it had been two days ago when D'Antoine had left for the *Nicol Bay*.

It was just two days, but it felt like two weeks, and all D'Antoine wanted to do was climb into bed and sleep, without dreaming about what he had just seen.

CHAPTER 8

The Port Hedland Races

> There are about 65 white men living in Broome, the majority of whom appeared to be extremely panicky, and are very apprehensive of the position in which they find themselves.
>
> Charles Snook

Even before the last survivors had been pulled from the waters of Roebuck Bay, plans for the evacuation of Broome were being hatched by the USAAF command and some of the local inhabitants. In some cases, some planned to evacuate just themselves, leaving the others behind to fend for themselves and anyone else in the town. Those who lived in Broome, including those in authority there, assumed that the servicemen and civilians who had faced the Japanese in the NEI and Malaya knew from that experience what to expect from those Japanese. It was a false assumption. In the campaigns fought thus far in Southeast Asia, raids such as the one just experienced by Broome were often followed up by the landing of Japanese troops to seize the strategic location, a point which was made repeatedly after the Zeros had flown away.

For those in Broome, this theory rapidly became an accepted fact. No-one could deny that Broome had become a key point in Allied planning in the past two weeks. Some of the people predicting a Japanese invasion were the same who had watched Japanese reconnaissance aircraft fly over the town the previous a/fternoon and said that there would be a full-blown Japanese raid on the town within 24 hours. They had been correct then, and if they were correct again, a Japanese invasion fleet was somewhere below the horizon, and would soon be steaming into Roebuck Bay.

Finally, there was the evidence in front of them. The Japanese raid had lasted barely fifteen minutes and was very destructive, but it had also been very targeted. Every aircraft in Broome at the time of the raid, with the exception of Jack Lamade's little Seagull, had been destroyed in the air, on the ground or on the water. But only aircraft were destroyed. Broome's two key strategic assets – its airfield and its jetty – were still intact. It was almost as if they had been deliberately spared so they could continue to be used by the Australians and Americans until they were available for use by Japanese occupation troops. In the face of all this seemingly overwhelming and incontrovertible evidence, flight from Broome before the Japanese landed was the only sensible survival strategy.

So, throughout Broome in the hours after the Zeros' departure, evacuation plans were made by military and civilian alike. The plans they made fell into three broad categories: formal, semi-formal and informal. The formal were those put in place, sanctioned and operated by the authorities then operating in Broome, primarily Colonel Richard Legg and his USAAF administrators. The semi-formal were authorised and sanctioned, but by the military and civilian authorities. The informal were those when an individual, or sometimes a small group, decided to simply up and leave before the Japanese arrived. The problem was that the confused lines of communication and command in Broome meant it was difficult for anyone to efficiently organise their escape. The result was a sometimes unedifying and undignified scramble southwards – the Port Hedland Races, an undeclared contest to get as far and to go as fast as possible to avoid capture, or worse, by the Japanese.

*

As Biddy Bardwell would later recount, when the Japanese started attacking the flying boats out on Roebuck Bay, 'all the native population on the foreshore came tearing inland. My native maidservant, greatly agitated, demanded that I should "go bush"'. Biddy chose not to go bush, instead seeking cover in her own air-raid shelter, which she found already occupied by an old and smelly ne'er-do-well from around town. Biddy went to her sister's house, which was nearby, and where she finally took cover in a 'tiny dell' between some oleander bushes in the garden. There she remained until the danger passed.

Broome's local population that had been living alone or in small groups scattered along the foreshore had rushed inland.

While many were Aboriginal, many others were Malays or Koepangers. For most, there was a controlled panic. They feared the worst, an imminent Japanese invasion, hoped that the Americans or someone would do something about it, but made preparations to flee the area all the same.

The Aboriginal people who fled tended to keep going away from the town. They knew the country well and had relatives in places like Beagle Bay and other missions across the northwest. That afternoon, the local inspector of Aborigines, Laurie O'Neill, scribbled a hurried note to his department head in Perth, noting that almost all his Aboriginal charges had gone bush, so he helped out at the hospital and buried the dead instead. He also noted that one of his own assistants, an Aborigine named Torres, had stayed behind to drive the truck that carried people and supplies between Broome and Beagle Bay.

The Malays and Koepangers had nowhere else to go. After the raid they simply returned to their shacks and camps around the bay. Those who had any real concerns relocated to one of the many campsites along Dampier Creek just that little bit further away from town.

The European population of Broome also tended to go bush, in the short term at least. One long-term resident, Bill Iverson, recalled that many of the town's residents just let their pet birds out of their cages, grabbed a few valuables and walked away from their homes. Within hours, the road to Port Hedland was lined with broken-down cars. Iverson and one of his mates walked around the town, shutting the doors of government buildings and private residences alike.

Most of the Europeans who fled had no long-term interests in or commitment to the town. If not exactly transient, they were in Broome for the duration of their posting or their job, and then they were off to somewhere else. Those Europeans with businesses or valuable assets in and around the town stayed, making adjustments as the circumstances demanded. In the coming days and weeks, they would move out of town each morning to be a safe distance away during those hours when a Japanese air raid was a possibility, generally the three hours either side of midday. The more pragmatic among them also established their own little food dumps out in the bush.

*

The formal, official and authorised evacuation of Broome involved American and Australian military authorities and Australian civilian representatives. At times, the exercise was only marginally less chaotic than the rush of the native population from the foreshore.

The Australian civil administration in Broome broke down almost immediately after the Japanese raid. Ralph Doig, a senior bureaucrat in the Western Australian Premier's Department who was given responsibility for the civil side of Broome's administration, assessed the immediate impact and put his recollections down on paper:

> The people of Broome panicked immediately. Shot straight through and grabbed any transport they could get. It was mainly men, the women and children were already gone from Broome. We received word from the Army that the State

public servants who were still in Broome had left their posts, so a message was sent to them immediately that they were to get back and stay on the job and await further orders. Even one of the police inspectors had moved out and had gone bush as the first step towards moving south.

While Doig was in Perth trying to get a clear picture of what had happened, in Broome Police Inspector James Cowie – the officer identified in Doig's recollections – was also setting his observations down on paper:

> The members of the RAAF . . . have disappeared. They seem to have taken all machine guns and defence weapons with them, and the place is really defenceless, as most members of the Home Guard have also cleared out. The police are doing what they can and are arranging to get an old motor truck and car in reasonable running order to take all out if finally we must go. However, they will hold on to the last . . . the Officials and others now left in Broome are living in a sort of helpless anticipation of future happenings now that all form of Defence is gone.

Cowie would remain in Broome, but be curiously absent from most of the major decision-making meetings held there. His health was an issue – he would accumulate several medical certificates from Dr Jolly – but he was also in receipt of personal directives from Police Commissioner Hunter in Perth to remain where he was and to do all he could to maintain morale and good order.

Even the Broome Road Board joined in the chorus of voices calling for assistance and support from Perth. In the afternoon following the raid, Sam Male, in his capacity as chairman of the Roads Board, sent a telegram directly to State Premier Willocks:

> We demand that aerial transport be sent to Broome to evacuate civil population who desire to leave. Alternatively adequate Australian fighter protection be afforded to avoid repetition of this morning's occurrence. Roads impassable.

To some extent, the Road Board's plea for assistance in the evacuation had been superseded by events before it was sent. By late afternoon that day, both the official and semi-official evacuations were well underway.

*

Jimmy Woods became involved in the evacuation when he landed his Electra in Broome as part of his regular mail run. His intended path was Broome and Port Hedland to Carnarvon and Geraldton and onto Perth where he would refuel, turn around and make the return flight to Wyndham. But seven minutes after Woods took off from Wyndham in his MacRobertson Miller Airlines Lockheed Electra, that airfield was attacked by a squadron of Japanese Zeros that had also flown across from Penfui in Timor. Unlike what Miyano's men had done in Broome, these Zeros shot up the Wyndham airfield, destroying a fuel dump. Fortunately, no aircraft were present. Woods was blissfully unaware of what had happened at the airfield he had just left as, following instructions, he had switched off his radio for the duration of the flight. He was surprised to see rising smoke while some distance out from Broome, and even more surprised when he was instructed to circle Broome for 30 minutes while a number of fires were extinguished and the runway cleared of all debris.

Woods landed at 11 a.m. and soon afterwards met with Richard Legg. The two men quickly came to an agreement over the role Woods and his Electra would play in the evacuation. The Electra, a ten-seat passenger aircraft, had neither the range nor the capacity to play anything but a supporting role to the large American aircraft, the B-17s and B-24s, which Legg expected to begin flying in later in the day. Woods began a shuttle run between Broome and Port Hedland evacuating, in the first instance, civilian and military personnel whose needs for either medical treatment or support were best met in Port Hedland.

Half an hour after he landed, Woods took off again, bound for Port Hedland, an hour's flight to the south, with 22 passengers crammed into his Electra. Among them were Dr Jolly and a few of the lightly wounded from the Dutch flying boats, several RAAF support personnel whose services were no longer required in Broome, and a number of civilian residents of the town, including Biddy Bardwell, who argued almost until the wheels left the ground that she should be allowed to stay in Broome.

While flying over the Eighty Mile Beach, around 150 kilometres south of Broome, Woods spotted the remains of a Dornier flying boat on the beach. It was the X-36, burnt by its crew to prevent it falling into Japanese hands. As Woods' Electra circled the wreck, the X-36's crewmen emerged from their hiding places among the sand dunes and waved to him. Woods scribbled a note to them on an air-sickness bag, which he attached to a piece of white cloth and dropped to the Dutchmen below, telling them that assistance would soon be on the way.

At Port Hedland, he unloaded his passengers and collected some water and emergency supplies. Flying back to Broome, he dropped these off for the Dutch aircrew, before landing at Anna Plains Station, further north towards Broome, where he told the station owners about the Dornier and its approximate location. The following morning, Wednesday, 4 March, Woods flew another full load of evacuees to Port Hedland, again calling in at the Anna Plains Station on his return. There, he learned that the station's boundary riders had been unable to locate the aircraft and its crew. Woods drew a detailed map of the wreck site, loaded up some medical supplies, food and water, and took off again.

He flew back to the Dornier and dropped off the supplies with a note saying a rescue party would arrive the next day.

*

Lester Brain did not slow down, despite the dengue fever, the heat and the general disruption caused by the Japanese raid. His was probably the most difficult of all the roles in Broome as he was responsible to several masters – Hudson Fysh and the Qantas senior management team, the departments of Defence and Civil Aviation, and he was also expected to coordinate his and QEA/Qantas' actions as closely as possible with those of Colonel Legg and the Americans. Most of the Australians in Broome, especially those directly involved in the evacuations from Java and now from Broome, looked to him for the leadership that had so far been conspicuously absent.

Following Brain's directions, the QEA flying boat *Camilla* touched down on Roebuck Bay at 11.30 a.m. With the permanent anchorages destroyed, she had to rely on her own anchors, which proved sufficient for the short time the *Camilla* would be there. Brain acted quickly; the *Camilla* was immediately loaded up with passengers, including nineteen US Navy personnel evacuated from Java and seventeen QEA staff under Malcolm Millar. An hour after her arrival, the *Camilla* was en route to Port Hedland where Millar oversaw a QEA evacuation shuttle service from Broome to Perth, similar to the one he had established at Tjilatjap. This led to yet another argument between Brain and Legg. The main issue between the two was that one was military and the other civilian. Lieutenant Colonel Legg did not think any civilian, no matter how senior or experienced, could tell a senior officer anything when both were in a war zone, which Broome now was.

When Brain returned from the search-and-rescue mission on Roebuck Bay and had organised for the reception, loading, refuelling and departure of the *Camilla*, he went to the schoolhouse to find Legg. The two men had clashed several times in the few days since Legg's arrival in Broome, but Brain attempted to be diplomatic, asking the American politely if there was anything that either he or Qantas could do to assist the Americans. Lester Brain, more than most, was attuned to the nuances of the relationship between Australia and the United States in the South West Pacific. He was, as well, a realist and a diplomat. He would, and did, take a lot of gratuitous advice from Legg in particular. He would then do what he believed best for Australia and Qantas, in that order.

Legg could see his new command, and with it his career, disappearing very fast if he lost any more men and material than he already had. Legg's reply was a curt, 'Give us 24 hours to get out of this goddammed place and you can have it.'

Brain, who found the comment bordering on the offensive, turned to leave, but Legg spoke again, this time in a more conciliatory tone. He asked if either Qantas or QEA had any aircraft in the area. Brain told him the *Camilla* was due to return soon and that he had just completed arrangements for its loading and departure. Legg asked him to cancel those arrangements and to direct the *Camilla* to conduct an aerial search off Cable Beach for possible survivors from the B-24 *Arabian Knight*.

Brain refused, saying the *Camilla* would be used to evacuate service and civilian personnel to Port Hedland, and then fly any wounded who required treatment directly to Perth. It was a long-range aircraft, he said, better suited to that kind of work than to air-sea rescue.

A short and sharp argument then ensued, with Brain unwilling to alter what he thought was the most appropriate use of the only QEA aircraft now available in the northwest. But he held out an olive branch of sorts. He needed the rest of the day to sort out his own staff, facilities and stores, to decide who and what would stay or go. If nothing had been heard of the *Arabian Knight* by the following morning, he would organise a limited seaborne search for survivors. It wasn't much, but it was all that he could do – and it was certainly more than the Americans themselves were prepared to do.

*

After his meeting with Legg, Brain realised that Hudson Fysh and Qantas needed to know that another QEA flying boat had been destroyed by enemy action. He walked through the strangely deserted streets towards the post office, not knowing if anyone was there or if he would be allowed to send a telegram in the current circumstances. A private telegram would be refused so, when he found the post office open and the postmaster himself in attendance, Brain asked to send a telegram to the Department of Civil Aviation in Melbourne.

Brain used a simple code to notify the department that Broome had been attacked by Japanese aircraft at 9.30 a.m. and that fifteen flying boats had been destroyed, including one QEA aircraft. What he would learn later was that the deputy director of Civil Aviation was amazed to receive the telegram – this was the first he had learned of the attack. When he telephoned around, no-one in Melbourne, then the base for Australia's defence establishment, knew of the attack either.

Worse was to follow. Most of the senior officers and officials were out at lunch; it would be another half-hour before any coordinated response could begin.

When Brain made his way back though town, he called into the hospital, which he found abandoned with signs everywhere of just how hurried its evacuation had been. All the wards were empty, beds unmade and mosquito nets strewn across the floor. The state of the surgery almost suggested that all, patient included, had just up and left at a moment's notice. Surgical instruments, stainless steel trays, dressings and bandages were scattered haphazardly, and it seemed that the instrument cabinets had been cleared out.

The food preparation and storage areas were also wide open, but in far less disarray. The pantries were still stocked with food, but no effort had been made to clean up the dirty dishes and food scraps which littered the eating area. It was, thought Brain, almost as if someone had waved a wand and all the people in the hospital had been swept away.

Brain worked all afternoon and well into the evening, making no concessions to either his fragile health or to his growing exhaustion. He was someone who took responsibility seriously, someone who would see something through to the end because he had been asked to do so. As a pilot, he knew that shortcuts usually had just the one outcome – disaster. What he had previously spent time doing, he now spent time undoing. Under his direction, fuel, aircraft spares, food, accommodation and transport had been established for the Java–Broome shuttle on the basis that the shuttle would involve a minimum of two QEA aircraft and around 30 air and ground crew. This operation now had to be dismantled; things that could be saved or salvaged would be, and everything else either destroyed or rendered unserviceable.

There were big and small decisions. Qantas had an account at Streeter and Male's general store for their own staff, and Brain extended that account to cover all evacuees – Dutch men, women and children, whether military or civilian, were able to select clothes to replace the rags they had been wearing, as were RAAF aircrew and anyone else who had lost everything in the morning's raid.

As Brain worked and walked his way around Broome, he watched evacuations taking place, and thought a lot of what he saw was just wrong. Many of those who led the evacuation were those who Brain believed should have stayed to the very end. Dr Jolly, the town's resident magistrate as well as its medical officer, had chosen to be evacuated with some of the wounded he had treated aboard Woods' Electra. At least another doctor, the RAAF's Flight Lieutenant Hamilton Smith, had arrived and could replace Jolly. The clerk of courts, the resident engineer, all customs officials and bank officials had simply walked away from their jobs to join the exodus south.

Brain found that James Cowie, the local police inspector, had suffered an unexpected recurrence of a long-standing heart condition that required specialised medical attention only available in the south. The Broome harbour master, a Mr W. Lawson, a Naval Reserve officer, also disappeared that afternoon. He was the custodian of all the naval codes, so when coded signals from the RAN began to arrive overnight and the next morning, they could not be read as the codes were locked securely away in a safe. Lawson had taken the only keys with him.

That night, after a hurried meal, Brain went for another walk around the deserted town. He walked away from the hotel where he was staying, along the road to the airport, stopping at the radio station. He knocked on the front door and waited. When there was no answer, he walked around to the back door and knocked there. There was no response either, and when he could hear no sounds from the inside, Brain realised that the radio station had also been abandoned.

He opened the door and walked straight in. Inside, a heavy hammer had been placed alongside the radio equipment, in readiness to smash all the radio and spares ahead of any invading Japanese. There was no one in place to wield the hammer. The radio operators were long gone, and the

Broome VDC member who had been assigned the task of guarding the station and its equipment was not there, either heading south with the others or hiding somewhere out in the bush. Lester closed the door behind him and walked back to his hotel. Another long, long day had just passed. It was time to refresh as well as he could, for tomorrow was sure to offer its own challenges.

*

Early the next morning, 4 March, 1942, Brain met three other men at the end of the Broome jetty. The three were Qantas engineer Jenkins, Shell Company employee Maurie Carseldine, the coxswain of the company's launch, and Flight Lieutenant Hamilton Smith, the RAAF doctor. The four men boarded the Shell company's launch and headed off to look for survivors from the downed *Arabian Knight*. Progress was easy in the relatively protected waters of Roebuck Bay, but soon after they turned out into the Indian Ocean, they began to experience difficulties. The launch was designed for use in shallow and calm harbour waters and the heavier swells beyond Entrance Point caused immediate and serious problems.

A succession of waves broke over the launch, almost swamping it and flooding the engine, which immediately stalled. To stay afloat, those aboard threw full 200-litre fuel drums overboard and bailed furiously while Jenkins worked to restart the engine. He was eventually able to do so, and the little launch continued on its way to the search area off Cable Beach. There it plied back and forth for an hour, making as thorough a search as was possible under the circumstances. They recovered a few items from the downed aircraft – burnt seat cushions, life-jackets and other debris – but could find no survivors. They returned to the jetty disappointed.

*

Under Richard Legg, the formal American evacuation proceeded at a lively pace, with the unstated assumption that everything would eventually fall in line with what the air force lieutenant colonel really wanted. Legg had a master plan in his mind, which he didn't share with anyone else. His aim was to have the evacuation completed by the night of 5–6 March – 48 hours hence – when he would, if necessary, destroy Broome and all its facilities to deny them to the Japanese. He was convinced that an invasion was almost certainly inevitable, and one of his first actions was to organise a lookout service to warn the town when an invasion fleet was spotted. An observer was placed in a church tower with orders to ring the church bell if they saw an approaching fleet. Because of the stresses involved, observers would be replaced after an hour on duty. He also called for two meetings to be held in front of the schoolhouse early that afternoon.

The first meeting comprised Dutch men, women and children, mainly civilians with just a sprinkling of MLD uniforms. They gathered at the base of the stairs that led up to the schoolhouse. Legg appeared at the top of those stairs, a short, stocky figure wearing the aviator's sunglasses that had been popularised by General Douglas Macarthur. Addressing those gathered before him, Legg announced that as a Japanese invasion was imminent, Broome was to be abandoned and would be destroyed to deny anything of value to the enemy. A road convoy would be formed to evacuate Broome's civilians, both locals and those who had flown in from elsewhere. That convoy would be made up of civilian vehicles and would travel down the coast road to Port Hedland, which was beyond the range of enemy aircraft.

The vehicles would travel at night and without headlights so the Japanese would not see them, and they would travel in small groups within the larger convoy. What remained of that day, and the first part of the next, was to be spent preparing the participating trucks and cars as well as collecting supplies for the journey.

The crowd stood, staring open-mouthed at what they were hearing, and wondering what the little man at the top of the stairs knew that they didn't.

*

Sometime later, Legg addressed the 93 US servicemen who had assembled at the Broome schoolhouse. His message this time was more in the tradition of military briefings. He had obviously been apprised of the realities of the situation in Broome, that locals were already leaving and that, if a convoy was to be formed to head south, it would be formed from a community of interest rather than at his direction. Men in uniform had already been seen participating in the formation of just such a convoy. It was believed that some were Americans, leaving of their own accord.

When his second audience came to order, Legg told them that he had received reports of USAAF personnel either leaving or preparing to leave Broome without authorisation. This was simple desertion and would be treated as such. He said that he had directed that a roadblock be established 35 kilometres south of the town, and all vehicles would pass through that roadblock. Any unauthorised service personnel who attempted to go south via the main road would be arrested there and returned to Broome under guard.

Legg went on to say that a number of transport aircraft were also expected to arrive in Broome at any time up to midnight. Unfortunately, he was not in a position to say how many aircraft would arrive and therefore could not also say either how many servicemen would be evacuated. More aircraft were expected during the morning on Wednesday. Because of the uncertainty surrounding the number of aircraft available, a priority list would be drawn for the aerial evacuations. Anyone whose name was not on the list by 2 p.m. that day should get out of Broome as quickly as they could. Until that time, any American caught leaving Broome by road would be considered AWOL (Absent Without Leave) at best, a deserter at worst. A civilian convoy was in the process of being formed and any who were not listed would be well advised to link up with that.

Soon afterwards, VDC captain Harry Macnee approached Legg to ask the lieutenant colonel about rumours the Americans were about to pull out of Broome, and also about a number of Americans he had seen leaving the airfield precinct in civilian cars. Legg suggested strongly that Broome was now a death trap and that he would be getting his men away as quickly as possible. When Macnee asked the basis for the assessment, Legg appeared annoyed to even be asked. He told the experienced soldier that he knew all about Japanese techniques; Broome would soon be bombed and then invaded by

Japanese paratroops. There were no anti-aircraft guns available and absolutely nothing in the town to stop the Japanese from doing what they wanted to do. The town should be evacuated temporarily the next day as a preliminary to a complete evacuation.

And with that Legg turned and left.

*

The official evacuation proceeded on two fronts, on land and sea, but it did not run smoothly. Records and reminiscences tell very different stories of what actually took place and often miss the flavour and feel of what really happened in favour of a bare recitation of facts. Among the conflicting and often contradictory recollections, a number of points stand out. The first is that the Americans' focus was primarily on the evacuation of Americans, something that was to be expected. The second is that Richard Legg was clearly spooked by the thought of an approaching Japanese invasion fleet, and that fear is reflected in a number of decisions he made. The third is that, again, the best work was probably done by those who had no direct responsibility for evacuations, men (all the women had left by now) who stepped into the vacuum created by those who chose personal safety above personal responsibility.

American bombardier John Minahan's recollections provide the best detail. The first of Legg's evacuation aircraft flew in on Tuesday afternoon, three B-17s which had travelled across the continent from Melbourne. Second Lieutenant Minahan recalls them being loaded with unwounded Dutch evacuees and then flown back to Melbourne. Those Dutch were probably the senior MLD, KNIL and civilian bureaucrats who had survived Roebuck Bay. It was not just Dutchmen who were aboard the flights. Australian airman Frank Russell later wrote that he, too, was flown to Melbourne aboard a B-17 that night, so it is probable that RAAF, RAF and USAAF aircrew were included on those flights.

Minahan does not mention, though, an incident that occurred during the afternoon. Smoke was spotted well out at sea, its source being something over the horizon, something that was obviously a ship as the smoke was moving. Rumour built on rumour. Because Zeros like those that had attacked Broome were known to have been flown off aircraft carriers in the past, some believed the smoke was from the approaching Japanese invasion fleet. This was soon dismissed because there was just a single source of smoke, so the story became a Japanese cruiser en route to Broome to bombard the town and soften it up for the invaders who were following. But then the smoke disappeared, and no one was any the wiser.

Another two B-17s arrived from Melbourne early the next morning and were quickly refuelled and loaded with US servicemen before being sent back. A B-24 also arrived from Perth, loaded with doctors, medical orderlies and medical equipment. It was twelve hours too late – all the wounded had been evacuated to Port Hedland, Perth and even to Melbourne. (There were some who were ill, mainly with dengue fever, but they were left in Broome.) The B-24 was quickly turned around and loaded with American servicemen. On its departure, the aircraft swerved off the runway and damaged part of its undercarriage in the sandy soil at the verge. That damage was repairable, but such was the paranoia about a Japanese invasion that the aircraft was stripped and destroyed to prevent it from falling into Japanese hands.

On Thursday, 5 March, a B-17 flew in from Melbourne and was loaded with Dutch evacuees for the return flight. Two more B-24s also flew in from Perth and most of the remaining Americans were placed aboard these aircraft, which returned immediately to Perth. The only US personnel remaining in Broome were Richard Legg and Jack Berry, the senior pilot whose aircraft had been destroyed in the Japanese raid. They had a fright that afternoon when a Japanese reconnaissance aircraft, probably the same Kawanishi Mavis that had been flying over the area regularly, again flew above the airfield then circled the town and Roebuck Bay before departing to the north. Legg and Berry remained under cover until it was just a speck in the sky.

*

In many ways, American accounts of the official evacuation of Broome tell only part of the story while hinting at things below the surface. They make no direct mention that the largest single evacuation from Broome in the wake of the Japanese raid was not aboard any American aircraft, for example, but a small Australian ketch, the *Nicol Bay*. This is not reflected in the official accounts, but the fact remains that on the evening of the raid, and after having worked hard before, during and after it, Harold Mathieson left Broome on the outgoing tide with up to 100 people crammed aboard. Because the boat had been requisitioned by the RAN, it is probable that Lieutenant Beau Davis was responsible for ordering the *Nicol Bay* to evacuate as many people as it could hold to Port Hedland and to remain there awaiting further orders. Lester Brain may also have been involved in the decision as he was the de facto senior Australian official in Broome.

Whatever its genesis, the result was that 100 or so evacuees were carried away from Broome aboard the *Nicol Bay*. There were apparently some RAF personnel on board, but the majority of the evacuees were Dutch civilians and service personnel, survivors of Roebuck Bay. They travelled as family groups and crewmates from the same aircraft, which may well have been the best thing that could happen to them at that point. After all that they had lived through in the previous 24 hours, what most wanted around them were familiar faces, even if those faces had only grown familiar during those same hours.

*

In his recollections, John Minahan also stated that in the days immediately after the raid, no aircraft arrived from Java. This is simply not true. No American aircraft arrived from Java, but several others did. A KNILM DC-2 arrived in Broome the day after the raid, the last land-based Dutch aircraft to escape from Java.

The next morning, 5 March, an MLD Catalina landed on Roebuck Bay. It anchored there and several curious crew members rowed to the jetty and walked into what appeared to them to be a deserted town. As they walked up an empty main street, Lester Brain emerged from the Qantas cottage, hailed the Dutchmen and invited them all inside for morning tea. He then explained what had happened, where they should go and who they should speak to about having their aircraft refuelled.

The last evacuation aircraft, two more MLD Catalinas, flew down to Roebuck Bay on the morning of Saturday, 7 March, the day before all Allied forces in Java surrendered to the Japanese. One of the two Catalinas had been abandoned earlier as it was so badly damaged that it was unlikely to ever fly again. With spares collected from other wrecked and abandoned aircraft, its Dutch pilot eventually made the Catalina airworthy. Since there was no radio and with every chance that it would fall apart in the sky, he flew the plane alone to Roebuck Bay where he landed without any problems.

Brain was unable to assist those aircraft and crews – by then, he too had left Broome. He was exhausted and needed a rest. During the afternoon of the Wednesday, having spent all morning searching for survivors from the *Arabian Knight*, he had wandered down to the hospital annex to see if he could be of any assistance there. Nothing seemed to have been done at the house since Dr Jolly and the more seriously injured patients had been evacuated. Like the hospital proper, the annex was a mess, appearing to have been abandoned in great haste.

Worse was to follow. On the verandah, Brain found a solitary Dutchman, slightly wounded, lying on a bunk that had been placed there. Nearby on a bed was the man's wife, badly wounded by machine-gun bullets. From the Dutchman, he learned that the couple had been treated by the American doctor, Dimmock, but that the woman had been considered too critically injured to be evacuated by air with the others the previous day. They had received no treatment at all that day. Brain subsequently arranged for Hamilton Smith to treat them both and ensured that they were evacuated by air the next day.

By then, Brain had only a few Qantas staff remaining with him. One of the main tasks he assigned them in the aftermath of the raid was to arrange for the evacuation of as many people as they could. He had ensured that Australian service personnel and the wounded were given some priority in the *Camilla*'s shuttle flights to Port Hedland. A second task had been to salvage anything of use by way of stores and equipment from the remains of the *Corinna* and the Qantas guesthouse, as it was unlikely that either Qantas or QEA would be returning to Broome soon in the foreseeable future.

Both tasks were completed by noon on Friday, 6 March. That afternoon, the *Camilla* flew to Roebuck Bay carrying 1.5 tons of potatoes and onions, and a load of medical supplies. It also carried more than a ton of gelignite to be used in the destruction of Broome and its facilities should that be necessary. When the *Camilla* flew back to Port Hedland later that afternoon, it carried Brain and his remaining Qantas and QEA staff. Although by then he was probably too tired to appreciate it, Brain had just completed one of the most significant deployments in his young company's history. He had also exemplified what care and compassion actually meant. With the assistance of the staff he gathered around himself, Lester Brain established and maintained the last civilian lifeline between Australia and the Netherlands East Indies when the latter was facing its hour of need. At Broome, and on Roebuck Bay, he took on any additional responsibilities he thought would bring the greatest chance of survival to the greatest number of evacuees. It was another job to him, but it was a job fraught with problems, not the least of which was his own physical health. At a time when many reputations were lessened in the face of adversity, Brain excelled himself and his reputation has not been tarnished by the passage of time.

*

Broome's Mobil Oil agent Ken Archer was always going to be one of the last to leave town. His family had been involved in the pearling business for decades and his role with Mobil Oil was just one of the many links he had with Broome. It was in that precise role that he was at the Broome airfield late on Wednesday night, more than 36 hours after the raid, checking that the fuel supplies were adequate for the aircraft expected to arrive the following morning. The Vacuum Oil Company agent had left some time earlier – that day or perhaps the day before – and had left 500 empty fuel drums stacked near the airfield's fuel point. That had attracted a lot of negative comments and Archer was determined that no such comments would be attached to him or to Mobil. He had a final look around the airfield before going home and found a naked man walking down the middle of the runway from the direction of Cable Beach.

The man was clearly in a bad way. He was solidly built but had recently been exposed to some hard conditions. He was unshaven and his hair was dishevelled. He was badly sunburnt and his lips were blistered, but he was conscious and coherent. He told Archer that he was an American air force sergeant and that his aircraft had been shot down just off Broome. His name was Melvin Donoho and he and his companion really needed help. Archer led him back to the airfield's hangar, still lit up because of the work that continued within, and after he was given water, food and clothes, Donoho told his story to Richard Legg, John Minahan (who had been called in), Archer and a group of incredulous American mechanics.

Donoho's story had the audience entranced. He said that he and Willard Beatty were the only two who survived the shooting down of their aircraft, the *Arabian Knight*. They had come together in the water and immediately began to plan their survival. The black plumes of smoke rising above Broome and Roebuck Bay provided an obvious reference point for them, and the two men had grabbed drums, containers, cushions, anything to support themselves as they paddled and kicked their way towards those distant targets.

They swam and drifted all that day and into the night without seeming to make any progress. They were held in a tight grip by tides and currents and it seemed they could do nothing to break that grip. At one point during the afternoon, the men were swept to within metres of a deserted beach, but were then swept straight back out to sea. The same thing was repeated several times over, and when it happened yet again, Beatty told Donoho that he doubted whether he could survive for much longer. Donoho, who was the stronger swimmer of the two, then started to spend periods of time floating on his back, using his legs to support Beatty, who was by now visibly weakening.

Morning became afternoon and afternoon became evening and still the men drifted aimlessly up and down the coast. They somehow survived the night together and early the next morning spotted the lighthouse at Gantheaume Point, the southern end of Cable Beach, just a few hundred metres away.

It could have been kilometres as they were again swept out to sea. At some time during the morning, the men agreed that if they stayed together, and continued to drift, they would both die. Their best chance of survival lay in Donoho striking out for shore alone. If he made it, he could direct a rescue party back to the area where Beatty would be floating.

With that, the men separated and were soon lost to each other because of the waves and currents. Donoho lost all sense of time and just concentrated on swimming and resting, swimming and resting, drawing closer to the beach but at a slow and frustrating rate of progress. Eventually, just after dark, his feet touched bottom and he staggered onto Cable Beach, probably somewhere around its southern extremity.

He made slow and painful progress along the beach until he thought he should be opposite the airfield and the town, and at that point left the beach and headed into the bush. By then, he was semi-delirious and walking like an automaton, but he became aware of a dim glow in the distance ahead and just concentrated on walking towards that.

Someone appeared out of the dark and gently led him towards and into the light – it proved to bc the interior light of an aircraft hangar – and he was soon swaddled in blankets, drinking water and eating a rich stew, and telling his story to Colonel Legg and Lieutenant Minahan.

When he was done, Donoho was led to a jeep and taken to the schoolhouse where he was put to bed. Early the next morning, he was woken, given a new set of army fatigues and taken back to the airfield where he was put aboard a B-17 for the long flight to Melbourne. Around the time his aircraft passed over Cable Beach, a search party there found the body of Willard Beatty, which had washed up in the general area where Donoho had swum ashore.

*

Late in the afternoon of Friday 6 March, a lone B-24 flew in from Melbourne carrying orders for Legg and Berry to now return to USAAF Headquarters in that city. The aircraft was rapidly turned around and departed again with the two Americans aboard.

Legg had been well-supported in Broome by his two USAAF lieutenants, Minahan and Rouse, and by the goodwill extended to him by the Australian authorities in the town. His legacy, if there was to be one, was of his focus on managing upwards rather than sideways and down. He was too conscious of what could go wrong if he made any particular decisions, too concerned of doing the wrong thing that he was not prepared to do the right thing when it was laid on a plate before him. He was, and will remain, a minor figure among those who rose to the top during those terrible hours at Broome. With Legg's departure, American responsibilities in Broome were now at an end.

As the last Americans, including Donoho, were leaving Broome on 5 March, the first returnees from the land convoy to the south were beginning to straggle back into town. If the air evacuation had been a qualified success, the land evacuation was a qualified failure, with the one blessing being that it did not cause any additional casualties.

The land evacuation commenced, continued and concluded in confusion. The devastation of the Japanese raid was followed by a brief period when Broome was awash with rumours of a possible Japanese invasion. These rumours seemed to be given substance by the formal announcements delivered publicly by Legg and others who were presumably in a position to know. Sam Male's telegraphed request for assistance to both defend and evacuate the town merely added an Australian overlay to a decision to abandon the town which had already been taken by the Americans.

The land convoy was never a complete entity in the way that convoys at sea were. Rather than being one discrete convoy, there were actually several convoys of men and machines: any support one may have offered another was soon just a moot point as the landscape, and the weather, turned the evacuation into a series of individual enterprises. The largest individual component of the 'convoy' was formed by and around Alec Bell or, more specifically, around the Bell Brothers' equipment and workforce. Those who were part of it realised that Colonel Legg's ideas about a convoy of cars and trucks travelling down the coast road at night without headlights were no more realistic than many of his other ideas.

Alec Bell and the locals had a much better understanding of the realities of the situation than Richard Legg and his senior officers. The northwest had just experienced three tropical cyclones and many other tropical storms, contributing to one of the wettest wet seasons in living memory. The road south was problematic for cars in good seasons; it would now most likely be impassable. Bell and his men therefore based their decisions on what was rather than on what they would have preferred it to be. Their convoy left Broome on the afternoon of 3 March. It was led by five large Ford trucks, each carrying several evacuees, and included the large, heavy-duty tractor that had been working at the airfield. It would be used to pull the trucks out of the mud when they became bogged, as they inevitably would. They aimed to go through to Port Hedland, but the most successful of them would only make it as far as Anna Plains Station, less than halfway there. That, too, was inevitable. What wasn't predictable were the many and varied experiences those who were part of that convoy would have.

*

Despite Legg's warning to his Americans to not jump the gun and thereby risk being classified as deserters, there were a number who took the opportunity to leave as soon as they could. One later described how a civilian contractor (Alec Bell) had offered him and his companions a lift aboard one of his trucks heading south to Port Hedland, 320 kilometres away. The American Frank Kurtz of the 19th Bombardment Group and several others from that unit accepted the offer when they were not on any evacuation lists, and climbed aboard one of Bell's trucks, which was loaded with food and water for the trip.

Just 35 kilometres south of Broome, the road they had been following simply disappeared, and there seemed to be nothing ahead but an endless vista of stunted scrub, broken occasionally by solitary trees and outcrops of rust-coloured rocks. The trucks soon became bogged, and the trip itself a nightmare of pushing and pulling through sand and bogs, with long detours around saltwater marshes. As they did so, the Americans were taught things about Australia and its laws, although 'lore' is probably the more appropriate idea.

One of the Americans later recalled that 'The Australian law is that any traveller can kill a sheep for eating, but he must skin it and leave the hide on a fence post for the owner.'

Eventually, the convoy could go no further. There was no road, not even any sign of a track. The recent storms had obliterated all traces of where the road had once run and all they could see ahead was an endless panorama of trackless bush. They turned around and started back to Broome.

*

The Dutch who were still in Broome after the *Nicol Bay* had sailed on the evening tide were also part of the mass heading south. Rudi Idzerda and the rest of the crew of the X-23 were offered a lift south by a group of Australians, an offer they accepted without too much hesitation. To the Dutchmen, the Australian bush seemed endless. The group that Idzerda and his crew were part of travelled through what seemed to be a trackless countryside with the aid of a compass and sometimes with reference to the sun. To Idzerda, they were well provisioned and confident, and he and the other Dutchmen got on very well with them, finding the Australians to be rough, hearty, uncomplicated and completely trustworthy.

However, their confidence in the Australians was not limitless. After getting caught up in some bad weather, it became obvious that something had gone seriously awry with the navigation. The discovery that they had absolutely no idea where they were coincided with the discovery that they were also getting short of petrol. Suddenly, and seemingly out of nowhere, an Aborigine appeared, a lone black man with long, dark wavy hair and a rich, full beard. After briefly communicating with the Australians using sign language, the Aborigine declined an invitation to ride in the car, but indicated that they should follow him. They bumped along behind him for an hour or so before he stopped and pointed to a telegraph pole that was clearly visible ahead.

They all knew that as long as they followed the telegraph poles they would eventually arrive at a settlement of some kind and so it was. The line ran past a fence and the fence led them, the next day, to the Anna Plains Station, where they were given a warm welcome. To the Dutchmen's surprise, the station was equipped with a primitive radio transmitter, for which current was generated by pedalling a stationary bicycle. It may have been primitive, but it was effective and the X-23 crew were soon collected by an aircraft. Their journey would end at an Australian naval base in Adelaide.

*

Most of those involved in the land evacuation of Broome failed to surmount the realities of climate and geography and straggled back to Broome within days of departing. The departures of 3 March arrived back in Broome during the afternoon of 5 March, and most of those who would return to Broome had done so by Sunday, 8 March.

The Broome they returned to was significantly different from the one they had left; it seemed smaller somehow, and less frenetic. The Americans had gone, which was part of the reason for the relative quiet, but there was now an air of resignation around the place, a feeling that what would be, would be.

The big American aircraft were gone, replaced by two RAAF Wirraways that had flown into Broome from their base at Pearce, outside Perth, on the morning of 6 March. What their pilots did not yet know was that one of their first tasks would be to search for a KNILM Dakota believed to have crash-landed somewhere to the north of Broome.

Nor were they to know that the crash site had been identified by some Aborigines who had left Broome on the eve of the raid. The Dakota, the *Pelikaan*, had been located on a beach at Carnot Bay and there appeared to be several survivors at the site.

CHAPTER 9

At the Edge of the World

It was all bush . . . it was hopeless.
Jo Muller

The survivors of the *Pelikaan* crash were in shock. First there was the violence of the Japanese attack and Ivan Smirnoff's stomach-churning aerobatics. Then the crash landing at water's edge and the continued strafing of the defenceless aircraft. The horrible wounds suffered by those who had been struck during the attacks and death. The increasing sense of desperation as they waited for rescuers who may not come, given that Broome itself seemed to be in strife.

The effects of this shock varied among the survivors. Most withdrew into themselves, for a time at least, looking off to some distant point on the horizon. One of them, the pilot Leon Vanderburg, sat down on the sand and started going through the contents of his sodden wallet. He removed all the banknotes and started placing them in neat piles on the sand in front of him. When one of the others asked Vanderburg what he was doing, he shot them a withering look and said he thought it was perfectly obvious. Indicating the little piles of banknotes in front of him, he said that one was for food, the other for water and the last was for cigarettes.

When Smirnoff joined the conversation, saying that he was still the captain and would decide how the food and water would be distributed, Vanderburg flew into a rage, cursed them all, and went to sit by himself. The incident brought home to Smirnoff the delicate state of everyone's nerves and how he would have to work to ensure they didn't kill each other before they were rescued. It also reinforced his belief that they were in a precarious – no, a desperate – situation.

*

Smirnoff had done most things correctly in the immediate aftermath of the *Pelikaan* being shot down. Some of his decisions had been borne of training and experience, and some had been instinctive. By early afternoon, he realised that their survival would now depend on planning and discipline. Jo Muller had managed to send out SOS signals before the radio battery had given out, and Smirnoff was confident those signals would have been received, if not by the radio operators at Broome, then certainly by one of the many Allied aircraft he believed were flying to and through the Broome region.

The most seriously wounded had been given what treatment he could offer and made as comfortable as possible among the sandhills, with blankets from the *Pelikaan* as makeshift beds and crude sunshades fashioned from parachutes. All were in a poor way. Daan Hendriksz had not regained consciousness, and Smirnoff knew he would not survive his wounds. Maria van Tuijn also remained unconscious, and Smirnoff believed that her wounds would also prove fatal. Little Johannes van Tuijn, just a baby really, was conscious but feverish. His leg wound was nasty but should not kill him, while Joop Blaauw, deep in a morphia-induced sleep, would survive his horrendous leg wounds if they were rescued and he was hospitalised soon enough.

The less seriously wounded should all survive with little more than minor scarring. Both Vanderburg and Pieter Cramerus had suffered shrapnel wounds, but they were really quite superficial. Smirnoff himself was probably the most seriously wounded among those who were mobile, with bullet wounds to both arms, one leg and his hip. He had been wounded more seriously in the previous world war; he had survived then and he would survive now. He was the captain, the leader of the little band. The braid on his cap and the pistol on his hip would sort out the rest.

The first thing Smirnoff did early in the afternoon was to undertake an inventory. Food and water, especially the latter, were the two necessities for survival where they were, and he sent Hoffman and Muller back to the *Pelikaan* to make a comprehensive search of the aircraft as soon as the tide had retreated enough to allow a safe passage into and out of the plane. They returned with a small water tank to hold drinking water for the crew, some tins of fruit and asparagus, and some half-rotten oranges left over from an earlier flight. The water tank contained around ten litres of fresh water, which Smirnoff announced would be rationed and distributed at the rate of several teaspoons per person per day. The fruit, asparagus and oranges would also be rationed as would the juice the fruit and asparagus were preserved in.

As afternoon became evening, other decisions were also made. The move back into the sandhills from the beach had been made because of the possibility of another attack by Japanese aircraft. When such an attack seemed less likely, the conditions in the sandhills became less attractive. It was very hot and very still back there, and sitting quietly, even in the shade, seemed to exacerbate feelings of isolation and thirst. There was always the chance of a (relatively) cool breeze on the beach, where it was also possible to sit in the water in the shade of the *Pelikaan*'s wings. The group decision was to stay on the beach as much as possible, even sleeping there overnight. Smirnoff decided that while the beach was certainly preferable to the sandhills, it was impractical to move the badly wounded backwards and forwards between the two. Not only would it cause unnecessary pain to the wounded, it would also be an unnecessary waste of energy for the fit.

However, it was necessary for someone to remain with the wounded at all times. Smirnoff would stay with them that first night, but it was a duty he expected them all to share.

*

The first night was one that Smirnoff would never forget. Like the others, he was thirsty, tired and despondent. His wounds hurt and, while they may not have been life-threatening, they certainly needed treatment. Infection and, ultimately, gangrene were always possibilities, so he continued to bathe his wounds in saltwater.

That night, he also had responsibility for the wounded and it was one that he took seriously. Daan Hendriksz was not a problem. Deeply unconscious and with very shallow breathing, he was mainly a background presence. Joop Blaauw drifted in and out of consciousness, calling out for water when he was awake and shifting around uncomfortably on his blanket when he was asleep. Little Johannes van Tuijn was the same, drifting between fitful sleep and waking periods when he seemed to be either screaming or whimpering. Smirnoff tried to help the little boy drink some water, but it took a lot of effort and the water was as likely to be spilt as it was to be drunk.

Maria van Tuijn was unconscious most of the time. Sometime during the night – Smirnoff thought that it was probably around midnight – she regained consciousness. Hearing her voice, Smirnoff moved across to sit on the sand alongside her. She asked Smirnoff about her son and seemed reassured when he said her little boy was asleep on her other side. She lapsed back into unconsciousness and, just a few moments later, with Smirnoff still beside her, Maria van Tuijn simply stopped breathing.

Smirnoff sat with her for a moment, thinking, then went into the sandhills and scraped out a small depression in the sand. He dragged Maria on her blanket to the depression he had dug and rolled her gently into it. He covered the body with the blanket and covered the blanket with sand. As he did so, Smirnoff recited the words he could remember from the Russian Orthodox Church's service for the dead. It wasn't much, but it would do until the morning when he would get the others help him make Maria van Tuijn's resting place a proper grave.

Just before dawn, Smirnoff realised that Daan Hendriksz had also stopped breathing. Again, he trudged back into the sandhills and scraped out a shallow grave into which he placed the remains of the young pilot. Another blanket, another thin layer of sand and another grave to be fixed in the morning.

He was tired and he was hurting, but he was the captain and he knew that he had to go on. He had seen many deaths in his time, but time did not diminish the impact of death when he again had to confront it. Maria and Daan had been his passengers, his responsibility and he felt that, in some way, he had let both of them down. He would keep his spirits up because that would help the others with theirs, but he had just buried two young people in graves he had dug with his bare hands. He must have wondered how many more he would have to dig.

*

The early morning sky suggested that Wednesday would be another hot day for the survivors. Smirnoff organised for a couple of the fitter men to throw more sand onto the mounds that covered van Tuijn and Hendriksz, and also supervised a final search of the *Pelikaan*. Nothing of any real value was found, but they did count more than 300 bullet holes in the fuselage and wings, and noted that the incessant pounding of the waves was starting to affect the aircraft. Cracks were beginning to appear along joints and welds, and it was obvious that if it remained where it was, the *Pelikaan* would soon break up.

Later in the morning, aircraft engines were heard flying high and coming from the north. When the aircraft appeared, several of the pilots recognised it as a Kawanishi Mavis flying boat, probably the same one that had made the reconnaissance flight over Broome two days earlier. The Kawanishi didn't deviate, but continued on a direct line south, towards Broome. An hour later, it returned, this time dropping down to make several slow, low-altitude passes over the *Pelikaan*.

Smirnoff and the others had taken cover in the sandhills when the flying boat dropped down towards them. Its last pass over the downed plane was a bombing run and the Japanese aircraft dropped five small bombs in a row, straddling the *Pelikaan*. None of them landed near the DC-3 and two that landed in the sand failed to explode. During the attack, Dick Brinkman covered Blaauw's body with his own, as much for reassurance as for protection; the crippled mechanic had been terrified by the sound of the engines.

After the Kawanishi left, Smirnoff called all the survivors together. Despite the two deaths, they would soon be in desperate need of water. He was one of those who had licked the dew off the bushes at the rear of the beach that morning and found it too salty to drink. He estimated that they had a day's supply left in the *Pelikaan*'s tank, perhaps two if they rationed it very carefully. After that, there was nothing, and in the climate they would die quite quickly if they weren't found.

What he proposed was to send out two men to explore the hinterland behind the beach where they had crashed. The men would search for creeks, springs, any form of fresh water and look for signs of human habitation. The rest of the survivors would find shade and do as little as possible during the day to conserve energy.

The two men he selected were the two men he trusted most, the *Pelikaan* crewmen Neef Hoffman and Jo Muller. He gave them strict instructions to go inland, seek high points from which to view the country, and return well before dusk so they didn't become either separated or lost.

Those who remained on the beach tried to do as little as possible. Depending on where the sun was and the state of the tide, they either sought shade under the branches of the shrubs in the sandhills or beneath the wings of the *Pelikaan*. Smirnoff distributed food and water, checked on the condition of Blaauw and baby Johannes – no change – and waited for Hoffman and Muller's return.

By mid-afternoon, when there was no sign of them, Smirnoff became concerned. He was even more so when the sun started to sink into the horizon and, when it grew dark, he was convinced that something bad must have happened. The two men eventually staggered into the makeshift camp, separately and in some distress, late at night. After a little food and some of the precious water, they told their story.

There was nothing inland from where they were. All they found was a seemingly endless plain that stretched as far as the eye could see in all directions. It was not completely featureless, there appeared to be low hills and rises, but the men could see no evidence of human habitation, native or European.

An examination of the coastal features appeared to offer better prospects so they set off to do that. If anything, the coast was even more disappointing. The area they tried to explore was comprised mainly of saltpans and mangrove swamps. At one point, they had to cross a tidal creek. Hoffman removed his shoes to do so and left them off as they crossed a sandy patch on the other side of the creek. Almost before he realised what was happening, the hot sand burnt the soles of Hoffman's feet and they blistered. The blisters burst and became so painful it was a real effort for him to walk. Although they had been just a couple of kilometres from the campsite, it had taken them several hours to cover that distance. Everyone in the camp struggled to sleep that night.

*

Smirnoff called them all together again in the morning and told them that he thought they would have been found and rescued by now. If they stayed where they were, they would all perish in the next few days. Their only hope of survival would be to split the party and send the fittest off to seek help. He believed Broome was no more than 80 kilometres to the south and he proposed sending two parties of two men each in that direction with whatever food and water they could spare. One party would consist of Jo Muller and Pieter Cramerus, and the other of Dick Brinkman and Hendrik van Romondt.

Before they departed, Smirnoff called the four men together, gave them half the food and water and told them that they were not to return to the campsite as doing so would only hasten the end for everyone. He also took van Romondt – still the biggest and fittest of them all – back to the *Pelikaan* and had him tear out some copper piping which Smirnoff planned to use to construct a small distillation plant to make fresh water from the seawater he would collect. They also carried away a kerosene tin for the same purpose. It was still early and relatively cool when the four men departed.

*

The two groups setting out for Broome from the *Pelikaan* campsite soon became separated, with van Romondt and Muller, the fitter pair, moving more quickly through the bush than Brinkman and Cramerus. After several hours, van Romondt and Muller were lost, almost out of water and starting to regret pushing as hard as they had. It was at that point they came across a soak, a small, muddy pool with water that was fresh, if a little gritty. Both men drank their fill, and then sat down to discuss what to do next. They had been walking now for several hours and it was the hottest part of the day. They agreed to find a shady place to rest for a couple of hours and then decide whether it was best to continue on or to perhaps return to the beach to bring the others to this spot.

Both men slept for an hour, perhaps two. The sun was still high in the sky, but when they returned to the soak they found that it had dried up and was just a patch of rapidly shrinking mud. Worse still, they were now out of water with no hope of replenishing their supply. Nature had made their decision for them, and the men now had no option but to continue on towards Broome.

For an hour, then two, they plodded south. As the sun started to sink, they realised they were now in real trouble, thirsty to the point of delirium, lost and struggling to put one foot in front of the other. Just as they thought they could go no further, a shadow appeared and a gentle voice spoke to them.

*

Among the Aborigines who left Broome to return home when the evacuations were ordered was a 25-year-old Bardi man named Jerry Dardan. Originally from One Arm Bay but raised at the Lombardina mission, Dardan had more recently been working as a labourer at the Broome airfield. When directed to travel to the Beagle Bay mission, Dardan and two companions named Joe Jinjarri and Paddy Torres decided to walk to the mission rather than travel on the truck that was evacuating the other Aborigines from Broome.

Late on the afternoon of 5 March, Dardan and his companions spotted two men in the bush ahead. By then, they were halfway between Broome and Beagle Bay and in an area where they would not expect to find other people. The three Aborigines went forward carefully, until they were close enough to see that the two men were struggling. Dardan walked towards them, noting that the men were very distressed and near collapse. He reached into his dilly-bag and took out the bottle of water he carried there.

*

After the men left the beach that morning, Smirnoff went to work setting up his small distillation operation. He filled the kerosene tin with seawater and set it on a small fireplace. He punched a hole in the lid, inserted the copper tube, which he looped and led to the water tank they had taken from the *Pelikaan*. It was crude, but it was effective, and Smirnoff thought that it might just help to keep them alive.

The pressure of not knowing what was to happen to them all was beginning to tell. They appeared to be perched at the edge of the world with little knowledge of either where they were or how long it would be before they were found or rescued. Alternatively, they were doomed to die here, alone and afraid. During the morning, several small altercations broke out over little things like who was sitting where, why they had to keep the fire stoked under the kerosene tin, and other things that normally would have been passed over without comment.

Little Johannes van Tuijn was at the centre of several heated exchanges. He would only sleep fitfully and, when he was awake, would whimper, those whimpers sometimes building into screams if he wasn't comforted. Dark comments would be directed towards the child when that occurred. Smirnoff did what he could, holding the baby, wetting his finger and trying to get Johannes to lick the water off it. He was rarely successful, and it seemed to Smirnoff that the child was slowly fading away.

During the day, massive banks of clouds built up and a heavy rainstorm struck the camp midway through the afternoon. Smirnoff quickly organised the others to grab the parachutes they had been using for shelters and use them to catch as much water as possible. Buckets, empty tins, anything that would hold water was pressed into service. The storm passed quickly and with the sunshine and blue skies came disappointment. Everything they had used to collect the rainwater had been affected by the salt spray thrown up by the waves. They had not collected as much water as Smirnoff hoped they would, and what they had was so brackish as to be undrinkable.

As they settled down for their third night on the beach, Smirnoff wondered just how much longer they could last.

*

Jerry Dardan called out to Joe Jinjarri and Paddy Torres that the men they had found were European and in a bad way. The three Aborigines gathered around the two Dutchmen and by sharing their food and water with the exhausted men were able to bring them back to a state of coherence and relative comfort. From Muller and van Romondt, the Aborigines learned the story of the *Pelikaan*, its crash landing and of the deaths and injuries among its passengers. They also learned that those still alive had very little food or water, and could not survive much longer in the tropical heat.

From the Aborigines, the Dutchmen learned that they had crashed between Broome and Beagle Bay, the only settlements for hundreds of kilometres around. They also learned that Beagle Bay was closer than Broome, and that Dardan and his two companions would head there now to raise the alarm and see if a rescue party could be organised immediately. Before they did that, however, they led the two Europeans to a more permanent soak – one today known as 'Dutchman's Well' – left them there, and told them to remain at that place. They would return but it would probably take at least a day. With that, Dardan and his friends disappeared into the gathering gloom.

*

For Smirnoff, Thursday night and Friday morning were perhaps the lowest hours of his life. The distillation plant he had built worked, but very slowly. If it was to produce enough fresh water to make a difference to their prospects, it would have to be in operation 24 hours a day. This, in turn, meant that someone needed to check that the fire was still alight and that the apparatus had not fallen over or fallen apart. Smirnoff allocated that task to those at the campsite, making sure the duties were shared evenly among them to avoid any more unnecessary arguments. Something woke Smirnoff during the night; when he looked around, he saw Heinrich Gerrits drinking from their freshwater tank.

When Smirnoff confronted him, Gerrits merely shrugged it off, said he had been thirsty, but also said it wouldn't happen again. Worse was to follow early the next morning just as it was light enough to see.

Up early as usual, Smirnoff looked around the camp, firstly checking on the condition of their two wounded, Blaauw and little Johannes. The child was in a semi-coma and Smirnoff doubted he would survive the day without medical assistance. Blaauw had simply disappeared. At some stage during the night, the mechanic had removed the makeshift splints from both his shattered legs and crawled away. It was easy to see where he had gone – downslope, towards the beach. He left an obvious trail which ended near the edge of the water, in what appeared to be a pile of discarded clothes. Looking closer, Smirnoff realised it was Joop Blaauw, and he was dead.

Smirnoff could only speculate on what Blaauw had been thinking, or if he had even been thinking at all. He knew that he could not leave Blaauw's body there but knew he was too weak to drag it back up the beach by himself. He went back to tell the others and to get help to bring the body back for burial. Help was eventually forthcoming, but it seemed to Smirnoff that there was more than a tinge of resentment attached to it.

*

Jerry Dardan led Joe Jinjarri and Paddy Torres to the Beagle Bay mission. The distance would have been the best part of 55 kilometres, but they made good time and were there before dawn on Friday, 6 March. The story they told spread like wildfire – a Dutch plane shot down by the Japanese with some people killed and survivors marooned on a remote beach. A camp among the sandhills at Carnot Bay. Small parties sent out to seek help. The poor state of the survivors and the urgency attached to organising their rescue.

The Pallotine missionary in charge of the Beagle Bay mission, the German Bishop Raible, took charge immediately. He would drive to Broome as soon as it was light to tell the authorities there about the Dutch plane and the survivors at Carnot Bay, and encourage them to organise some kind of food drop for those survivors.

While he was doing that, a rescue party would be fitted out at Beagle Bay to travel overland to Carnot Bay to bring the survivors back to the mission. There were no roads and no real tracks between the two places so the rescue party had to travel on foot, with one or two pack animals carrying their supplies. Raible nominated one of the younger monks, Brother Richard Bessenfelder, to lead the rescue party that also included Phillip Cox and Joe Bernardi, local Aborigines familiar with the area, and Gus Clinch, the Australian Army warrant officer who had been placed at Beagle Bay to keep an eye on the German monks there and to provide a military presence in the north-west. Dardan would guide the party back to where they left the Dutchmen at the soak, and then onto the camp at Carnot Bay.

Bishop Raible left in a truck for Broome shortly after sunrise, estimating that it would be around midday before he would be there to raise the alarm. The rescue party led by Brother Bessenfelder left later in the morning. Dardan thought it would take them most of the day to get back to where they had left the Dutchmen. After checking on them, they would push on, and hope to arrive at the Carnot Bay campsite sometime on Friday night or Saturday morning.

*

Smirnoff had come to the conclusion that they were fated to end their days where they were, dying either of thirst or starvation, or perhaps killing each other when one or more of them could no longer stand the sight of his colleagues. Their interactions were very brief now, each man looking inward rather than outward. For Smirnoff, where there was life there was hope, and he determined to continue doing whatever he could to keep them alive for as long as he possibly could, to keep pushing back that inevitable end.

That Friday morning, he spent a lot of time with little Johannes van Tuijn. The poor child seemed to be dying by inches. He no longer screamed, he seemed too tired to do that, but he would whimper quietly from time to time. Smirnoff spent an hour, more, rocking the child backwards and forwards in his arms, speaking softly to him of things that had been and things that might be. He tried to give the child little sips of water, but Johannes' lips were cracked and he now seemed to also be unable to swallow. When Johannes fell asleep, Smirnoff put him down gently on his bed and went for a walk along the beach. Because of Johannes, he did not want to stray too far from the campsite, so he walked down to some rocks not twenty metres from where the *Pelikaan* was being slowly broken up by the waves. He thought that, with luck, he might find some shellfish there. He found nothing to eat, but he did find his binoculars, wedged between two rocks and miraculously unbroken. He carried them back up the beach and set about thoroughly drying them.

Those binoculars were put to good use just a couple of hours later. Someone heard a noise they believed might be aircraft engines and looking south, Smirnoff thought he could see two little black specks, planes flying quite low over the beach and weaving from side to side as though searching for something. Those on the beach took cover beneath bushes in the sandhills. Through his binoculars, Smirnoff spotted the RAAF roundels on the aircraft – he recognised them as Wirraways – just as they spotted the *Pelikaan* wreck. By the time the Wirraways arrived over the wreck, Smirnoff and the others were out on the beach, waving furiously and shouting out at the tops of their voices.

The aircraft flew low with their cockpits open, and the pilots waved back to the men on the beach below. They then turned in a wide arc and flew low and parallel over the beach. As they did so, the pilots threw out a number of packages attached to small parachutes that landed in a line along the edge of the sandhills at the rear of the beach. As those on the beach scrambled back to retrieve the packages, the Wirraways made one more low pass over the *Pelikaan* before flying off again in the direction of Broome.

Smirnoff feared what would happen if the packages were opened immediately and their contents simply wolfed down. He insisted that they be gathered together before being opened. Whatever they contained, he said, those contents would be rationed as they still had no idea when they would be rescued. Two of the packages had scribbled notes attached to them. One of the notes read, 'Relief party be with you tonight with food and medical supplies. Good luck. MacDonald, RAAF'. The other read simply, 'Relief party arriving tonight from mission'.

One package contained a variety of tins of either fruit or fruit juice, some chocolate and packets of cigarettes and boxes of matches. Others contained medicine and dressings – sadly, of limited value now. Except, Smirnoff remembered, for little Johannes. After distributing the food among the others, and explaining that eating too much too quickly could well kill them, Smirnoff selected some condensed milk and a first-aid kit, and returned to the shelter where he had left the child on his blanket.

While he had been gone, Johannes had turned onto his side, curled up into the foetal position and put his thumb in his mouth. Smirnoff didn't have to touch the tiny figure to know that the child had quietly slipped away while he and the others were at the beach. Smirnoff may not have been able to save the little boy but there was one last service he could do for him. He tore Johannes' parachute shelter in two and used half of it to wrap the body in a tiny shroud. He carried the body out to the back of the sandhills where they had buried his mother and scraped a hollow in the sand. He had a moment's panic when he realised that he couldn't remember which of the three graves Maria van Tuijn's was. Then he thought that it didn't really matter anyway. If there was a heaven, mother and child had already been reunited there.

He lay Johannes in the tiny grave and piled sand over the body. As he did so, he muttered the half-forgotten words of the

Russian Orthodox prayers that he had learned as a small child a long time ago. His thoughts touched briefly on mortality and the many ways death could find you no matter where you were. Then he simply stopped, stood up and returned to the others on the beach. There were still things that needed to be done.

*

The rescue party from the Beagle Bay mission made good speed across the seemingly featureless plain. They were at the Dutchman's Well soak by evening and found the two men they had left there, van Romondt and Muller, waiting for them and still in reasonably good health. Scouting ahead, one of the Aborigines found the other team of Dick Brinkman and Pieter Cramerus, also close to the end of their endurance, and took them to join the others at the soak. Between them, the four Dutchmen were able to provide an accurate description of just where the *Pelikaan* had come down. Decisions were made by Richard Bessenfelder. When the Dutchmen were well enough to travel, one of the Aborigines would lead them back to Beagle Bay. The others would push on to Carnot Bay. Bessenfelder made sure enough supplies were offloaded, then he and the main party pushed on.

Around 3 a.m. on Saturday, 7 March, Ivan Smirnoff became aware of a dark figure moving among the sandhills and stood up, ready to call out a challenge. The figure disappeared, then reappeared close by, speaking in a soft voice and with inflections and accents that made it difficult to understand what he was saying. What Smirnoff understood, though, was that the figure was a scout attached to a rescue party that was on its way and would be there sometime around dawn, now just a few hours away. The figure disappeared as quietly as it had arrived. Smirnoff toyed with the idea of waking the others to share the news with them, but decided against it and lay down to try to get some more sleep himself.

Right on dawn, Brother Richard Bessenfelder's rescue party arrived at the makeshift camp. Those survivors were all awake – Smirnoff had woken them up shortly before the sun rose. Bessenfelder and Clinch examined the Dutchmen and provided what medical assistance they could, while the food and water they had brought from Beagle Bay were distributed among those who had survived. While this was happening, Phillip Cox, the Aborigine who had guided Bessenfelder's party to Carnot Bay, wandered down to the beach to examine the wreckage of the *Pelikaan* to find it riddled with bullets from one end to the other, and amazed that anyone aboard had survived.

Neither Ivan Smirnoff nor Richard Bessenfelder wanted to tarry at Carnot Bay; there was literally nothing there to sustain them and it was around a 40-kilometre trek to get back to Beagle Bay. They left as soon as they reasonably could but didn't push as hard on the return trip to the mission as they had on the outward leg. The party camped out in the bush that Saturday night and arrived back at Beagle Bay on Sunday afternoon. Van Romondt, Muller, Cramerus and Brinkman had already arrived, and all the Dutchmen would later recall a level of care and concern that far exceeded anything they had expected.

At the mission, the Dutchmen ate, drank, washed and were given new clothes to replace their rags. They were also given beds to sleep in. Two days later, a week after they had been shot down, the mission truck drove them back to Broome. Before they departed, a grateful Ivan Smirnoff presented Richard Bessenfelder with a pewter mug with the KNILM logo; it would remain one of the monk's most treasured possessions.

In Broome, they were given medical assistance and accommodated overnight at one of the hotels. The next day, they were flown to Port Hedland for medical treatment at the hospital. Later that week, the *Camilla* flew them to Perth from where the survivors went their separate ways. The long last flight of the *Pelikaan* was finally over.

CHAPTER 10

Scorched Earth, Empty Seas

> Unless aerodromes in the north west . . . are urgently required for our own advanced bases, the population should be withdrawn and anything of slightest value to the enemy destroyed.
>
> Official Report, 20 March 1942

The Japanese did not forget about Broome after the raid on 3 March. A follow-up raid was launched from Penfui the next day, but had to turn back when, just 80 kilometres short of Broome, the planes ran into a severe weather front. Further reconnaissance flights were ordered and another raid took place almost three weeks after the first, late in the morning of Friday, 20 March. There were major differences with this raid. The first is that it was undertaken by Mitsubishi G4M 'Betty' heavy bombers rather than just fighter aircraft. The second was that this time the town of Broome itself was targeted. There was also a third, quite significant difference. The marksmanship demonstrated by the fighter pilots was not duplicated by the bomb aimers aboard the Betty aircraft. Almost all the bombs that were dropped fell well wide of their intended targets. There was no significant damage to the town and only one casualty – a Malay man named Abdul Hamid bin Juden was killed by an errant bomb.

*

On 6 March, Radio Tokyo announced that Japanese naval aircraft had successfully attacked Broome three days earlier. The brief report was picked up in all the major Allied capitals, and ultimately reported in city and country newspapers across Australia. It was more of a communique than a news report, published under the headline 'Broome attacked' with a dateline of London, 6 March. It read:

> It was officially claimed in Tokyo today that the Japanese naval planes which raided Broome on Tuesday destroyed 28 flying boats. It was also claimed that at Wyndham which was machine gunned on the same day a hangar was set on fire and a transport plane burned.

The Japanese announcement came hot on the heels of the official Australian government response to the raid – in some weekly newspapers the two appeared in the same edition – and the two were a contrast in both style and content. Prime Minister John Curtin told his Australian constituents that:

> Rumours to the effect that loss of life in the Broome raid yesterday were very heavy is (sic) utterly untrue. It is not in the national interest to make any statement giving details of casualties at any particular place as this will give valuable information to the enemy. I can assure the Australian public, however, that while losses have been incurred – whether they be life or property – the raid was not of a kind to give that satisfaction to the enemy which he expected.

The words were Curtin's; the reasoning behind them was that of the Australian military chiefs of staff. When asked for advice on releasing any or all of the details of what had actually taken place at Broome, their formal response was:

> The Chiefs of Staff consider that it would not be in the national interest to make any statement giving the details of casualties at any particular place, as to do so would give the enemy valuable information. They also consider that to make a statement in relation to the raids at Darwin, Broome and Wyndham would establish a precedent which would require a similar statement to be made in the case of all future raids.

Given that the words used would have been carefully chosen, it would be easy to suggest a cover-up, an attempt to obscure the fact that military planning for the Japanese air raids on Darwin and the northwest was at best sketchy and at worst non-existent. The reality in March 1942 was that those chiefs of staff were in shock rather than in denial. Just two weeks earlier, most of an Australian infantry division had been surrendered to the Japanese in Singapore, a fortress city widely believed to be impregnable by most Australians.

In the three months since they entered the war, the Japanese had conquered an area that had taken the British, Portuguese, Spanish and Dutch more than 300 years to subdue. The Australian chiefs of staff and the Prime Minister were scared by the pace of the Japanese advance and by the capacity of the Japanese air forces to mount attacks on the northern half of Australia seemingly at will. The press release was not put out to deceive the people of Australia. It was put out to dampen fears and maintain morale while the military and civil authorities found out what had actually happened and made necessary arrangements to thwart what seemed to be a Japanese plan to seize a foothold in the northwest of the continent.

*

For nearly three weeks, almost nothing was done. In Broome, Harry Macnee, Beau Davis and Hamilton Smith were in daily contact with their various headquarters in Perth, and both Sam Male and Beresford Bardwell continued to pepper the Western Australian government with advice and requests. Laurie O'Neill did the same with the Department of Native Affairs, although some of his correspondence was of questionable value to the decision-makers in the south. In one of several missives he sent to Perth, O'Neill noted, 'though we were caught unprepared and our losses were heavy, we had the satisfaction of knowing that approximately about five of the attacking planes would not return to their base'.

Reports such as these obviously clashed with other reports coming out of Broome and, in a generous world, might explain part of the delay in sending senior officers to Broome to investigate and report. There were issues at Broome, but it seemed that the authorities in Melbourne, Canberra and Perth were incapable of making decisions about them.

On 20 March, around the middle of the morning, RAAF Wing Commander Charles Snook landed his Hudson aircraft at Broome airfield with his passenger, Major Clifford Gibson. Snook was to prepare a comprehensive report on what had happened recently, while Gibson was there to take charge of the defence of Broome and, indeed, of the entire northwest of the continent between Carnarvon and Wyndham. In one respect, the actual timing of their arrival was unfortunate. Barely an hour after their arrival, the second Japanese air raid struck the town. While not a great deal of damage was done, Snook's aircraft was damaged. For the rest of his time in Broome, Snook feared that someone, somewhere, had leaked details of his movements to the Japanese.

Gibson had been given an impossible task. The 43-year-old major was not a regular soldier; a lawyer, before enlisting in the AIF, he had been Western Australia's senior prosecutor. He must have been shocked by what he found in Broome. When the last of the Americans flew out on 6 March, the entire defence of Broome rested on six rifles. The RAAF had 40 boxes of ammunition, but this was for arming the Wirraways, while the Broome Volunteer Defence Corps still held 5000 rounds of rifle ammunition. Two Browning machine guns had been salvaged from American aircraft destroyed in the 3 March raid, but until Gibson could beg some ammunition from a visiting

US aircraft, the guns were for display purposes only. Gibson also had a truck and two cars at his disposal.

Snook's job was never going to be all that much easier than Gibson's. The 51-year-old had seen service in the previous world war, but seemed more suited to an administrative rather than a frontline role, and those still in Broome very definitely believed that they remained in the frontline of war.

Prime Minister Curtin's statement on the raid may have been for the general public and designed to maintain morale, but in Broome it had the opposite effect. Long accustomed to being isolated and ignored, the statement simply reinforced those beliefs. The evacuation of the last American and Australian personnel on 6 March was only partly alleviated by the arrival of the two Wirraways and their RAAF support staff. The townspeople did not want inferior aircraft and a pair of middle-aged administrators. They wanted guns and planes and tanks, whatever was needed to really protect the town and deter the Japanese.

The return of the stragglers from the failed land convoy added more voices to the chorus calling for something, anything, to be done. In the absence of state and federal authorities, a number of prominent locals stepped into the breach. By Saturday, 7 March, all of the town's basic services – electric light, sanitation, the ice works – were functioning again after those responsible for their operation had simply walked away. The town's two major stores, Dyson's and Streeter and Male's, were open for business. There were some restrictions to bringing the town back to the level of service it had provided before the raid, though, as both the Koepangers and wharf labourers refused to work during the daylight hours.

A local evacuation committee had also been formed under the auspices of the Broome Roads Board.

Tensions still remained high in the town. A report from the RAAF's senior officer in the town before Snook's arrival, probably Flight Lieutenant Davis, dated 10 March, stated baldly that civilian morale in Broome had 'seriously deteriorated' since the return of those who had been part of the land convoy to the south. Those returnees had demanded that Davis and Harry Macnee of the VDC arrange for the immediate evacuation of all civilians from Broome. While Davis was content to simply report this to the Air Board in Perth, Macnee took it further. He sent an urgent telegram to Western Area command headquarters, also in Perth, requesting both the proclamation of martial law and the forwarding of troop reinforcements. Neither request was acceded to.

Two days later, the sitrep (situation report) from Broome was more optimistic. It reported briefly on the operation of the evacuation committee, and noted that the work of the committee meant that the 'discontented population' was now 'temporarily satisfied'. All the town's essential services remained operational, although the report's author believed that the freezing works would most probably be shut down. A stocktake of all food and fuel supplies held in the town would be completed that day. The report concluded by saying that all the wounded Dutch refugees, the seriously ill and the aged, plus all the town's 'wilful' residents had now been evacuated to Port Hedland.

The pendulum swung back the other way when Davis again put his name to a sitrep to the Air Board on 16 March. He said that the Board's decision to withdraw the RAAF medical officer Hamilton Smith and other RAAF personnel was causing real consternation in Broome. A meeting that day had set up what he called a 'special committee', and that committee had decided that unless troops for the defence of the town and a replacement doctor were despatched immediately, an organised evacuation of the town, and indeed the district, would be ordered by the committee. What Davis did not mention was that the twelve RAAF personnel then in Broome had decided to stay to assist the locals until their replacements arrived.

*

That was still the situation on the ground when Snook and Gibson arrived four days later. Snook talked to all the people who had any real knowledge of Broome and the region, but the report he submitted was predicated on the basis that Broome, and the entire northwest, were expendable because there were more important battles to be fought elsewhere.

The wing commander noted that there were only about 65 white men then living in Broome and that most of them were 'very panicky' and concerned about their isolated and exposed position. The defences available were limited. The town's major businesses had disappeared and, apart from those involved in maintaining the town's essential services, there did not appear to be any good reasons for the other civilians to remain in Broome. Snook did note that it would be difficult for them to get away owing to the almost complete lack of transportation in the town.

After noting that the runways at the airfield had been mined so they could be destroyed if the circumstances warranted it, Snook offered the opinion that the entire town and all its facilities would be taken by a Japanese destroyer and 100 soldiers, and they would do it 'with the greatest of ease'.

Snook then turned to the real reason he had been sent to Broome and offered recommendations for what should now happen:

> Unless aerodromes in the North West such as Broome, Wyndham, Derby, etc., are urgently required for our advanced bases, the population should be withdrawn and anything of the slightest value to the enemy destroyed. The seasons have been good; provided an early start was made it should be possible to drive the cattle south. I suggest the above scorched earth policy owing to our own apparent lack of equipment, there being no machine guns available.

Snook's is a strange document, full of internal contradictions and possibly written to support a policy that had already been determined. As Snook was submitting his report, Beau Davis was ordered to remove all the pearling luggers from the northwest.

When the Japanese invaded, they would find nothing but scorched earth and empty seas.

*

The Japanese air raid highlighted the need for the Broome pearling luggers to be relocated away from the northwest. If, as many suspected, the raid was the forerunner of a Japanese invasion, the luggers would be ideal vessels to carry bands of Japanese soldiers up and down the coast. Early in March, government regulations placed all small coastal vessels under military control so there were no legal impediments to cleaning out the region's ports and harbours. The main problem Beau Davis now had was that he had no crew to sail the luggers anywhere at all.

As Davis continued to condemn and burn luggers in the creeks and bays between Broome and Wyndham, a large part of his workforce headed south. They were the Koepangers and Malays who had formed the bulk of the crews on the pre-war pearling fleet, and had been working as labourers at the airfield while the luggers were laid up for the wet season. Along with most of the other workers, they headed south with the land convoy, but returned in dribs and drabs in the days that followed. Their return gave Davis his workforce just as the pressure started to build for him to put his evacuation plan into action. First, though, he had to make some modifications to that plan.

Because the luggers Davis had selected for evacuation and relocation were all working vessels, some thought was given to relocating them to ports where they could be put to productive use. Davis was asked to consider sailing some of them to Darwin and Colombo in Ceylon (Sri Lanka). These plans were never formalised as the potential crews refused point-blank to even consider undertaking such dangerous journeys.

The second issue was the competence of the crews themselves. All were good sailors, but were not qualified as anything beyond deckhands. Up until the war, most of the luggers had been captained by Japanese, but they were obviously no longer available. Davis had serious doubts about the ability of the lugger crews to navigate their way through potentially dangerous seas all the way south to Fremantle, a journey that would probably take a couple of weeks to complete even if everything went well. The crewmen themselves were not apparently too concerned, believing that if they stayed together and remained within sight of land, nothing too bad would occur. The RAN also said it would send a small vessel under the command of Commander Geoffrey Branson to shepherd the fleet south.

Davis was given a month to prepare the 45 luggers he had selected to make the voyage south. He completed the task in just under the allocated time and his fleet prepared for departure on 22 March. He might have delayed longer had he known what lay ahead, as the fleet set sail on a voyage that turned into an unmitigated disaster. The lugger fleet was divided into three separate flotillas and led out of Roebuck Bay by Branson's naval vessel. As they approached Port Hedland, they sailed straight into a cyclone and were scattered across the ocean. Five luggers sank off the port in the storm on 25 March, and a further eight were pushed deep into the mangroves that fringed Port Hedland's harbour.

A decision was made by Commander Branson and Lieutenant Dais to try to refloat those luggers. That decision wasted a lot of time and used up a lot of goodwill. Because of the tidal range in the northwest, work to refloat the vessels could only be undertaken at low tide when the men had a foothold in the mud. The daytime heat and humidity among the mangroves also made it preferable to work at night. Sandflies and mosquitoes were in plague proportions and the sighting of sea snakes and sharks near the boats at high tide didn't help. The fleet eventually set sail again, only to be struck by another tropical storm at Cossack, near present-day Karratha.

Another five luggers were lost. A further two went down in rough weather near Geraldton and, finally, three were blown ashore and broken up at Scarborough, just to the north of Fremantle, on 30 June.

The final number of people and vessels lost may never be known. Some luggers simply disappeared, lost when blown far out to sea or broken up on some previously unknown reef. Some may even have been deliberately run aground by a frightened crew who then just walked away to resume their lives elsewhere. It would seem that fewer than half – and perhaps as few as a quarter – of the luggers made it all the way to Fremantle. Crew losses were also heavy, and the dozen or more Koepangers and Malays who died were as much victims of the poor planning that characterised all the Broome evacuations as they were of the elements. The seas had been emptied, but the cost was high.

*

Complete plans and individual proposals for the implementation of a scorched earth policy were put forward by both civil and military authorities, examined in Broome, Perth and Melbourne before most were rejected outright. Some of the gelignite that the *Camilla* had flown into Broome after the attack was used to mine the runway there, and a proposal was floated to demolish the airfields at Wyndham, Port Hedland, Derby and Drysdale as well. The Air Board in Perth considered, and then rejected, that proposal. The Army suggested blowing up the Wyndham meatworks and all utility plants throughout the entire northwest, suggestions also rejected by Western Area command in Perth.

In the end, and at last, common sense prevailed. There would be no scorched earth policy. Broome and the smaller towns and settlements would not be abandoned and destroyed, but left as they were. A small garrison would remain in Broome, but otherwise the measures adopted were precautions designed to address possibilities rather than pre-emptive responses to those same possibilities.

Luggers continued to be either pressed into service or destroyed, depending on their condition, but other precautions were proportional to the threat. The lighthouse keeper at Cape Leveque, to the north of Broome, was ordered to turn his light off lest it be used as a reference point. He was also given a radio and an aircraft recognition guide and ordered to report any suspicious activity. Throughout the northwest, all properties and outstations equipped with pedal radios were given photographic recognition guides containing details of Japanese, Dutch, American and Australian aircraft, with a code to describe each, and instructed to telephone in any sightings.

The land-based equivalent of the empty seas policy was also attempted. All over the northwest, mobs of cattle were brought together into large herds that were then driven across the top end of Australia to Queensland, and from there down into the southern states. Around 100,000 cattle were involved in the operation and some of the drovers were on the road for months.

The farmers left behind prepared themselves for what might happen as well as they could. For several weeks at Wallal, their property on the coast between Broome and Port Hedland, the Lacy family braced themselves for a possible

Japanese invasion by evacuating their homestead every night. They slept in a special camp they had built in the bush, over a kilometre inland from the main home, where each family member had their own camp bed made out of cyclone wire mesh and a mosquito net. Every morning at sunrise, the family was given the all-clear to return to the homestead by their Aboriginal houseboy who, in turn, had been given it by the Aboriginal night watchmen who guarded the homestead overnight. After a few weeks, the Lacy family moved back into their home. The Japanese were either coming or they weren't, and it didn't matter too much either way.

Broome was given a garrison of 50 soldiers, a figure that remained constant for the rest of the war. Occasional RAAF flights and RAN and civilian ships visited Roebuck Bay, but mostly the little town just bathed in the sun and battled through the various wet seasons that came and went.

Broome was now part-ghost town, a shadow of what it had once been. In May 1942, the total civilian population of Broome comprised 30 Europeans and 27 Koepangers and Malays, most of whom worked in some support role for the military. All were waiting for an invasion that never came.

CHAPTER 11

The Ghosts of Roebuck Bay

War is the tragedy of what might have been.
James Bradley, *Flyboys*

The Japanese were satisfied with the air raid on Broome and its results. The attack was part of a two-pronged strike – the second target being the airfield at Wyndham – directed against facilities they believed were being used to evacuate key personnel from Java and fly in vital supplies to those still fighting the Japanese on the island. If those Western Australian towns could be used in a defensive support role, they could certainly be used in an offensive role should circumstances change, making them important military targets. Japan's only success in Wyndham was in blowing up a fuel dump, but the fifteen flying boats and eight land-based aircraft they destroyed at Broome was seen as a significant victory.

At Broome, only military targets were attacked in the 3 March raid. Almost without exception, all the aircraft attacked were military aircraft, the exception being the *Corinna*, the QEA flying boat that had been part of the evacuation effort from Java. It may not have been camouflaged, but the *Corinna* was as legitimate a target as any of the other aircraft there that day.

Despite their obvious successes, the Japanese did not have it all their own way. The most successful in the unit which carried out the attack, Warrant Officer Osamu Kudo, was shot down and killed when his Zero crashed down into the sea off Cable Beach. Neither Kudo nor his aircraft were ever recovered. Another of the attacking Zeros also failed to return to the squadron's base at Penfui. Private Yasuo Matsumoto's aircraft was slightly damaged in the attack. Realising that he would not make it back to base, Matsumoto put his Zero down in the sea near a small uninhabited island just to the south of Rote Island, just twenty kilometres off the southern coast of Timor.

It took Matsumoto two hours to swim to the uninhabited island. He was later taken across to Rote Island by local fishermen and stayed with them until he was picked up by a Japanese patrol boat and taken to Kupang, where he rejoined his squadron on 20 March. His comrades warmly welcomed him back; they all thought he'd died.

Six of the seven Zeros that returned to Penfui had bullet holes from ground fire in them, and another one of the pilots, Sergeant Masalei Okazaki, was slightly wounded.

The Japanese admiral, Yamamoto, the architect of the Pearl Harbor attack, allegedly said before war broke out that, should Japan initiate hostilities, their forces would run amok in the Pacific for six months, but then the industrial might of the United States would begin to inexorably slow them down and ultimately destroy their capacity to wage war, and so it was. Slowly at first, then with a gathering impetus, the Allied forces firstly matched and then overtook Japan's forces in the Pacific. When they did so, the war would have only one possible outcome. Had Japan not surrendered after the atomic bomb attacks of August 1945, a significant portion of the population would have starved to death. The Japanese will remained strong but, just as Yamamoto had predicted, they were no longer physically capable of waging war.

The fate of those who took part in the Broome raid on 3 March provides a sanguine illustration of Japan's declining war fortunes. The Babs reconnaissance/observation aircraft that accompanied the Zeros on the Broome raid was caught and shot down by American fighter aircraft near Darwin on 22 March. There were no survivors.

Lieutenant Zenjiro Miyano, the leader of the Zeros in the Broome raid, went on to become a fighter ace, with sixteen confirmed combat victories. On 16 June 1943, Miyano was leading a force of 24 Zeros over Guadalcanal when they were attacked by a superior force of American fighters. Miyano did not return from the mission and neither he nor his aircraft were ever seen again. He was posthumously promoted two ranks to commander.

One by one, the other Zero pilots from the raid fell to the Allies' growing air strength. The only Japanese pilot who attacked Broome to survive the war was First Air Private Yasuo Matsumoto. He would later describe the success of the Broome raid thus: 'Our greatest fruits of battle were beyond expectations.'

*

Strategically, the Japanese air raid on Broome was of only marginal significance; the loss of aircraft and minor damage to the airfield had no lasting impact on the Allies' capacity to resist the Japanese but, tactically, it was an outstanding success. When news of the raid filtered back to Dutch headquarters in Bandung, further evacuation flights were directed to either Port Hedland or Derby. That order, too, soon became moot. Two days after the last MLD flying boat departed Tjilatjap (Cilacap), a major Japanese air raid destroyed what remained of the facilities there. The next day, all remaining Allied forces on Java surrendered to the Japanese.

A trickle of aircraft flew out of Java after the raid, but the main evacuation route had been severed. The destruction of the flying boats had one more consequence. Both the *Corinna* and the A18–10 had been earmarked for further evacuation flights to both Java and Timor. These flights were to rescue particular, high-value RAAF and RAF personnel, high-ranking officers and a number of men with important technical skills. With no suitable aircraft available, those flights were never made and those who were to be rescued became prisoners of the Japanese.

Broome was attacked three more times during the war. The second raid, on 20 March 1942, inflicted some damage and one person was killed, but by then Broome was virtually a ghost town. Another attack took place in August 1942, and that one, too, had few consequences. The final Japanese air raid on Broome was one year later, in August 1943, and resulted in neither damage nor casualties. It was almost as if the two August attacks were as much about seeing what the Allies were up to in Broome, and checking that the town and Roebuck Bay were not being used as a base to launch an attack on the Japanese-held islands of the Netherlands East Indies. They weren't, because by then the Allied focus was on New Guinea and the islands of the Pacific.

The reputations of several of Broome's leading citizens were tarnished by the 3 March raid. The competence of Australian military planners and the general feeling towards Americans and their priorities. Coming on top of the disaster that was the Japanese air raid on Darwin, Australia's top leaders, civil and military, looked for scapegoats. In the case of Broome, the most obvious scapegoat appears to have been General Eric Plant, the commander of the 5th Military District, the command responsible for Broome. Plant himself would later report that:

> A considerable amount of activity by the US Air Force took place at Broome without any information being received here, and from reports received since, this activity and its sudden cessation had most to do with the chaotic conditions there.

If his aim was to deflect criticism of the shortcomings of his military command, the ruse did not succeed.

It was an admission that the general in charge didn't know what was going on in an important part of his command, and it was this alone that justified Plant's transfer to an administrative position on the east coast of Australia and his replacement by Gordon Bennett, the general who had fled Singapore just hours before the surrender to the Japanese. Coincidentally, Bennett had passed through Broome as he was being repatriated back to Australia.

Many lesser ranked officials also suffered opprobrium because of their actions. One of them was Police Inspector James Duff Cowie. Like many others, he had recently suffered from the dengue fever that he had first contracted in 1941 and had actually applied for a transfer from Broome on health grounds. That application was approved on 28 February, but Western Australian police protocols required Cowie to remain in place until his replacement actually arrived to take over.

Cowie was seen around town during the afternoon after the raid but then, as far as those in town were concerned, he simply disappeared. Cowie and the police commissioner in Perth, David Hunter, had exchanged a series of telegrams in which Cowie said that he could do no more in Broome and Hunter said that, until instructed otherwise, all police officers in the northwest were to remain at their posts while the current crisis continued. Cowie flew out of Broome aboard a Dutch flying boat on 6 March and travelled down to Perth where he was admitted to hospital for a complete health check, apparently at Hunter's direction. A police board of inquiry was formed, and it recommended that Cowie be dismissed from the Western Australian Police Force for leaving his post as the district police officer for the Roebourne and Kimberley districts without the authority of the police commissioner and without lawful excuse.

The Western Australian Legislative Assembly subsequently ordered a judicial review of the board of inquiry's findings and recommendations. It was held in Perth a year after the original inquiry, in late March 1943, and both Dr Jolly and Harry Macnee gave evidence on the state of Cowie's health in early March 1942. The key point, though, seemed to be Cowie's claim that there was no doctor available to treat him in Broome after Jolly flew out to Port Hedland on the afternoon of 3 March. Evidence showed that at least one American doctor – Dimmock – was still in Broome for a short period afterwards and that Flight Lieutenant Hamilton Smith, the RAAF doctor, was also available from that afternoon. Evidence was offered that Cowie was aware of all this.

The judicial review's decision, handed down in late March, upheld Cowie's dismissal. James Duff Cowie's 32-year police career was over. He reappeared briefly again in 1946 as a prices investigation officer, investigating offences against the postwar price control legislation, but thereafter was lost to history.

Dr Alexander Jolly also felt slighted by Cowie's dismissal, in which he felt his professional medical advice had been discounted. At his appearance before the 1943 judicial review, Jolly testified that he had asked the British Medical Association, then Australia's peak medical body, to investigate his conduct at Broome. They had completely vindicated his actions. Perhaps rumours about Jolly's early exit from Broome persisted for, in October 1944, he enlisted in the AIF and, as Captain Alexander Jolly, served in the 2/2 Casualty Clearing Station, a unit that was expected to operate very close to the frontline. Jolly was demobilised in November 1946 and disappeared from public view until March 1949. Then, as a member of the Communist Party of Australia, he was arrested and subsequently fined for addressing workers outside the Midland Junction railway workshops without permission.

*

Harold Mathieson survived the war. After carrying 100 evacuees from Broome to Port Hedland aboard the *Nicol Bay*, Mathieson was ordered to sail the ketch south to Fremantle where he and the *Nicol Bay* spent the rest of the war, working out of the Boom Defence Depot. In the immediate aftermath of the raid, several of the Dutch survivors presented Mathieson with an inscribed revolver and other mementoes for what he had done for them. At war's end, the Netherlands government awarded Mathieson the Gold Medal of the Order of Orange Nassau for his rescue efforts on Roebuck Bay. The medal was presented to Mathieson in a ceremony at the Broome Boom Depot by the Dutch Consul in Perth in late October 1945. The Consul read out the citation which accompanied the award:

> To the captain of the ketch Nicol Bay for having directed his ship to some burning and sinking aircraft belonging to the Netherlands Navy during an enemy attack on Broome, March 3 1942, bringing to safety and care several wounded Dutchmen who were then in extreme life danger, thereby showing initiative and judgement as well as extraordinary personal courage.

After the war, Mathieson and the *Nicol Bay* returned to civilian employment, and resumed their pre-war lighter role among the ports and inlets of the northwest. The *Nicol Bay* ran onto an unmarked reef near Cockatoo Island in King Sound and was wrecked on 5 September 1959; fortunately, there were no casualties. Afterwards, Harold Mathieson retired and moved to Perth, where he died in May 1963.

One of the *Nicol Bay*'s deckhands, Charlie D'Antoine, worked from before dawn until after dusk on the day of the raid, in and on the water and later on the jetty and at the cemetery.

D'Antoine stayed in and around the northwest for the remainder of the war and was reunited with his mother and siblings in Derby when the war ended. By then he was working for Australian Iron and Steel Limited on Cockatoo Island in Yampi Sound and it was there that he learned that his actions on 3 March 1942 had been recognised by the Royal Humane Society of Australia with a Certificate of Merit for his bravery.

In late September 1945, the Netherlands Embassy in Canberra awarded Charlie D'Antoine the Silver Medal for Humane Assistance. The citation read: 'This distinction has been accorded to you for your actions in connection with the saving of lives from burning and sinking Netherlands Navy planes on March 3, 1942.'

D'Antoine received two further medals from the Dutch, one from the government and the other from the KNIL, the Royal Netherlands Air Force, but neither he nor Mathieson received any official recognition from the Australian government or any of the Australian armed forces.

*

Three weeks after the raid, Lewis Ambrose was flying another QEA flying boat, the *Corinthian*, from Brisbane to Darwin via

Groote Eylandt. The aircraft was on loan to the RAAF, and carrying a number of servicemen when it crashed on landing in Darwin harbour, possibly as the result of a collision with a submerged log. The aircraft was written off and two American servicemen were killed. Ambrose's injuries were so severe that he was hospitalised for five months. Ambrose remained with Qantas after the war. Between 1952 and 1954, he was the airline's London manager, and after that, manager of QEA's Far East operations for four years. In 1958, he was appointed general manager of all Qantas operations in Europe and the United Kingdom. He retired at the end of that posting.

After flying out of Broome on 6 March, Lester Brain spent time in Perth and Sydney before moving to Brisbane where he was appointed manager of all Qantas operations. These included a major maintenance base Qantas established at Archerfield that serviced both RAAF and USAAF aircraft. On 10 November 1944, Brain was at the controls of the *Coolangatta* when the flying boat crashed on landing at Rose Bay in Sydney Harbour. One passenger was killed and five passengers and crew received serious injuries. His co-pilot on that flight was Keith Caldwell, whose A18–10 had been destroyed on Roebuck Bay.

Brain remained in the RAAF Reserve and was promoted to wing commander in 1944. He stayed in the service until July 1947. That year both he and Lewis Ambrose received letters of commendation from King George VI for their work in Broome in February–March 1942.

Brain worked for Qantas after the war and while still in the RAAF Reserve. After he resigned in 1955 he remained within the aviation industry. He was awarded the Order of Australia in 1979 and died in a motor vehicle accident the following year. He was 77 years old.

John Oram, the senior steward who was Brain's right-hand man during their time in Broome, enlisted in the RAAF on Anzac Day 1942, perhaps as a result of what he had seen in Broome and on Roebuck Bay. He served in the RAAF until 1949 when he was discharged from the service as Flight Lieutenant J. C. Oram, DFC and bar. Oram had served as a Lancaster pilot flying missions over Europe. Both DFCs were awarded for bravery during those operations. He made his home in Melbourne, where he married in 1948. Oram died in Parkville, an inner Melbourne suburb, in 1966; he was just 53 years old.

Captain Jimmy Woods, the MacRobertson Miller Airlines (MMA) pilot who narrowly missed being shot down at both Wyndham and Broome, worked tirelessly in the days after the raid, providing a one-man shuttle service between Broome and Port Hedland, organising the rescue of the crew of the X-36 and generally offering all assistance he could. For his efforts, Woods was subsequently made a Knight of the Order of the Orange Nassau by Queen Juliana of the Netherlands. He left MMA in 1948 to form his own company, 'Woods' Airways', which used war surplus Avro Anson aircraft to fly passengers between Perth and Rottnest Island, the shortest scheduled passenger flights in the world. From then until his last flight on the route he had pioneered fourteen years earlier, Woods made an incredible 13,000 flights between the island and the mainland. Captain James Woods, MBE, died on 9 May 1975. His ashes were scattered on the water between Perth's City Beach and Rottnest Island.

Herb Plenty was the young RAAF flight lieutenant who tried to convince anyone who would listen that the overflight by the Mavis on 2 March meant that an air attack would be launched against Broome the next day. Plenty survived the war as Wing Commander H.C. Plenty, DFC and bar, and he remained in the RAAF when hostilities were over. He held a number of senior postwar positions, including commanding officer of the RAAF Communications Unit at Point Cook and, later, commanding officer of the RAAF's Central Flying School at Sale in Victoria. Plenty passed away on 13 May 2013 at the National Capital Private Hospital in Canberra.

Andrew Ireland was the 22-year-old, Scottish-born RAAF corporal and armourer who was blown into the water with the dinghy he was trying to inflate when the A18–10 exploded in flames. Ireland spent several hours on Roebuck Bay rescuing as many survivors as he could, and later helped with the recovery and burial of the dead. For his efforts, Ireland was subsequently awarded the British Empire Medal and the Distinguished Flying Medal for bravery in March 1943. He was demobilised in March 1946 with the rank of warrant officer. Andrew Ireland passed away in 2001.

One of Andrew Ireland's crewmates who also worked hard at rescuing survivors on Roebuck Bay was 23-year-old Frank Russell. Russell was flown to Melbourne the night after the raid aboard an American B-17 and, in a telephone conversation from there with his mother, related a story he had heard about the pilot of a Zero shot down at Broome. The pilot's body had been recovered, he said, and on examination it had proved to be a woman. On 21 May 1944, while he was still serving with No. 20 Squadron, Pilot Officer Frank Russell's Catalina flying boat was shot down by Japanese aircraft. There were no survivors. Russell's short life and service are commemorated by a plaque in his father's old church in Cooma.

The Bardwells, Beresford and Biddy, are remembered by a street name in Broome. Their son, David, joined the RAAF and survived the war. Both Beresford and Biddy eventually retired from their various roles in Broome and moved to Perth where Beresford passed away in 1961. The irrepressible Biddy Bardwell died at her home in Swanbourne on 1 October 1971.

Catherine Milner was one of those evacuated from Broome shortly before the attack. Two of her children, James and Joan, both volunteered for the air force during the war, James finishing as a flight lieutenant and Joan as the squadron officer in charge of Western Area command. Catherine returned to Broome after the war, but with her children all adult and living elsewhere, it was no longer the home it had once been. She sold the Sun Theatre and retired to Perth.

Captain Harry Macnee, DCM, MC, of the Broome VDC, was a genuine hero in two world wars. He continued to serve in the 2nd Battalion of the VDC until he was discharged in February 1946 at 59 years of age. Like many others, Macnee moved to Perth after the war, settling in the suburb of Nedlands and working as a pearl buyer. In 1946, he was an industry representative at a conference held in Canberra to chart the future of pearling in Australia. He was appointed to the State Transport Board in 1947 as the board's rural representative, a position he held for the next five years. Harry Macnee passed away on 28 October 1960.

The Americans who played a significant part in the events at Broome that day all survived the war. Jack Lamade and his ill crewman, Tubbs, flew their Seagull down to Port Hedland without incident, and then continued all the way down the coast to Perth, where they arrived on 7 March. Later in the war, Lamade became the commander of the US Navy's Combat Group 7 aboard the aircraft carrier, the USS *Hancock*. After the Battle of the Leyte Gulf, he was awarded the Navy Cross for his leadership during that battle. John Dietrich 'Jack' Lamade died in Williamsport, Pennsylvania, the town of his birth, in April 1985.

Dr Charles Stafford, killed when Osamu Kudo shot down the B-24 *Arabian Knight* off Cable Beach, was posthumously awarded the Silver Star for his medical work in Java before he was evacuated to Broome. The wreckage of the *Arabian Knight* has never been found.

Lieutenant Colonel Richard Legg remained in the US Air Force after the war, serving as the commanding officer at the Otis Air Force Base at Cape Cod in Massachusetts before his final posting, in 1956, as the vice commander of an air force division.

Both of Legg's deputies during the Broome operation, lieutenants John Minahan and John Rouse, also remained in the air force after the war. John Minahan relocated to Melbourne and married an Australian girl named Mavis Monahan in East Melbourne on 26 May 1942. The Minahans made their home in the US after the war. Minahan retired from the air force in 1965.

John Rouse was also posted to Melbourne and he, too, married an Australian girl named Honor in May 1942. Rouse went on to a distinguished war service career, twice being awarded the Silver Star for gallantry. Promoted regularly in the postwar air force, Rouse rose to the rank of brigadier general and when he retired in 1967, it was as the commanding officer of the Pacific Air Force Base Command, located at Hickham Field in Hawaii. Honor Rouse joined her husband in the US after the war. The couple had four children, a son born in 1950 and triplet daughters born in 1954. One of those daughters, Sharon, studied in Holland and married a Dutchman. As Sharon Vos, she is one of the best-credentialled age-specific long-distance runners in the US. Rouse passed away in 2005 at 90 years of age.

The surviving aircraft and aircrew from PatWing 10 were relocated to Perth's Matilda Bay from 7 March 1942 until September 1944 when the units was relocated to the Admiralty Islands. While at Matilda Bay, the unit grew to a strength of over 60 aircraft and 1200 personnel, and it was one of the few American units involved in the Pacific War from the first day to the last.

*

The group most affected by what happened in Broome and Roebuck Bay that day were the Dutch men, women and children who thought that the problems in their lives were behind them when they touched down in Australia. None of those who survived the day, neither the MLD aircrew nor the evacuees – de Vluchtelingen – could ever forget what they saw, heard, smelled and touched that day. That so many of them went on to live full and productive lives is a testament to the human spirit.

The shrapnel that struck him was never removed from Henk Hasselo's body. The sergeant pilot of the X-1 was transferred to the RAF for the duration of the war, most of which he spent flying Catalinas out of Ceylon. After the war, he married an Australian girl and also resumed his MLD career in the NEI. When the Dutch NEI became the independent nation of Indonesia, Hasselo brought his family back to Australia. For the rest of his working life, Hasselo was a pilot with Australian National Airlines.

Bastiaan Sjerp, the X-20 pilot who saved his baby son, David, by strapping the child to his chest and then floating on his back, also continued as a wartime pilot. In 1947, still an MLD pilot, he was awarded the Flying Cross for sinking the Japanese destroyer *Shinonome* off Miri in Borneo in the opening days of the war. He was subsequently awarded a second Flying Cross for his service in Europe later in the war. When Sjerp retired in 1964, he was the commander of all Dutch naval aviation. He died twenty years later, in June 1984, aged 69 years.

Rudi Idzerda survived the war after training as a fighter pilot. After the war, he remained in the MLD, eventually reaching the rank of rear admiral and flag officer. He later wrote his memoirs, *Adventures of a Flying Dutchman*.

Theo Doorman followed his late father's career path, joining the Dutch Navy and serving for several years before retiring as a lieutenant commander and pursuing other interests.

The Koens family travelled on to Port Hedland from Broome, and were then flown to Melbourne, where they stayed for several months. Both Pieter and Elly learned English in that time. The Koens were sent overseas to the US and eventually moved to Canada, where they settled permanently.

A. J. and Hendrika de Bruijn, who were aboard the MLD Catalina Y-70 and lost their daughter Arina on Roebuck Bay later adopted Willie Aggelen, who was also aboard the Y-70 and who lost both her parents. She was saved by the wounded man who slipped beneath the waves shortly before Willie was rescued.

*

The legend of Ivan Smirnoff continued to grow in the postwar world. When Margot Smirnoff, living in Sydney, learned that her husband was missing and believed dead, she organised a memorial service for him. Afterwards, she gave away all his clothes and shoes to Dutch evacuees who had fled the NEI with few, if any, possessions. She thought that Smirnoff would not be needing them again and that he would like his friends wearing them and thinking of him. When she learned that he was alive and after he returned to Sydney, Margot organised a welcome-home party and invited all their friends. Everything Margot had given away was returned to Smirnoff at the party.

Smirnoff spent the war flying transport aircraft for the KNIL. Afterwards, he moved back to KLM and by 1948 held the world record for flight time, having racked up over 28,000 flying hours. When not flying for KLM, Smirnoff was loaned out to other aviation concerns. In 1948, for example, he was on loan from KLM to the Atlas Supply Company of America, flying the company's 'Skymaster' aircraft on a world sales tour.

Smirnoff and Margot returned to the Netherlands after the war. Cancer claimed Margot in late 1945, but Smirnoff kept flying for KLM until 1949 when he retired to the Spanish island of Majorca. He remarried and wrote an autobiography, *The Future has Wings*.

Smirnoff passed away on Majorca on 23 October 1959. He was 61 years old.

Pieter Cramerus, another of the *Pelikaan* survivors, retrained as a fighter pilot and was eventually posted to a Spitfire squadron in England. There, he flew over 400 reconnaissance and combat missions and was shot down one more time during these. Cramerus moved to the US after the war, settling in Houston, Texas. He subsequently became an American citizen, bought a ski lodge and retired to a ranch in Montana where he pursued his twin passions of bird-hunting and fly-fishing. When the ranch became too much to handle, Cramerus moved to Denver, Colorado.

Daan Hendriksz did not survive the last flight of the *Pelikaan*. The military pilot left behind a young widow, Jacqueline, who was pregnant with the couple's first child. Jacqueline was taken prisoner by the Japanese and held in an internment camp for the rest of the war. Seven months after her husband's flight, she gave birth to a little boy she named Daan. Both Jacqueline and little Daan survived the war, and back in Holland after it ended, Jacqueline remarried. She and her new family later migrated to Australia.

Sergeant Leon Vanderburg also survived the *Pelikaan* experience and the war and he, too, migrated to Australia, passing away in Victoria in 1975.

The Aborigines involved in the rescue of the survivors from the *Pelikaan* had their actions recognised by the authorities. Jerry Dardan was rewarded by both the Dutch and Western Australian governments. The Dutch presented Jerry with a valuable hunting knife and money that was placed in a savings account opened on his behalf. The Western Australian government presented him with a new tomahawk, a new billycan and a blanket. Joe Jinjarri and Paddy Torres were also given new blankets.

Parts of the *Pelikaan* still exist in the Broome Museum, at Smirnoff Beach at Carnot Bay and at Waterbank Station near Derby. When the RAAF salvage team went to the aircraft in 1942, they dismantled and removed the engines, the controls and the control surfaces. Some of these that can be seen at Waterbank and in the museum today. Everything else was left where the aircraft finally slid to a halt on the beach on 3 March 1942. In the postwar years, the site attracted both the curious and treasure hunters. It was probably the latter who, in 1975, blew up the remains of the *Pelikaan*, leaving just the few parts that are visible today.

*

Gus Winckel was treated for his burns primarily by Dr Dimmock, the USAAF flight surgeon, and was back in the air the day after the attack. For two days, he flew shuttle flights between Broome and Port Hedland in a borrowed Lodestar, before flying down to Perth. There, he was asked to make one last flight to Java to evacuate some senior RAF officers trapped in Bandung. On 6 March, he departed Perth and, travelling via Broome where he refuelled, flew into Bandung that night. There he landed on a road lit only by jeep headlights, refuelled and flew fourteen passengers to safety in Perth.

Winckel was subsequently based at Moruya on the south coast of New South Wales, where he was part of a squadron that flew reconnaissance and anti-submarine patrols up and down the coastline. On 5 June 1942, just days after the Japanese midget submarine attack in Sydney Harbour, Winckel and his crew were flying an anti-submarine patrol off the coast when, to their surprise, they spotted a submarine on the surface, moving at speed and leaving a strong wake behind. They attacked the submarine with bombs and sank it. That success provided a highlight in what had been an otherwise bleak year for Australia. Winckel and his crew were personally congratulated by Prime Minister Curtin.

After the war, Winckel was awarded both the Bronze Cross with Honourable Mention and the Gold Cross for his wartime exploits. He migrated to New Zealand, married and raised a family, and eventually retired to Burleigh Heads in Queensland.

Winckel died on 17 August 2012 from complications arising from a broken hip he had suffered six weeks earlier. He left behind a 92-year-old wife, Yvonne, and three sons, Shayne, Jean-Paul and Michael. He also left behind memories of outstanding courage and service to both his country and to humanity.

There are two streets named after Gus Winckel in Broome, one of which leads to the airfield where he made his one-man stand. A statue of Gus also stands in the main street of Moruya, placed there to recognise not only his wartime service, but that of all the airmen who flew their lonely patrols out of Moruya.

*

Within a short while, the sea took most of what had been left behind in Roebuck Bay. Just a few weeks after the Japanese aircraft flew away, another Dutchman passed through Broome and walked out at low tide to see where so many of his countrymen had died. In his diary, he described how he looked out on the sand and mudflats, searching for souvenirs, anything to remember the other evacuees who had died there, so near their journey's end. What he found was a place of eerie silence with a few sad mementos of what had transpired in that place. 'Rotting suitcases with men's, women's and children's clothing, bags, hats, shoes covered by a thin layer of mud in the barnacle-encrusted destroyed airplanes.'

Soon, even that was gone and just the frames of the great flying machines were left.

The bodies of the Dutch men, women and children killed in the attack and buried alongside the beach at Roebuck Bay did not rest there for long. In April, they were joined by the four victims of the *Pelikaan*, and in August–September 1942, all the bodies were reinterred in the Broome War Cemetery. After some pressure from the Dutch authorities and the families of the dead, the remains were once again removed from their resting place in January 1950. The bodies of four Dutch naval personnel and 31 Dutch civilians were reinterred in the Netherlands oor Lagegraven, a shrub-lined section behind the Garden of Remembrance in the Perth War Cemetery. The Dutch community in Perth holds a service there each May to commemorate the end of World War II in Europe and the sacrifices of the Dutch. The service includes placing a rose at the headstones of the 35 Broome victims buried there.

The remains of the other Roebuck Bay victims were repatriated to Indonesia and the Netherlands. Those reinterred in Indonesia rest in the Dutch Cemetery of Honour, located in the Menteng district of Jakarta.

*

Postwar Broome was never going to be the same as pre-war Broome; too much had happened and too much had changed. Of the 52 luggers that worked out of Broome before December 1941, only six survived the war. In Broome itself, only ten of the houses in the town were occupied by the original inhabitants at both the start and the end of the war. Pearl shell never made a comeback either, although pearls did. Broome was well placed for the renewed pearl market, as it was well placed for the mining boom that started in the 1950s and has continued to this day. It is equally well placed as a stopover for the 'grey nomads', the retirees who travel far and wide to see their country.

In 1967, the long jetty at Broome was demolished, its replacement being another very long jetty, but this one is much closer to the mouth of Roebuck Bay.

Today, the remains of some of the flying boats on the seabed of Roebuck Bay and of the *Pelikaan* at Smirnoff Beach on Carnot Bay are visible when the tides are low enough. The Western Australian government declared the Broome flying boat wrecks heritage sites on 17 April 2003. This was the first time that submerged aircraft wreck sites that had been located were formally protected as heritage sites in Australia.

*

No-one can say exactly how many people were killed in the Japanese attack on Broome. There is general agreement that 48 Dutch evacuees died there sixteen men, twelve women and twenty children – and that another 32 were missing and believed to have been killed in the attack. Another half-dozen RAF aircrew were killed as were nineteen of the Americans aboard the *Arabian Knight*. That gives a total of 105, to which the four dead aboard the *Pelikaan* must be added. The RAAF doctor, Hamilton Smith, noted the high proportion of dead to wounded when he arrived in Broome the afternoon of the raid. A general rule of thumb for combat casualties is three wounded to one dead. It seems that at Broome, that figure was closer to one to one, bringing the total casualties to just over 200.

For many years, it was accepted that, in a fourteen-day period from mid-February until 3 March, around 8000 evacuees – mostly Dutch women and children – were airlifted from Java to Broome and beyond. Even the official war historian, Paul Hasluck, fell in line; he did add a rider to this though: 'The figure of between 7–8,000 evacuees passing through Broome was originally from the observations of an official of the Broome Road Board.'

That figure was always problematic. It seems as though the various aircraft movements somehow became conflated, and that it was assumed that any aircraft flying in from Java was packed with evacuees. This was simply not the case. The largest number of evacuees in Broome was the 200-plus who were there on the morning that the Japanese struck. Recent work by Dr Tom Lewis and Peter Ingman has balanced the picture. They posit a figure of 1350 evacuees, of whom some 400 were Dutch.

*

Over time, the Japanese air raid on Broome on 3 March 1942 came to assume its place in the roll call of significant war events in twentieth-century Australian history, something of a footnote to the story of the Japanese push into the southwest Pacific. Broome was not the major disaster that Darwin was, nor was it a raid that captured the public imagination that the midget submarine raid on Sydney Harbour did. But it was not insignificant, certainly for those who were there.

On the sixtieth anniversary of the raid, David Sjerp returned to Broome for the first time since his evacuation. He was far too young at the time to have retained any memories of what had taken place and at first felt nothing about Broome or what the memorial service would mean. While in Broome, he took the opportunity to walk out to the remains of the flying boats in Roebuck Bay, exposed by the very low tide. As he stood looking at the rusting metal poking through the sand and mud, he felt a numbness creep over him, almost a feeling of disassociation, that there was nothing, absolutely nothing here for him. The next day, alone in his hotel room, Sjerp was struck by a wave of emotion that took his breath away.

That same year, Theo Doorman also returned to Broome for the service. He could still clearly recall the day of the attack and what he had done to survive. He could also remember the fates of others who didn't survive and confessed that what he had seen had given him nightmares for years afterwards.

Others came back for the seventieth anniversary in 2012. Pieter and Elly Koens, then aged 83 and 80, were there, the memories of their family's survival still fresh in their minds. Henk Hasselo was there, as was Frits van Hulssen. Gus Winckel wanted to be there but ill health prevented him from travelling. He was represented by two of his sons.

The day was very similar to that which dawned on 3 March 1942 – very warm early on, with the promise of even hotter conditions as the sun rose. It was the tail end of the wet and the day promised to be fine throughout. The main service was held early, at 8 a.m. in Bedford Park where a small memorial to the events of 3 March 1942 has been placed. It is opposite the spot where the steam railway once ran down to the long jetty, and not far from where Keith Caldwell, Rudi Idzerda, Old Adam and others watched the silver fighters diving down onto the helpless people below. There were dignitaries and there were speeches and, for some of those present, there were memories of that terrible day.

At 4 p.m. a smaller service was held at the Broome Museum. Piet and Elly Koens, still called that although she had been Elly Doeland for many years, were there to present their mother's passport to the museum. It was the passport their mother Sara had lost in Broome that day and which was returned to her when the family were living in Melbourne months afterwards. It was appropriate that part of the Koens' history find a resting place overlooking the place where they had fought together to live.

One of the unsung heroes they had gathered to honour that morning was Maurie Carseldine, the Shell Oil man who took his launch out to rescue survivors on 3 March 1942 and again the next day to look for Americans who may have survived the shoot-down of their aircraft. Carseldine had not spent a lot of time in Broome – a few weeks at most – but he had a souvenir from his days there.

Sometime after the raid, Carseldine was at the airfield, his primary workplace, and while walking around the place spotted a small group of coins someone had dropped, probably as they were looking for cover during the raid. He picked them up. There were sixteen in the little collection, and there was no real pattern, no sequence to the coins. They were from all over – India, Brazil and Holland, one very old with '1857' the only legible writing on it. A couple appeared to have been burnt and one was certainly misshapen. Carseldine took them with him when he left Broome and, years later in Brisbane, let his daughter Carol play with them.

He had always thought to return them to Broome as a memento of that terrible day but, in the way of things, he never quite got round to doing it. Maurie Carseldine passed away in 2002. What the parent was not able to do, the child did, and that afternoon, Carol Carseldine donated her father's coins to the Broome Museum.

Soon afterwards, the sun dipped down towards the horizon over the Indian Ocean and night fell over Broome and Roebuck Bay. The special guests would soon depart Broome, many of them leaving with the knowledge that they would probably never return. Seven decades earlier, they, and many others like them, had arrived in Broome, seeing that arrival as the start of a brand new life. One hundred of them would never leave. They would perish in and on the waters of Roebuck Bay. They were long gone, too, but the memories of who they were and how they died would never wash away.

EPILOGUE: JACK OF DIAMONDS

Mid-March 1942

After medical treatment in Broome, Port Hedland and Perth, Ivan Smirnoff was eventually cleared to rejoin his wife and KNILM in Sydney. While passing through Melbourne, he was visited by two men dressed in suits at his hotel. One introduced himself as a police detective, while the other was a senior official of the Commonwealth Bank. They asked Smirnoff about the package that was entrusted to him just before he took off from Bandung.

Smirnoff told them about the *Pelikaan* and how the package was swept away while he and the survivors were marooned. The men revealed that the package contained some valuable silver coins, some high-denomination NEI banknotes, and a small fortune in cut diamonds.

Ivan was both surprised and shocked by the news,

particularly because he felt that the bank – and the government – could have trusted him with knowledge about what the package contained exactly. Questioned at length, Smirnoff nonetheless maintained his explanation of what had happened, and his account was corroborated by the other *Pelikaan* survivors.

*

At around the same time as Smirnoff and the other *Pelikaan* survivors were being interviewed about their knowledge of the mysterious package, a beachcomber named Jack Palmer was sailing his lugger into Carnot Bay. Palmer was well known in Broome and throughout the northwest. He was the kind of drifter who had always been attracted to the region, someone who may have had a colourful past and who appreciated the freedoms that came with being a long way away from the centres of governmental authority. Palmer made a living doing a little bit of this and a little bit of that. He would work ashore, generally in Broome, for long enough to fuel and provision his lugger, and then sail away for days, weeks or months, until he had either found something of value or needed to replenish his supplies.

On this latest voyage in March 1942, Palmer's crew consisted of two young Aboriginal boys and they were slowly sailing north from Broome to Beagle Bay where he thought there might be some work available because of the relocation of so many of the Broome Aborigines to the mission there. The detour into Carnot Bay was just to have a look around to see what might be there. Palmer quickly spotted the wreck of the *Pelikaan* at the edge of the beach, and anchored just out on the other side of the breakers before leaving the boys aboard while he rowed the lugger's dinghy ashore.

Palmer moved quickly through the interior of the aircraft, looking for anything that had an intrinsic value. There were some discarded items of clothing in the main cabin, which he threw into a pile near the door. He would give them to his crew later as part-payment for their work. He only took things that could be prised loose and carried without too much effort; he would leave the heavy salvaging to the professionals. The tide was low and as he looked into the various spaces in the aircraft that had been opened up by the pounding of the waves, he spotted something wedged between the fuel tank and the metal of the fuselage.

It took a bit of work to get the package out and Palmer looked closely at it when he had done so. He thought it may originally have been wrapped in thick paper or even cardboard, but that had been thoroughly soaked and was now little more than lumps of mush held together by stamps and a formal red seal. This he easily tore apart and threw on the sand. What he then held was a quite large leather wallet containing a number of internal pockets. He did not know what those pockets held, but suspected it might be valuable. He decided to wait until he was back on the lugger before opening it.

Palmer rowed back out to the lugger, gave the clothes he had found to the boys, and retired to the cabin where he carefully opened the wallet. The coins and banknotes were a windfall, but it was the diamonds that thrilled him. There were dozens – no, hundreds – of them, and while most were quite small, there were a number of decent-sized stones. Palmer knew his beachcombing days were at an end, and the days of living hand-to-mouth were all behind him now. All he needed to do was to keep his mouth shut and his plan his next moves carefully.

*

But, in fact, Jack Palmer did neither of these things, and from this point onwards it becomes difficult to separate fact from fiction. Shortly after making his discovery, Palmer sailed away to the north, eventually reaching Beagle Bay where he anchored near two other luggers that had pulled up on the beach. He recognised them both; they were owned by his acquaintances and fellow beachcombers, Jack Mulgrue and Frank Robinson.

Palmer just couldn't help himself. He blurted out his find, and showed the diamonds to the men after swearing them to secrecy. To seal the bargain, he gave both men a few diamonds.

With that, the 'Dakota diamonds' assumed a life of their own. Palmer used diamonds to purchase sexual favours from Aboriginal women at the Beagle Bay mission, and it seems that the others may have done the same. Diamonds also seemed to have been used to purchase supplies and some were given away as gifts to friends and acquaintances. Frank Robinson later claimed he buried his in a bottle in the sand at a place called Little Creek. They were recovered by an Aboriginal woman named Connie Jurida who, unaware of their real value, used some to pay for tobacco.

The Beagle Bay mission became the epicentre of diamond activity. The Aborigines, who were the recipients of many of them, were generally aware that they had come from the Dutch aircraft that had been shot down at Carnot Bay but had little, if any, idea of what the stones were actually worth.

Some were simply passed down to children who used them as playthings. When, later, they heard that police would be coming to enquire about the whereabouts of some missing diamonds, many people at the mission panicked. The stones were thrown away, as if tainted, into the sea, into the creek and down lavatories.

The police involvement came about because of Jack Palmer. In mid-April 1942, Palmer walked into Major Cliff Gibson's office in Broome and told the somewhat bemused army officer that he wanted to enlist in the Australian Army as it was his patriotic duty to do so. As if to convince Gibson of his patriotism, Palmer produced a salt shaker, removed its lid, and tipped the contents onto Gibson's desk. Dozens of diamonds spilled out. Thus it was that on 14 April 1942, Jack Palmer became W87102, Private John Palmer of the 19th Garrison Battalion. He was immediately earmarked as the coastal observation man to watch the seas and skies from Gantheaume Point, where Gibson could keep an eye on him. Gibson confiscated the diamonds and despatched them by courier to Perth.

An army investigation team was formed in Broome under the leadership of Lieutenant Laurie O'Neill, the former policeman and Inspector of Aborigines now in army uniform and heading up a field security unit. Because he was now in the army, Palmer did not have to be taken into custody, merely placed under O'Neill's command, and he cooperated with O'Neill as the investigation got underway; to an extent, anyway. O'Neill's team returned to the crash site at Carnot Bay. Parts of the aircraft had been removed by a RAAF salvage team (Palmer had actually returned there when this was happening), but the mainframe was still there, and while searching carefully around it, O'Neill's team recovered some brown wrapping paper with part of a red seal attached to it.

From the time he tumbled the diamonds on to Gibson's desk, Palmer had given one explanation about how they came into his possession and would not deviate from it. He admitted to finding the package containing the diamonds when he was scavenging on and around the *Pelikaan*. He also admitted that he gave some of them to his friends Jack Mulgrue and Frank Robinson. But, he said, when he had opened the wallet beside the *Pelikaan*, most of the diamonds had fallen out and disappeared into the shallow water around the aircraft. The only diamonds he had were those he had been able to grab before they fell into the water.

As Private Palmer spent his lonely days out at Gantheaume Point watching for enemy aircraft and submarines, diamonds started turning up in the most unlikely places. Beagle Bay residents still used them as barter items – at least until the investigation team arrived. A Chinese trader in Broome produced one and there were rumours that Palmer and the others had buried most in petrol tins they had secreted in places known only to themselves across the northwest. A few small stones were even found in a matchbox left in a train carriage in Perth.

Finally, in May 1943, Jack Palmer, Jack Mulgrue and Frank Robinson were arrested and charged with the theft of the diamonds. The trial, in the Western Australian Supreme Court, began almost immediately before the chief justice of the court, Sir John Northmore, and a jury of six. A number of witnesses, including Cliff Gibson and Ivan Smirnoff, were called and after several days of evidence and arguments, the jury retired to consider its verdict. They returned a short time later to announce that they found all three defendants not guilty.

*

Jack Palmer celebrated Christmas 1943 with an army discharge certificate. He never returned to beachcombing. For the rest of his life, Palmer was known as either 'Diamond Jack' or, inevitably, 'The Jack of Diamonds'. He lived the life of a man of independent means. He moved to Broome and bought a house. In the 1950s, he bought a large blue Chevrolet. He never revealed where he got the money for either the house or the car, and for the rest of his life he always had enough money to buy a few rounds of beer for his mates, or the services of a woman for a few hours.

In 1958, Palmer was admitted to Broome Hospital and diagnosed with a terminal illness. One of his nurses there was Vera Dann who, as a young girl at the Beagle Bay mission, had played with some of the Palmer diamonds. Dann was a day nurse at the hospital and she noted how Palmer had a small padlocked case that he placed under his pillow every night. One day, he had it open when Dann entered the room and she saw that it was literally packed with banknotes. One morning soon afterwards, Dann arrived to find that Palmer had died during the night. The briefcase was not there and was never seen again.

*

The diamonds, or at least stories about them, would not go away in the postwar years. A number of diamonds were allegedly found in the fork of a tree in Broome. In another Broome story, a handyman was hired to do some minor repairs to a house. When the owners returned several hours later, the repairs had not been done and there was no sign of the handyman. However, a hole had been excavated in the fireplace and a box-sized compartment uncovered. The fireplace had been rebuilt during the war, around the same time as diamonds began to circulate in the community.

The stones eventually recovered by the authorities were valued at just over £20,000, or ten per cent of the total value of the diamonds carried aboard the *Pelikaan*. Extrapolating from those figures, and using today's values, it means that more than $25 million worth of diamonds are still sitting somewhere out there, perhaps in the northwest. Maybe even in Broome itself . . .

ENDNOTES

Chapter 1. The Port of Pearls

Page

9. 'By the 1940s, Broome had become a nondescript town . . .': John Bailey, p. 294.
11. Broome still has Australia's largest Japanese cemetery . . .: Oliver, p. 24.
11. A large number . . .: Adam-Smith, p. 264.
13. Their Commanding Officer and . . .: Harry Macnee had also won both the Distinguished Conduct Medal and Military Cross for bravery in the field, and had been wounded twice. Originally from Northcote, Victoria, where his grandfather was one of the district's pioneers, Macnee and two friends went to Western Australia while in their late teens in the first decade of the twentieth-century. After working as a labourer, he headed north to Broome where he worked as first mate aboard the *Eva*, the mothership to one of Broome's pearling fleets. After distinguished war service at Gallipoli and on the Western Front, Macnee returned to Perth. Macnee invested

in a small fleet of luggers and did reasonably well until the price crash during the 1920s. He still had at least one lugger in 1928 but increasingly focused on life ashore. He had several pearling investments, and became the Broome coroner, but a lot of his time went into military matters, the militia and the RSL.

Both were jobs he shared with Lou Goldie, one of very few Jewish Australians to ever make their home in Broome. Goldie had arrived in Broome from Sydney in 1912, and he established himself as a pearl buyer and valuer. He, too, fought with distinction in the Great War and, after being wounded on the Western Front, was sent to England for treatment and rehabilitation. There he met and married Doris Spragg, the daughter of England's leading manufacturer of diving suits. Back in Broome, Goldie continued in the pearling industry and also brought the first decompression chamber from England to the pearling town. The Goldies had three children. From 1928–39 he was a member of Broome's Road Board.

15. That pearl later sold . . .: *Daily News*, 2 March 1932.
18. A further sixteen luggers . . .: It being the wet, most of the luggers had been beached and stripped down in Dampier Creek or around Roebuck Bay. The crews had also been paid off.
20. The Japanese launched a massive air raid on Darwin. . . .: (AA) A 1196/247.
22. The influx from Broome . . .: Wills, p. 87.
24. Qantas sent Lewis Ambrose . . .: see Bennett-Bremner, in particular p. 79, for the background to this.
24. While Millar and his small staff . . .: Lester Brain had been the Qantas chief pilot since 1934. He was also appointed Head of Operations for QEA, and was a RAAF Reserve member, and had 20 years flying experience.
26. To coordinate the ground operations . . .: The New Zealand-born

Oram had been chief steward on the initial Sydney to Southampton QEA flight.

28. 'The position of Java . . .': Bennett-Bremner, p. 85.
31. He seconded some American . . .: Tyler, p. 71.
31. Rouse decided to bury . . .: see Rorrison.
33. 'Unfortunately, and in the words of . . .': Tyler, p. 71.
33. 'A keen diarist, Minahan . . .': ibid.
33. On the afternoon of Sunday . . .: In a number of accounts of the Japanese raid on Broome, Legg's name is spelt 'Legge'. Most contemporaneous accounts do not include the second 'e' and I have gone with their spelling.

Chapter 2. The Flying Dutchmen

Page

37. 'Two Douglas airliners . . .': Van Appeldoorn, p. 207.
44. With the destruction of what remained . . .: As well as the aircraft we are following, a number of Dutch submarines also made successful escapes to Fremantle.
47. The Y-67 Catalina carried . . .: Doorman had been a very successful naval officer, one of the pioneers of Dutch naval aviation. In 1938, he was appointed Commander of Naval Aviation in the NEI and in May 1940 he was promoted to rear admiral.
54. Van Romondt was a technician . . .: Australian Archives have an arrival card for a Maria Gertrude Blaauw, born 1917, who arrived in Broome on 20 February 1942. Perhaps Joop was flying to join either his wife or his sister.

Chapter 3. Ground Zero

Page

57. 'The atmosphere of expectancy . . .': A9695/68.
58. The American bombardier John Minahan . . .: Tyler, p. 71.
58. 'The school they had taken over . . .': ibid. p. 67.

60. 'This place looks . . .': ibid. p. 66. La Guardia Field was New York City's main airport and at that time was probably the busiest civil airport in the world.
63. Later, Harold Mathieson . . .: Tyler, p. 41.
64. The more nervous residents . . .: ibid. p. 91.
64. The other keen diarist . . .: ibid. p. 90.
65. 'At first, he thought . . .': AWM PR 30/30
65. Back at the powerhouse . . .: One of the engineers later spoke to Margaret de Castella about the incident which is recorded in Bain, Chapter 16.
66. Plenty was thanked . . .: Tyler, p. 2. Herb Plenty had enlisted in the RAAF in Port Pirie the day after World War II broke out. He was posted to Malaya with No. 8 Squadron, flying Hudsons. Early in the fighting, he was shot down, but made his way back to Singapore with his crew four days later. Around the time he flew into Broome, his parents were informed that he was missing in action.
69. They therefore decided to . . .: ibid. p. 41.
73. With its starboard engine . . .: Rorrison, p. 224.
75. Brain had set up . . .: (AA)A 9695/63.
76. Around 100 metres . . .: Lawton, p. 92.
76. No-one really knew . . .: Edwards, pp. 128–9.
77. In Edson Kester . . .: There were only three of these B-24 variants in the southwest Pacific. By coincidence, one of the others, General Brett's personal aircraft, was also at Broome that day.
77. It was almost 50 metres . . .: Tyler, p. 67.
77. Another Japanese aircraft . . .: After the events of 3 March there were persistent rumours that a Japanese spy had signalled a Japanese reconnaissance aircraft from the long jetty that night, giving details of the numbers and location of Allied aircraft in Broome. I could find absolutely no evidence to support this.

78. 'Before his evacuation . . .': Stafford had also recently become a father for the first time, his wife giving birth to a daughter in December.

Chapter 4. The first strike: the attack on Roebuck Bay
Page

81. 'We had just gone ashore . . .': Idzerda, p. 39.
83. 'Planes with suns on wings . . .': While this description is based on several written accounts, the most important is an interview Biddy gave after she was evacuated from Broome, published in the *Northern Times*, 13 March 1942. It is also found in Tyler, p. 5.
84. He must have been . . .: Cadigan, p. 145.
85. When he realised . . .: This is one of several anecdotes recorded in the Lawton article.
88. Nineteen-year-old gunner/armourer . . .: In 1966, Doug Dick changed his name by deed poll to Doug Dickson.
88. 'I knew then it was . . .' Rorrison, James, 'Nor the years contemn,' p. 253.
89. When he looked back . . .: www.pacificwrecks.com. Dick would later claim that the non-swimmer Russell, wearing nothing but shorts and a tin hat, was ten metres past the wing tip when he saw him, 'cutting through the water at 14 knots'. See also A 9695/62 and 68.
93. 'The other survivors . . .': Shores, p. 313.
93. As Bowden thought . . .: Wills, p. 31.
94. A bit further away . . .: Merv Prime includes three Dutch evacuees with the name 'Van Der Plaasche' in his booklet. Juta specifically recalled Van Der Plas, and I have gone with his recollection here.
95. She called out to him . . .: Wills, pp. 24–5.
95. They climbed through that . . .: Jung/Peters, p. 39.

96. Before Juta could react . . .: Wills, p. 25.
96. Her efforts were becoming . . .: ibid.
98. They never reappeared . . .: Tyler, pp. 26–9.
98. Somewhere within the flames . . .: Wills, pp. 30–1.
105. It was a world of loud colours . . .: Xav, 'They came in the morning,' in Gregory, p. 146.
107. They flew in hard . . .: An old pearler named G. M. Lister, whose camp overlooked the bay. Quoted in the *Northern Times*, 13 March 1942.
107. It was just seven minutes . . .: Rorrison, p. 250.

Chapter 5. The Second Strike: the attack on Broome Airfield

Page

109. 'As the fighters turned . . .': Tyler, p. 75.
112. There were no trenches . . .: Tyler/Minahan.
112. 'It happened as he ordered . . .': www.pacificwrecks.com.
113. He understood that his Lodestar . . .: Winckel would later recall, 'When I looked at my plane I was very angry . . . it was like my mother, my sister. It was a beautiful plane, you know. You get attached to something like that.' Worth, p. 142.
113. Winckel's left hand . . .: See Cornell, p. 53, for Winckel's thoughts at the time.
115. *It's all over* . . .: www.pacificwrecks.com.
116. When the water . . .: No-one who was there and survived ever spoke in detail of Kudo's end and his aircraft. I have written what I believe is the most plausible end for it.
118. 'The pilots appeared . . .': A 9695/70.
119. With limited ammunition . . .: Shores, p. 313.
120. 'Mr. Knight and myself . . .': James, p. 400.

Chapter 6. The Last Flight of the *Pelikaan*

Page

121. 'Smirnoff put up . . .': Coupar, p. 172.
123. Smirnoff half-turned and screamed . . .: Coupar, p. 171.
124. Daan Hendriksz was hit . . .: In all the written recollections of the attack, Hendriksz's wound is the only one that is not described. He did not regain consciousness after being struck, so it may well have been a serious head wound.

Chapter 7. Roebuck Bay

Page

131. 'When the Japs have finished . . .': Tyler, p. 50.
133. He trusted himself . . .: Rorrison, p. 256.
134. They decided to swim . . .: ibid.
134. They found it had . . .: ibid.
135. 'Some of the wounded . . .': AWM PR/Russell.
136. No Japanese bombers were sighted . . .: Rorrison, p. 261.
137. They were closer . . .: Fysh, p. 151.
138. Bastiaan and David Sjerp . . .: Jung/Peters, p. 45.
138. 'After getting about half . . .': Tyler, p. 50.
139. With another Shell employee . . .: A 9695/62.
139. Shouts and screams . . .: Fysh, p. 149.
140. Then they turned . . .: Idzerda, p. 40 and Prime, p. 33. The woman was probably Mrs Amsterdam, the wife of Lieutenant Commander Amsterdam of the MLD. The Amsterdam's lost all three of their children and were both badly burnt in the attack.
141. The Koens were picked up . . .: Nonja Peters, p. 117.
142. By then, he had also . . .: Wills, p. 32.
144. He stood up and looked . . .: Jung/Peters, p. 45.
144. He had not gone far . . .: Henk later learned that the boy was Jacques van der Zande.

145. It was Robin Hunter . . .: Wills, p. 32.
146. Once on dry land . . .: Jung/Peters, p. 44.
147. The man was crying . . .: Tyler/Kurtz.
147. Then he led them . . .: Connell, p. 54.
147. John Oram . . .: As the QEA evacuation operations were wound down, John Oram was cleared to return to flight duties.
148. These, too, were taken . . .: Rorrison, p. 277.
149. Legg's reply . . .: Tyler/Rouse, p. 67.
149. 'Colonel Legg did, however, provide . . .': Rorrison, p. 262
150. Armbruster was one of . . .: Rorrison, p. 277. Armbruster would also say that, for him, 3 March 1942 was the most horrible day of the war.
150. When asked if they would . . .: ibid. John Rouse would later suggest, quite pointedly, that 'instead they (the Dutch officials) went down to the hotels and drank beer all afternoon'. Tyler/Rouse, p. 68.
151. Distraught, he dug . . .: Edwards, p. 138. The story is also recounted in Tyler/Rouse, p. 75.
151. Other stories surround . . .: ibid.
151. When authorities learned . . .: In some cases only body parts were recovered. A finger with a wedding ring was the only remains of Johannes Blommert found, and this was buried with appropriate reverence. Jung, p. 161
151. 'The doctors . . .': Tyler/Minahan, p. 67.
153. He joined in straightaway . . .: A 9695/66.
153. Smith's second patient . . .: ibid.

Chapter 8. The Port Hedland Races

Page

155. 'There are about 65 . . .': A 9695/67.
157. As Biddy Bardwell . . .: Northern Times, 13 March 1942.

158. That afternoon, the local . . .: Born in 1908, O'Neill was also a member of the Broome VDC who would transfer across to the AIF in November 1942. In both the VDC and the AIF, O'Neill appears to have held field security positions. Prior to joining the Native Affairs Department, O'Neill had been a policeman in the northwest.
158. He also noted that . . .: James, p. 400.
158. Iverson and one of . . .: Lawton, p. 92.
159. Ralph Doig, a senior bureaucrat . . .: Penglase/Horner, p. 97.
160. While Doig was in Perth . . .: Choo, p. 141.
161. In the afternoon . . .: Edmonds, 'A Lesson in Efficiency', in Gregory, p. 172.
164. This led to another argument . . .: Bennett-Bremner, p. 79.
165. Legg's reply was . . .: Rorrison, p. 263.
165. It wasn't much, but . . .: ibid.
166. Most of the senior officers . . .: op. cit., p. 264.
166. When Brain made his way . . .: Bennett-Bremner, p. 99.
168. The clerk of courts . . .: James, p. 400.
168. He was the custodian . . .: Lester Brain heard later that the harbour master was arrested in Port Hedland and subsequently court-martialled. Rorrison, p. 265.
169. Lester closed the door . . .: Rorrison, p. 265.
170. They returned to the jetty . . .: Subsequent searches along Cable Beach turned up many similar items.
170. Because of the stresses involved . . .: Rorrison, p. 266.
170. Legg appeared at the top . . .: Paul Hasluck, in Australia's official war history, would describe Legg as 'a rather melodramatic type'.
173. John Minahan's recollections . . .: Tyler/Minahan, p. 75.
174. Frank Russell later wrote . . .: AWM PR/Russell. Russell also noted that he received pants and shoes to replace those he had lost in the water at a local store, and had charged the purchases to Qantas.

174. But then the smoke . . .: The smoke came from the funnel of a freighter, the SS *Chungking*, originally bound for the Philippines with a cargo of pears and potatoes. Caught short by the Japanese advances, it reversed course and headed for Australia with the aid of a school atlas. Arriving off Roebuck Bay, it was unable to raise the harbour master, who had already decamped. The *Chungking* then continued its voyage south. Bain, Chapter 16.
177. From the Dutchman . . .: ibid.
180. The black plumes . . .: Rorrison, p. 263.
180. 'He said that he and . . .': This is just one of several versions of the fate of Willard Beatty, whose relatives are still trying to determine what actually happened to him. In one version, his body was never recovered, in others he was alive when washed ashore but died either on the spot or in hospital in Perth after being flown there. Unfortunately, there are no formal records covering his death and/or his burial, so stories about his fate are all speculative.
183. It was led by five large . . .: Bell Brothers also left two of their trucks behind for use by those remaining in Broome.
184. The trucks soon became bogged . . .: Tyler/Kurtz, p. 78.
184. One of the Americans later . . .: White, p. 197.
186. 'This journey would end . . .': It was also the start for a whole new series of adventures for Rudi Idzerda, and he recounted them with some panache in his book, *Adventures of the Flying Dutchman*.

Chapter 9. At the Edge of the World

Page

189. 'It was all bush . . .': Wills, p. 58.
191. They returned with a small . . .: Tyler/Vanderburg, p. 84.
197. Everyone in the camp . . .: ibid.

198. Among the Aborigines . . .: Like several other names in this story, Jerry's name has been spelt several ways. Occasionally, Jerry will end with an 'ie', while variants of Dardan include Dardon and Dardin.
202. When Smirnoff confronted him . . .: Wills, p. 68.
202. He left an obvious trail . . .: Wills, p. 64.
208. Those survivors were all awake . . .: Something that was not mentioned then, and may not have been raised subsequently, was the fact that the dead had not been buried deep enough and the strong smell of decomposing bodies had spread well beyond the campsite. The smell had made it easy to find the survivors.
208. While this was happening . . .: Verheijke, Emma, (Ed.) *Broome 3 March 1942 – 3 March 2012*, p. 27.
208. Van Romondt, Muller, Cramerus . . .: They were also objects of natural curiosity. One of the Beagle Bay residents, Tony Ozies, would always recall meeting Ivan Smirnoff and feeling the machine gun bullet that was still embedded in his left leg. Ibid, p. 27

Chapter 10. Scorched Earth, Empty Seas

Page

211. 'Unless aerodromes in the north west . . .': A 9695/67.
212. 'It was officially claimed . . .': Northern Times, 7 March 1942.
213. 'Rumours to the effect . . .': Most major Australian newspapers published this in their 4 March editions. See, for example, the *West Australian*. Many of the newspapers also carried a communique issued the previous evening by Drakeford, the air minister. It mentioned that 'Details of the attack on Broome are not yet complete, but no casualties are reported', *Argus*, 4 March 1942.
213. 'The Chiefs of Staff . . .': A 816.
214. Though we were caught . . .: James, p. 400.
216. There were some restrictions . . .: A 1196/247, Document A22.

217. He sent an urgent telegram . . .: A 1196: Military document dated 7 March 1942.
217. The report concluded . . .: ibid. Document dated 12 March 1942.
218. A meeting that day . . .: A 1196/247.
219. Snook then turned . . .: A 9695/67; see also Tyler, p. 67.
221. The RAN also said . . .: Geoffrey Charles Fremantle Branson was one of those interesting characters that wars throw into the spotlight. A former Royal Navy officer, Branson had escaped from Hong Kong ahead of the Japanese, finishing in Australia where he was commissioned into the RAN. He was based at Fremantle, the port city named after one of his lineal ancestors. Branson would be Mentioned in Despatches for his work with the RAN during the war.
222. The seas had been emptied . . .: The full story of this maritime disaster has not yet been told. Both Wise and Lawton provide some detail about what happened.
223. Throughout the northwest . . .: Adam-Smith, p. 268.
223. Around 100,000 cattle . . .: Not only did the transcontinental transfer of the cattle deny them to potential invaders, it provided the inspiration for the UK's Ealing Studio to produce its first film in Australia, 1946's *The Overlanders*, starring Chips Rafferty.
223. For several weeks at Wallal . . .: Lacy, p. 334.
224. In May 1942 . . .: Choo, p. 141.

Chapter 11. The Ghosts of Roebuck Bay

Page

225. 'War is the tragedy . . .': Bradley, p. 338.
228. He would later describe . . .: www.pacificwrecks.com
228. 'A considerable amount . . .': Bain, chapter 16.
231. They had completely vindicated . . .: Full coverage of that review, and the evidence submitted to it, is in the quite

extensive reporting in the *West Australian* of 24 and 25 March 1943.

232. 'To the captain . . .': *Daily News*, 2 November 1945.
233. 'This distinction has . . .': ibid, 26 September 1945.
236. The pilot's body had been recovered . . .: AWM PR 90/30.
244. In his diary . . .: The diary was kept by H. Neeb, and the entry was dated 5 April 1942. It is quoted in Jung, p. 193.
247. 'The figure of between . . .': Hasluck, p. 145.
247. Recent work by Dr Tom Lewis . . .: Lewis and Ingman, p. 141.

Epilogue: Jack of Diamonds

Page

251. The men revealed . . .: Those who have researched the story of the 'Diamond Dakota' all give a contemporary value of £300,000 pounds for the diamonds. On today's values, the same diamonds would be worth $30 million.
255. The stones were thrown away . . .: Prospero/Embassy, p. 27.
257. The briefcase was not there . . .: ibid.

BIBLIOGRAPHY

Adam-Smith, Patsy, *Australian Women at War*, Penguin, Ringwood, 1996.

Australia under fire, 1942, Australia Post, 1991.

Bailey, John, *The White Divers of Broome*, Pan Macmillan, Sydney, 2002.

Bain, Mary, *Full Fathom Five*, Artlook Books, Perth, 1992.

Balagai, Remi, et al., *This is your place: Beagle Bay Mission 1890–1990*, Beagle Bay Community, 1990.

Bennett-Bremner, E., *Front-line Airline*, Qantas Foundation, Longreach 1996.

Bradley, James, *Flyboys*, Little Brown, USA, 2003.

Cadigan, Neil, *Man among Mavericks: The story of Lester Brain*, ABC Books, Sydney, 2008.

Chan, Gabrielle (ed.), *War on Our Doorstep*, Hardie Grant Books, South Yarra, 2003.

Connell, Daniel, *The War at Home*, ABC Books, Crows Nest, 1988.

Coupar, Anne, *The Smirnoff Story*, Jarrold's, London, 1960.

Edwards, Hugh, *Port of Pearls*, Self-published, Swanbourne, 1984.

Ewer, Peter, *Wounded Eagle*, New Holland, Sydney, 2009.

Fysh, Hudson, *Qantas at War*, Angus & Robertson, Sydney, 1968.

Gillison, Douglas, *Royal Australian Air Force*, Australian War Memorial, Canberra, 1962.

Gomm, Kevin, *Red Sun on the Kangaroo Paw*, Chargan, Perth, 2010.

Gregory, Jenny, *On the Homefront*, University of WA Press, Nedlands, 1996.

Hasluck, Paul, *The Government and the People 1942–45*, Australian War Memorial, Canberra, 1970.

Hurst, Doug, *The Fourth Ally: The Dutch forces in Australia in World War 2*, Self-published, Canberra, 2001.

Idzerda, Rudolf, *Adventures of a Flying Dutchman*, Woodfield, West Sussex, 2006.

James, Jan Kabarli, *Forever Warriors*, Self-published, Perth, n.d.

Jung, Silvano, *Australia's Undersea Aerial Armada*, PhD thesis, Charles Darwin University, 2008.

Lawton, Kevin, *Tales from Broome, 1883–1983*, Self-published, n.d.

Lewis, Tom, and Ingman, Peter, *Zero Hour in Broome*, Avonmore Books, Kent Town, 2010.

Macklin, Robert, *The Battle of Brisbane*, BWM Books, Canberra, 2000.

McKernan, Michael, *The Strength of a Nation*, Allen & Unwin, Crows Nest, 2008.

McKinlay, Brian, *Australia 1942: End of Innocence*, Collins, Sydney, 1985.

McMillan, Andrew, *Catalina Dreaming*, Duffy & Snellgrove, Sydney, 2002.

Messimer, Dwight, *In the Hands of Fate: The Story of Patrol Wing 10*, US Naval Institute, Annapolis, 1985.

Oliver, Pamela, *Raids on Australia: 1942 and Japan's plans for Australia*, Australian Scholarly Publishing, North Melbourne, 2010.

Parnell, Neville, *Flypast: A record of Aviation in Australia*, Civil Aviation Authority, Canberra, 1988.

Penglase, Joanne, and Horner, David, *When the war came to Australia*, Allen & Unwin, St Leonards, 1992.

Peters, Nonja (ed.), *The Dutch Down Under: 1606–2006*, University of WA Press, Crawley, 2006.

Prime, Mervyn, *Broome's One Day War*, Broome Historical Society, Broome, 2007.

Rorrison, James, *Nor the Years Contemn: Air war on the Australian front 1941–42*, Palomar, Chapel Hill, 1992.

Sandler, Stanley, *World War 2 in the Pacific: An Encyclopaedia*, Garland Publishing, New York, 2010.

Shores, Christopher, Cull, Brian, and Yasuho, Izawa, *Bloody Shambles*, Grub Street, London, 1992.

Stanley, Peter, *Invading Australia: Japan and the battle for Australia 1942*, Viking, Camberwell, 2008.

Tyler, William, *Flight of Diamonds*, Hesperian, Carlisle, 1987.

Van Appeldoorn, Jan, *Departure Delayed*, Robertson & Mullens, Melbourne, 1945.

Verheijke, Emma (ed.), *Broome: 3 March 1942–3 March 2012*, Embassy of the Kingdom of the Netherlands, Canberra, 2012.

Weller, Helen (ed.), *North of the 26th*, Nine Club, East Perth, 1979.

White, William, *Queens Die Proudly*, Hamish Hamilton, London, 1944.

Wills, Juliet, *The Diamond Dakota Mystery*, Allen & Unwin, St Leonards, 2006.

Worth, Bob, *1942*, Pan Macmillan, Sydney, 2008.

Articles

Lacy, Gray, 'The Wallal of Yesterday', in Weller, *North of the 26th*, op. cit.

Lawton, Kevin, 'Broome People', in Weller, *North of the 26th*, op. cit.

Prior, Flip, 'Japanese felt full force of Wild Bill's Anger', *West Australian*, 3 March 2012.

Piper, Robert Kendall, 'The flight of the Diamond Dakota', *Canberra Times*, 25 October 1981.

Wise, F.J.S., 'Tasks of a civilian in war years', in Weller, *North of the 26th*, op. cit.

Newspapers

Daily News

Canberra Times

Charleville Times

Northern Times Carnarvon

The West Australian

Websites

'The Japanese Air Raid on Broome', www.awm.gov.au/exhibitions, accessed 10 October 2013.

'Remembering Charlie D'Antoine', ABC Kimberley podcast, 2 March 2012.

'Air raid horror recalled on 65th anniversary', www.abc.net.au/local, 11 March 2007.

www.network54.com, accessed 11 September 2013.

www.pacificwrecks.com, accessed 12 September 2013.

Articles on websites

Boer, Peter, 'The Depot Squadron of the KNIL Army Aviation Corps', www.academia.edu, accessed 19 September 2013.

Jamison, Bob, 'The Flying Dutchman: Really', www.jamison-wildlife.com, accessed 16 September 2013.

Kimenai, Peter, 'Japanese Air Raid on Broome', www.go2war2.nl, accessed 11 September 2013.

Kroupnik, Vladimir, 'Incredible adventure of the Russian airman Ivan Smirnoff in Australia', www.australiarussia.com, accessed 16 September 2013.

Mailer, Robert, and Collins, Ben, 'Broome war hero Gus Winckel dies aged 100', www.abc.net.au/local, 20 August 2013.

Message Stick, 'Broome Hero (4.11.05)', www.abc.net.au, accessed 27 September 2013.

Meyler, David, 'Eyes in the Sky: The Flying Boats of the MLD', www.avalanchepress.com, accessed 12 September 2013.

Mills, Vanessa, 'Surviving the Japanese Zero attack on Broome's Roebuck Bay', www.abc.net.au/local, 14 November 2011.
Henk Hasselo, https://www.youtube.com/watch?v=Ni9EUMe7GMo, accessed 30 September 2013.

Australian Archives

A 9695/62 Interview with Sergeant D.F. Dick, RAAF.
A 9695/63 Interview with Sam Male and Alan Morgan.
A 9695/65 Letter from the Chief of the Air Staff to General Officer Commanding, United States' Forces in Australia.
A 9695/66 Report from Flight Lieutenant Hamilton Smith, a doctor, on conditions at Broome.
A 9695/67 Extract of a report by Wing Commander C.W. Snook on Broome.
A 9695/68 Broome raid, 3 March 1942.
A 9695/70 Report on aerodrome attack by Wing Commander I.J. Lightfoot.
A 9695/71 'Salvage of equipment from Broome', dated 15 April 1942.
A 816 56/301/57 Statement re censorship by Chiefs of Staff.
A 1196 15/501/244 A series of reports on Broome to civil authorities.
A 1196 15/501/247 A series of reports on Broome to military authorities.

Australian War Memorial

PR 00298 Frank Russell papers.
PR 90/030 Norm Keys papers.

ACKNOWLEDGEMENTS

Living in Canberra offers many attractions for a writer, with access to the Australian War Memorial, the National Library and the National Archives being the most obvious. It is also a culture-rich environment, and I would like to acknowledge such institutions as the Canberra Writer's Centre, the Honest History organisers and both Paperchain and Alexander Fax – the best little bookshop I have found – for the ongoing support they offer writers.

While I had some knowledge of the events in this book, my interest became my passion after visiting Broome with friends in 2013. There, I was introduced to the work of Merv Prime, Dr Silvano Jung, Dr Tom Lewis and Peter Ingman, all of whom have preceded me in making personal a piece of Australian history often overlooked. The Broome Historical Society and museum continue to provide focus and support to the story; Elaine Rabbit and her volunteers have done a wonderful job with the museum, which I can highly recommend to anyone who has the opportunity to visit it while also visiting one of the most beautiful and memorable parts of our country.

On a more personal level, my agent, Sophie Hamley of Cameron Creswell, and the editorial staff at Pan Macmillan have all contributed mightily to my ability to write the stories I do. At Pan Macmillan, I would especially thank Alex Craig and Sam Sainsbury for their professional assistance.

Writing can be a sometimes lonely and self-focused pastime. My wife, Pamela, my children and grandchildren bring me back to the real world through their ability to make me understand that life is to be lived and not just written about. A welcome to Jed James Fowlie, who joined the clan just in time for Christmas last year. Thanks, also, to a small group of special friends, Messrs. Mellios, Watson, Pattie and Macaulay, who have kept me from getting ahead of myself on many occasions.

Ian W Shaw
Glenrowan

'I am a widow's son outlawed, and my orders must be obeyed.'
Ned Kelly: criminal, underdog, icon.

On 26 June 1880, the notorious Kelly Gang rode into Glenrowan. It was to be their last stand.

In this impeccably researched account, Ian Shaw vividly details the action and violence of the 41-hour siege, creating immaculate portraits of the real heroes – and the real villains.

There's soulful Joe Byrne, toasting the success of the gang moment, bleeding to death the next. And the two younger gang members – Dan Kelly and Steve Hart – who prefer to die rather than surrender. The murderous Sergeant Arthur Steele prepared to fire upon innocents to further his own ambitions. And the hostages in the inn, trapped between the law and the outlaws.

Above it all sit the enigmatic figure of Ned Kelly – vainglorious, cunning and brave. A figure revered by the people and demonised by the authorities. Ned's daring and deeds made him famous. Glenrowan made him immortal.

Ian W Shaw
On Radji Beach

On 12 February 1942, Singapore was just days away from its fall to the Japanese. As the city burned, hundreds of desperate people scrambled to the docks to flee. Amongst them were 65 Australian Army nurses, who boarded a coastal freighter, the *Vyner Brooke*.

But theirs was a doomed voyage. Japanese bombers attacked and sank the vessel off Sumatra. Those who survived drifted for up to three days before making landfall on one of the many beaches on Banka Island.

A group of survivors, including 22 nurses, gathered at Radji Beach. They voted to surrender, but the Japanese patrol that found them divided them into three groups and the executions began. In the last group were the Australian nurses, who died in a hail of bullets as they walked, abreast, into the sea.

Miraculously, there was one survivor, Vivian Bullwinkel, who in spite of a bullet wound endured 13 days in the jungle before surrendering to another Japanese patrol. She was reunited with the other surviving *Vyner Brooke* nurses in a makeshift camp on the island. Three-and-a-half years later, only 24, she made it home.

Meticulously researched from the diaries and papers of some of the nurses who survived, this is a moving account of the fate of every nurse who boarded the *Vyner Brooke* that day.